LIVING

YOUR

DREAMS

LIVING YOUR DREAMS

Gayle M. V. Delaney, Ph.D

HARPER & ROW, PUBLISHERS, San Francisco
Cambridge, Hagerstown, Philadelphia, New York
London, Mexico City, São Paulo, Sydney

FIRST PAPERBACK EDITION

Library of Congress Cataloging in Publication Data

Delaney, Gayle M V
Living your dreams.

Includes bibliographical references and index
1. Dreams   I. Title.
BF 1091.D38   1979   154.6'34   78-20590
ISBN 0-06-250201-8

86 87 88 89 90   10 9 8 7

To the man of my dreams,

STEVE WALSH

ACKNOWLEDGMENTS

Thank you, Jim Fadiman, for having moved me to write this book and for having seen to its publication. Patty Garfield, thank you for your patient and careful help at every stage of its production. John Vitale and Alan Vaughn, you were good to plough through the first draft and give me your thoughts and ideas. Loma Flowers and Bill Alexander, you tamed the cheerleader in me; and Ida Rubin Cullen, you said just the right thing about rearranging the chapters and expanding the one you had so looked forward to. Robert McGinn, our philosopher in residence, thank you for your leads. Bob Castle, you kept me sane by keeping me skating, and your kindnesses saved me so much stress.

Dreaming friends, thank you for sharing your night lives with me. You have taught me a lot. Gin Beers and Bill Delaney, you set me up for all this, didn't you? Well, I thank you; it has been wonderful. And Steve, your loving presence was just what I needed. It still is.

CONTENTS

Preview

The movies of your mind can confuse or frighten you; or they can give you insights into your personality and help you solve specific problems in your life. This book presents an effective technique which will help you to go to sleep tonight with a personal or professional problem in mind and awaken in the morning with a dream that will provide new understanding necessary to solve that problem.

The most important thing you will find in these pages is a new method of dream interpretation which is elegantly simple and extraordinarily accurate. The method, called dream interviewing, minimizes the interpreter's distortions and maximizes the dreamer's ability to discover the highly personal and specific meaning of the dream. With practice, both beginners and professionals will discover that dream interviewing techniques will shorten the time necessary to understand a dream and will heighten the dreamer's appreciation for the practical application of the intuition, objectivity, and creativity so abundant in the sleeping mind. You needn't wait years for the good fortune of helpful and beautiful dreams; you can call them forth tonight, or almost any night you wish, by incubating them.

Dream incubation is the process of eliciting, at will, dreams that are helpful in solving problems, healing illness, or guiding the dreamer into new dimensions of experience. It has been used in various forms since ancient times. In this book, you will learn a modern method of dream incubation, developed by the author, which you can practice on your own with very little effort and surprising success. As you discover that you really can direct your dreams to help you out with daily, as well as other-worldly, concerns, you will experience a new sense of partnership between your conscious self and your "unconscious" self. In fact, like others before you, you will probably notice that in sleep you are not so much *un*conscious as conscious in ways that differ from your normal, waking consciousness.

Part I, "Tonight," provides instructions on recalling, recording, and incubating your dreams. We all dream four or five times a night; and by learning a few simple tricks, you can recall many of your dreams quite easily. Though keeping a good journal of your dream life is not indispensable to dream study, it is an extremely useful and rewarding way to get the most out of your explorations. The detailed instructions on writing a dream journal in the Appendix will provide you with a convenient framework in which to record and consider your experiences with both dream incubation and normal, spontaneous dreaming. Specific step-by-step instructions on how to choose the subject of a given night's dreams will be found in the second chapter. You will notice that throughout the book dreams are given titles in parentheses following each dream account for easy reference.

Part II, "Screenplays: How to Choose and Use Them," explores different ways of using dream incubation to improve the quality of your relationships with your friends and enemies, business associates, and family. Your dreams can give you specific insights into these relationships as well as into your relationship to your body, mind, and heart. They can tell you what is really going on in your marriage and what is behind the conflicts you experience with your children. They can give you clues as to why you might be suffering more than necessary from a certain illness. Your dreams can also show you how to improve the self-image you carry in your heart and project to the people around you. Many examples of other dreamers' experiences using incubation will illustrate both the uses of incubation and the practice of my favorite method of interpretation, which I call *dream interviewing*.

You will learn how to interpret both your spontaneous and your incubated dreams by using a very direct approach which does not require a therapist or detailed knowledge of any particular dream theory. In dream interviewing, you ask the producer of the dream to tell you what it means. Since you produce your own dreams, you know what each symbol represents. Dream interpretation is a matter of learning to ask yourself the right questions that will jog your memory and remind you of what a part of you knew all along. The instructions on dream interviewing are preceded and followed by many detailed examples of its use. I have made it a point to present many dreams just as the dreamers first consciously experienced them and then to proceed with a detailed account of how the dreamers arrived at an understanding of them.

Practice with your own dreams and those of others is the key to learning the art of dream interpretation. I think it is important in a study of others' dreams that readers be presented with the raw material of the dream and of the dreamer's associations to it. This way readers are better able to see how a particular method of interpretation can be applied to their own dreams. Both simple and complex dreams are discussed in detail.

As you read the dream stories of many different people, you will learn how to see your own dreams more clearly and how to listen to the words of the dream producer within you rather than depend upon the theories of dream specialists. As you learn to appreciate the reality of your dream world, it will become one of your most treasured sources of insight and inspiration in your daily life.

Part III, "Day Dreamers and Night Trippers," explores ways to use dream incubation to summon our creative muses and our inner wisdom. The usefulness of some forms of apparent extrasensory perception in dreams will be discussed in terms of how they have proved helpful to dreamers who needed information not available through their normal senses at the time of their dreams. Taking psychic dreaming a step further, we shall consider examples of spontaneous and incubated dreams in which the dreamers felt they encountered future children, deceased relatives, and existence on other planes of reality.

Throughout the book, and especially in Chapter 10, "Startrekking," we shall investigate the various degrees to which it is possible to be conscious while in the sleep state. Dream incubation can serve as an effective tool in increasing your intuitive awareness of the meaning of dreams and as a launching pad into other states of consciousness involved in lucid (conscious) dreaming and astral travel. You will learn how to use incubation to enhance your awareness of these altered states of awareness.

You will also find suggestions for eliciting dreams which will give you important feedback on the quality of your experiences with different disciplines of self-discovery. You will read the stories of dreamers who asked for and received important insights into the usefulness of various forms of self-development and exploration, such as psychoanalysis, growth groups, and meditation.

Your exploration of dreams can become a more lively and humorous pursuit when it is shared with one or more friends or family members. Studying your dreams with others will tend to accelerate your progress in understanding your dream life. In Part IV, "Getting Your Show on the Road," you will find guidelines for forming dream groups and suggestions for exercises and reading which can be incorporated into both your private and shared dream explorations.

My students and I have used the techniques of dream study presented here with great benefit. The understanding and joy gained from our dream work has permeated our lives and significantly expanded the spectrum of our experience. I wish you no less, dear reader, and hope you will enjoy living your dreams.

*Q*uidquid luce fuit, tenebris agit: "What occurred in the light, goes on in the dark." But the other way around, too. What we experience in dreams—assuming that we experience it often—belongs in the end just as much to the over-all economy of our soul as anything experienced "actually": we are richer or poorer on account of it, have one need more or less, and finally are led a little by the habits of our dreams even in broad daylight and in the most cheerful moments of our wide-awake spirit.

Suppose someone has flown often in his dreams and finally, as soon as he dreams, he is conscious of his power and art of flight as if it were his privilege, also his characteristic and enviable happiness. He believes himself capable of realizing every kind of arc and angle simply with the lightest impulse; he knows the feeling of a certain divine frivolity, an "upward" without tension and constraint, a "downward" without condescension and humiliation—without *gravity!* How could a human being who had had such dream experiences and dream habits fail to find that the word "happiness" had a different color and definition in his waking life, too? How could he fail to desire happiness differently? "Rising" as described by poets must seem to him, compared with this "flying," too earthbound, muscle-bound, forced, too "grave."

Friedrich Nietzsche, *Beyond Good and Evil*
Trans. Walter Kaufman
New York: Vintage Books, 1966, p. 106, section 193.

PART ONE

Tonight

You Were Born to
Be a Star

It was a beautiful night. The stars glittered excitingly in a navy blue satin sky. Oh, those stars! They twinkled with the spirit of an Irish Setter wagging his tail with joy at the return of his master. Here I was, in Hollywood. I felt welcome and happy and full of expectations that something good was about to happen.

The next thing I knew, I was being led into the spectacular home of Otto Preminger. I had never seen it before. Now, as I sat in the main living room, I savored its beauty. The room was decorated in the best Art Deco style. There were circular mirrors, palm trees, and blue silks covering great furniture forms. Everything was designed with symmetry and yet surprise. I was surrounded by luxurious and brilliant design reminiscent of some Fred Astaire and Ginger Rogers movie set.

I awaited the entrance of the great movie producer. What would he say to me? Why was I invited to come here? Would he say, "I want to make you a star"? Would I be able at last to ice skate and dance my heart out in the movies? I kept waiting for Mr. Preminger to walk into the room. I waited, and waited, . . . and waited.

Slowly, slowly, I began to realize that this marvelous house belonged to me! Somehow Otto Preminger's house was mine! ("Otto Preminger")

Upon awakening, I understood the dream in a flash. Otto Preminger is, to me, the greatest of movie producers. That his house was really mine meant that I was the Otto Preminger of my own dream productions.

For some time, I had accepted the belief that my dreams were productions of some mysterious forces from unknown worlds of instincts, archetypes, and myths. I called these dream-making forces "my" unconscious. But to tell the truth, some dreams seemed so strange that, as far as I was concerned, they could have come from anybody's unconscious. I had the feeling that dreams were sent to us by the gods or by some agent or part of ourselves that was very wise but often very strange and inscrutable.

We Create the Whole Show. In the weeks that followed my Preminger dream, I found that, when I reminded myself that I was the producer of my own dreams and that I had chosen the script, the setting, and the actors, and directed and organized the whole dream show, the lights went on! Almost all my dreams and their meanings became very much more accessible to me. I stopped looking at dreams as something I received and started experiencing them as something I created. When I worked under the assumption that I produced a dream with great care and skill in order to get a message across to my waking self, it was much easier to understand why the dream images acted as they did. I had cast the stars in the Preminger dream to convey a sense of welcome which actors or stars would normally express at the return of their producer. My dream images were welcoming me home. I had forgotten that I was their producer. I had spent several years in Jungian analysis trying to understand my dreams. I had accepted the belief that I needed an expert to help me. What I really needed was a more immediate sense of my role in the creation of my dreams *and* the belief that, with a few pointers and some practice, I could better appreciate and understand my dreams than anyone else could.

In the six years that have passed since this dream, I have been teaching people who are curious about their dreams various ways to deal with them. In our "Dream Meetings," the dream producers gather, not only to interpret their dreams, but also to learn how to produce dreams on a chosen night that will help them resolve problems or answer questions that face them in their daily life.

Before I go any further, let me suggest the theory or model of dreaming we have used in our dream meetings. This model includes the following basic assumptions:

1. *We are the producers of our own dreams.* You may sometimes catch yourself, while still asleep, actually choosing dream images, sets, and actors and forming the dream. This can happen when you manage to become aware of both your sleeping consciousness and your normal waking consciousness at the same time. This may have already happened to you. If not, you will find instructions on how to achieve it in Chapter 10. As you work with your dreams, you will become aware of the fact that there is no clear dividing line between "conscious" and "unconscious." Far more is available to our waking consciousness than most people realize. Many activities, such as blood pressure, heart rate, and dreaming have been considered exclusively unconscious functions. These are now recognized to be susceptible to conscious awareness and direction.[1] We *are* conscious while we produce our dreams. Our dream consciousness is different from our waking consciousness, but it is possible to become aware of it and watch it in action. As you will see later, you can even learn to direct the action of a dream while dreaming.

2. *We are the writers of our own screenplays.* Your dreams are your productions, your own works of art. If you assume that you wrote the scripts, you will find that, instead of shivering in the memory of a cold and snowy dream scene, you will be more likely to ask yourself, "Why did I 'write in' a blizzard here? What am I trying to express with it?" Thus, apparently given dream elements are opened up to your understanding. If you assume that there are no coincidences in your dreams and that you carefully wrote the entire screenplay with attention to each detail, you will find that every element of the dream will intrigue you and offer you clues to its meaning.

3. *We are the directors of our dream shows.* Not only have you written the parts for the actors in your dreams, but you direct their action. You encourage them to express their roles as fully as possible. The particular qualities of joy, anger, or laughter expressed by your dream actors have been very deliberately planned to elicit in your waking self certain memories and feelings.

4. *We are the stars of our dream scenes.* This probably seems obvious. You are, after all, the central character in most of the dreams that you recall. But have you appreciated your performances as your mother-in-law or your grammar school playmate? Do you remember the time you co-starred as Richard Burton or the time you sang as Edith Piaf? You may have been missing some of your best performances by not recognizing that it was you who played the part of most of your dream characters!

Of course, you as script writer–producer have created supporting roles for your close friends and family. When they play themselves (more or less), you tend to use them in a scene to represent some feelings you have about them. Sometimes you have them play themselves in order to illustrate the dynamics of your relationships with them.

Most of your dream characters, however, represent parts of you. For example, you may cast a ferocious caged cougar to illustrate the anger that you have not allowed yourself to show at work.

You were born to be a star. Look closely and you'll see that you star in every dream, even those in which you thought you were only a spectator.

What will looking at dreams with these attitudes do for you? You will find the actions of your dream images less perplexing. You will start to ask yourself questions that will lead you to understand why you dreamt a particular dream scene. You will be less likely to pass over certain key elements that might otherwise have seemed inconsequential. You will enjoy your dreams more. By taking responsibility for the production of your dreams, you will tend to believe that you must be able to understand them. A belief in your ability to learn to interpret your own dreams will speed you on to your goal.

Directing Our Dreams. If we produce our own dreams, might we be able to direct dreams from the waking state?

Yes. It *is* possible to direct your dreams by conscious intent. You can set yourself a question before you go to sleep and awake in the morning with an answer to your question. Suppose that you are having a lot of conflict in your relationship with your mate. Your fighting and your resolutions to be understanding are getting you nowhere. You can learn to direct your dreams to answer a question such as, "What are the dynamics of our conflict?" Or you might ask questions like these: "Why do I always pick men who are dead ends?" "What can I do to improve relations with by brother?" "What next job wise?" "Why can't I lose weight?" "Where can I find the information I need for this project?" "What did the otters in my last dream represent?" These and many other questions have been answered in dreams for myself and the dreamers in the Dream Meetings.

You probably have noticed that "sleeping on a problem" sometimes solves it or leads to its resolution. You can learn to ask your dreams to help you with your problems or answer your questions in a way that will give you results when you ask for them. You can choose and use your dream scenes in several ways; one way is by incubating your dreams.

Dream incubation is not new. Many cultures throughout history have had dream incubation rituals. The ancient Egyptians, Phoenicians, Hebrews, Babylonians, and Greeks all practiced this art,[2] although by methods very different from the one you will learn in this book. Dreams were usually incubated after specific rituals of purification, such as fasting and bathing. Dreamers were instructed to sleep in temples or other sacred settings under the direction of priests or holy people. The expectation was that a god or benevolent spirit would cause the dreamer, or *incubant,* to have a dream that would solve or lead to the resolution of physical or mental illness. In some cases, the dreams might guide the dreamer in making important decisions. If the incubated dreams failed to produce an immediate cure or resolution, the incubant might then take his dream to the priests or wise ones for interpretation. The Ojibwa, an American Indian tribe from the Great Lakes region, have used dream incubation in initiation rituals.[3] The initiate would be instructed to set himself apart from the tribe and build himself a ritual nest. He would stay in his nest in the wilderness, fasting, until he received from the spirits a dream indicating his role and function in his society.

Such rituals can be considered forms of sacred dream incubation. Here, the word *sacred* is used as Emile Durkheim,[4] the turn-of-the-century French sociologist, has suggested—that which is sacred is "set apart" from our daily experience and is related to or a representation of something "other" than ourselves, usually a divine force or a god. Things sacred may or may not be organized into practices we would recognize as religious. The ancient forms of incubation described above are sacred practices in that they call for the incubant to sleep in a special place, set apart from the usual one, pray for and expect a helpful dream to come from a sacred being, and, at times, consult with a holy or wise person regarding the meaning of the dream.

Because sacred dream incubation tends to be a rather complicated and lengthy undertaking, I began a search for a more practical, secular method of using dreams for specific problem solving. In 1969 when I came across the dream-related ideas of Edgar Cayce,[5] I found a much simplified form of dream incubation: Just pray to God for an answer and expect a dream!

This "technique" was a lot more practical than temple ritual, and I did get some very helpful dreams using it. For me this method worked about five times out of ten. There was a problem connected with it, however:

For people who did not believe in the power of prayer, this form of incubation was useless.

I began experimenting with my own dreams and hit upon a method of dream incubation that regularly worked for me. But would it work for other dreamers? Several psychologists and dream researchers have suggested prayer or just "asking your dreams" before sleep for an answer to difficult questions.[6] Some used hypnotic suggestion with patients in therapy.[7] Dr. Henry Reed, an inventive psychologist, even re-created a temple ritual for the incubation of dreams.[8] However, I wanted to teach others how to incubate dreams on their own without the help of a therapist, hypnotist, or priest. It soon became clear that just asking, hoping, or praying for a helpful dream, though useful sometimes, was not a very dependable approach. I began to consider the incubation of dreams not as a sometime gift but as a skill that could be learned and perfected through practice and step-by-step instruction. After some exploration and experimentation in the Dream Meetings, we hit upon a specific procedure for incubation that is brief, easy to follow at home alone, even by people new to dream study, consistently productive of "successfully" incubated dreams which deal with the incubated issue, and easy and rewarding enough to encourage the dreamer to use incubation regularly.

Our Allies and Our Teachers. When you begin to incubate your own dreams, you will find that, instead of confounding you, your dream experience will be one of your most dependable allies in helping you out of your predicaments and into new fields of discovery.

At this point, you may be asking why we should go to our dreams for guidance and inspiration. After all, if we ourselves write, produce, direct, and star in our dreams at a level of awareness so near consciousness that we can at times observe the process, what do our dreams have to offer that our waking consciousness hasn't? Why should we consider our dreams any wiser than our conscious selves?

The model of dreaming presented here suggests that dreams are like home movies we produce *in response* to profound experiences we have in a different state of consciousness. In the sleep state, we operate with altered states of consciousness in which we can perceive and understand events that do not necessarily involve images nor follow our usual ideas of space and time or cause and effect. We embark upon experience that involves perceptions that are direct and immediate. We "tune in" to areas of our being that have been called the subconscious, the unconscious, the inner self, the higher self, the source of our being or God. Almost everyone who has studied dreams agrees that they lead to experience with parts of ourselves that are equipped with information and wisdom far greater than anything we are aware of in waking consciousness.

According to this model, the dreams themselves are not the same as the *experiences* with our inner resources. They are instead translations of these basically nonphysical, nonmaterial comprehensions into terms we can understand. We, the dream makers, translate direct experience that is imageless and time- and spaceless into images and sequences that make sense to our three dimensional, physical world–oriented consciousness. From insights we gain and lessons we learn while in deep sleep, we move back toward the dream state in order to roll a movie that will summarize and translate them into images. We form dramas and comedies which we can remember and relate to our daily life of objects and events in movement through time and space. This dream-making process is what scientists measure as REM sleep.[9]

The goal of a serious writer-producer-director in making a film is to express an experience or convey a meaning or message as clearly and with as much impact as possible. The producer tries to make this expression understandable and acceptable to the audience, because he or she wants to sell the production, have it remembered, enjoyed, and valued. The writer-producer-director seeks to touch the life of the audience and add new dimensions of awareness to that life.

These are *your* goals almost every time you produce a dream scene. You skillfully choose just the right image from your subconscious storehouse of memory and association to get across as much of the essence of the original experience as you can. You choose images and events that will make enough of an impression on your conscious self to encourage morning recall and encourage a fascinated, or at least interested, study of your work. But you are also careful not to dramatize or exaggerate too much for fear that you won't sell the movie. If you frighten or shock too much, your conscious self may refuse to accept the show and simply forget it before awakening. Sometimes you make mistakes in judgment; some dream shows are better than others.

I see dreams as your best effort to present to your waking self the underlying dynamics of what is going on in your life. Your dream self will draw from experiences with sources of enormous energy and wisdom. It will translate these inspirations and comprehensions, using your present subconscious network of beliefs, opinions, associations, and memories to bring you new insights into yourself and the world you know. The dream producer in you does its best to make your life work better for you, to enrich the depth of your feeling and understanding, and to expand your sense of identity to include the experience and awareness of greater realities in which you also have your being.

In the dream state, you can have access to valuable information on the state of your body, mind, heart and spirit. You also have access to insights on the nature of your relationships with those you love and hate, to experiences of yourself in other times and places, as well as to strength and abilities you have not used. The dream state also provides you with an arena in which you can "screen test" various possible future actions and compute their outcomes. Dreams offer you what can never be expressed in words. They offer you an *experience* of understanding, not a lecture or book describing the experience.

Tapping the Wealth of Your Dreams. You can tap the wealth of your dream life with practice and some guidance to get you started. This book will be a good beginning and will lead you to other resources to light your way. Later, you will not need the help of "experts" or analysts. You will soon realize that only you can live the reality of your dreams. They are composed of a unique web of rich association and memories known intimately only by you. And after all, they are meant to remind you of deeper, richer experiences in which you, and not your analyst, participate.

Every dream is a work of art. Incubated dreams, spontaneous dreams, nightmares, and funny dreams are all important. Dreams that come to you in drama form and need interpretation are as important in their turn as those very special dream experiences which need no interpretation and which seem to change you overnight. Some people tend to devalue their normal dreams once they have or even read about lucid dreams and those which seem to put us in almost direct contact with other new and beautiful realms of experience. These are the dreams where we may know that we are dreaming and find that we can create our dream scenes while we dream them. Some of these dreams, which are recorded in history, present the dreamer with a new invention, a masterpiece of music or sculpture, or even a mystical glimpse of the nature of the universe.

Our dream life is full and varied. You will in time produce and review many kinds of dreams. Rejoice in them all.

You may be wondering when I'm going to start talking about all the painful, embarrassing, awful things dreams are supposed to tell you about yourself. Dreams do make us look at ourselves. Sometimes they point out characteristics or behaviors that we'd rather not deal with even though they trip us up in life and may make our lives as series of "poor me" stories. But your dreams will never humiliate you. Your attitude toward your dream or your interpretation of it may leave you feeling embarrassed, ashamed, or guilty, but such feelings are not necessary. If you will remember that your dream maker's main goal is to help you out and to further you, you will be able to appreciate the fine humor with which you are typically shown your weaknesses. Only when you really ignore your dream producer, forget to take the productions to heart, will your dream producer resort to intense nightmares as the only way to convince you that you are in great need of some new understanding if your life is to go well.

Even then your attitude will make all the difference. If you can let go of the need to judge things as good or bad, black or white, you will perhaps be able to find great (and pleasurable) excitement from the very intensity of frightening or horrible dream experiences. To intensely feel pleasure or pain is to really live. Trying to block out painful or unpleasant experiences of the day or night leads to a muting of all your feelings and to a distancing from life itself. When you awake from a nightmare and find yourself wanting to forget it, try to remember all the suspense mysteries and murder thrillers and horror movies you've seen and enjoyed. Remind yourself that there is pleasure in such intense feelings of fear and anxiety. You may have lost your appreciation for such things, but you surely had it as a child. That child is within you now. Cultivate your instinctive drive to taste all of life.

As you learn to trust in your dreams and recall more of them, you will discover that most of your dreams are funny or pleasant or interesting and surprising. Many dreams will try to tip you off to treasures you have yet to discover in yourself. Here are examples of a few dreams that do just this for their dreamers. These examples will start you thinking about your own dreams as well as provide a preview of a method of interpretation called dream interviewing, which we will explore later.

One day, Ardell, a lovely midwestern woman in her early sixties, related this dream:

I was in bed with Bob Hope. He didn't realize that he was in bed with me. I kept real quiet so as not to embarrass him. Later I was telling Dorothy about his sweater. She said we would see it in the picture. I said that there wouldn't be any pictures. ("In Bed with Bob")

Ardell had no idea what the dream might be about. She had not worked with her dreams before and couldn't imagine what she was doing in bed with Bob Hope! Asked, "Who is Bob Hope?" Ardell said, "He is a good, kind man. He is a funny comedian whom I like and admire very much." Our dream interview continued along these lines:

Gayle. How might you have embarrassed Bob?

Ardell. I was sure that he had gotten into the wrong bed. If he had realized that he was in bed with me, he would have been very embarrassed. So I kept very still so as not to disturb him.

G. How were you so sure that he had made a mistake?

A. I just assumed it. After all, why would Bob Hope want to get into bed with *me?*

G. Whom did you expect him to want to find in bed?

A. A pretty, young, glamorous girl, I suppose. Certainly not me!

G. So you just assumed your impression to be true without verifying it?

A. Yes, it seemed obvious.

G. That's too bad. I'll bet that if you had talked to Bob, he would have told you that he knew very well who was in bed with him. Since you produced this dream show, it seems safe to assume that the role you cast Bob Hope in is purposeful and not a mistake. Part of the role you cast for yourself included the feelings that Bob had made a mistake. That feeling indicates that you hold a belief about yourself that says, "I am not attractive or exciting enough to attract someone who is like Bob Hope."

A. Well, I know I wouldn't attract Bob Hope himself. Someone like Bob Hope? I don't know.

G. Who is Dorothy?

A. A very good friend.

G. It seems that she's telling you that the sweater is important and that you'll be able to see it in the picture. You say that there won't be any pictures. Why?

A. I don't know.

G. Do you remember what the sweater looked like?

A. Yes. I guess I do have a picture of it from the dream memory! It was white with a little green alligator on it, like a golf shirt.

G. Do you know anyone who wears a shirt like the one Bob Hope wore in your dream?

A. No, I can't think of anyone.

G. Are you sure you can't think of *anyone?*

A. . . . I can't.

G. I saw someone you know well wearing that very shirt yesterday!

A. Who?

At that point, George, Ardell's husband of forty years, pulled the shirt in question out of his suitcase.

A. Oh, George! Are you my Bob Hope?

Ardell's dream self was trying to help her see the Bob Hope in her husband. She had not fully appreciated the funny, humorous, "star" qualities in George. What had prevented her from fully appreciating and enjoying the Bob Hope in him? The dream gives us a hint. In the dream, Ardell didn't relate to Bob because she was so sure that she was not "enough" for him. Her own lack of self-confidence kept her from relating to him. Since Ardell believed that she could not attract someone with the qualities she ascribed to Bob Hope, she had difficulty appreciating similar qualities in the man who was attracted to her, her husband.

Ardell's Bob Hope dream was followed that same night by a dream in which "the gold was all lost on a ship coming from Africa." The gold, which usually represents something very valuable in our personality, came from Africa. Ardell thought of Africa as an underdeveloped part of the world full of primitive people, dark jungles, and adventure; so it is from the darker, underdeveloped areas of herself, her shadow, that the gold came. In fact, there is a Jungian proverb that ninety percent of the shadow is pure gold. Ardell never realized her wealth because the ship sank before it reached her own country, or her consciousness. Why did the dream writer-producer sink the ship in this scene? In her book *The Dream Game*,[10] Ann Faraday personifies this part of the dreamer, calling it the "secret saboteur." We may never see the saboteur in the dream itself, but we know he or she is there whenever obstacles and difficulties anonymously frustrate us. If we assume that Ardell wrote and produced every scene in her dream, and did so with great discrimination, it follows that she wrote the part for the secret saboteur. Thus, Ardell had access to the knowledge that would explain her acts. Why did Ardell have the secret saboteur sink the gold shipment? She had no idea.

Luckily, she had remembered the preceding Bob Hope dream, which, as dreams of the same night often do, gave us a clue. Ardell suffered from some beliefs that she held about herself. She believed herself to be "only" Ardell. Her lack of self-confidence grew lately as her life changed, as her work as mother of six children ended, as she aged. Her old sense of identity was inevitably changing. Like so many women in her position, Ardell saw herself as less attractive and less needed than when she was younger. What now? Ardell had not become fully aware yet of the riches of her own personality; of Ardell who is not only mother, daughter, wife, but Ardell, the individual who is uniquely and beautifully herself. Ardell didn't yet know the woman who was attractive enough for Bob Hope. We can guess that she didn't recognize these parts of herself because she hadn't looked for them. Her gold shipments had sunk back into unconsciousness (the ocean). Perhaps if she had been on the lookout for the ship, she could have saved it. Of course, in order to be on the lookout for the ship she would have had to believe that it was on its way and be looking in the general direction of Africa.

Bob Hope played a starring role in the dream show of another producer, one of the experts in the study of dreams and the parapsychology editor of *Psychic Magazine*. His name in the daytime is Alan Vaughan, though by night he, too, assumes many roles. Alan dreamt:

I was in Frank Sinatra's office. I go to interview Bing Crosby, but I can't find him anywhere in the huge sports arena where I am searching for him. Bob Hope comes up to me and says that he'll help me find Crosby. ("Looking for Crosby")

Over the telephone, our dream interview followed these lines:

Gayle. Alan, who is Frank Sinatra? Pretend I come from another planet and have never heard of him. Tell me who he is and what he's like.

Alan. O.K. Well, let's see. He's a very popular singer. I think he's a bit too egotistical, too self-important. He's too self-important.

G. Fine. Who is Bing Crosby?

A. He's a millionaire. He's very, very good at his art, singing, acting, etc. He's the sort of guy who comes into town for a bargain matinee for the fun of it like everyone else. He's an honest man. I like him a lot.

G. Who is Bob Hope?

A. He's a very successful comedian. Again, a good, honest man. I don't like his politics much. Very 1940s style.

G. Do you like him? How do you feel when you watch him?

A. Yes, I do. When I watch his films I really enjoy that 1940s style of light and easy humor. It leaves me feeling great, light and humorous.

G. What is a sports arena, and what was the one in your dream like?

A. A sports arena? Well . . . a place for sports events. The dream one was very big.

G. I wonder if the sports arena might represent your professional activities since it was so big? That's the kind used for "pro" sports, right?

A. Yes, that would fit. There were lots of things going on in the arena, and it sort of reminds me of my professional life just now. It really fits when I think that I'm in the process of negotiating with a television station which may produce a program on ESP that I'd like to do.

G. O.K. It sounds like we're on the right track. Now then, Bing Crosby could represent your professional ideal. He's a millionaire who has made it without compromising his good character.

A. Yes, he has the kind of success I would consider ideal. I suppose I want to interview him to find out more about him. But I can't find him.

G. The dream scene opens with you in Frank Sinatra's office. That's where "you are coming from" when you go looking for Crosby. Can you feel the part of you that is like Frank Sinatra?

A. Yes . . . I can.

G. Wouldn't you guess that the part of you who is too self-important would set up a professional life from his control office that is a bit too busy, and that would make contacting a nice guy like Crosby difficult?

A. Yes, yes, it would. My Sinatra self would have a hard time finding or getting along with a Crosby. He probably would consider himself too important to act as an interviewer anyway.

G. Yes. Now, in the dream you only "come from" Sinatra's space. You are busy looking and searching for Bing. So who is it that can help you find your Crosby self?

A. Bob Hope! He can laugh at himself, so he can see himself better than Sinatra. When I can laugh at myself, get into my 1940s state of mind, full of light humor, I'll find Bing, or my prized professional style and goal.

G. How old are you, Alan?

A. Just turned forty! I suppose the decade of my forties might bring with it a sense of light and easy humor about myself. I guess that, if I develop my Bob Hope characteristics in my forties, I will mature professionally toward my Bing Crosby goal. That's a good dream to remember.

It was now up to Alan to encourage the development and manifestation of his Bob Hope self in his everyday life. His dream provided him with vivid and lively images of his goals, of the obstacle that was giving him trouble, and of the way to overcome it. He could hold these images in his mind during the day. He could catch Sinatra in his obstructing act and call in Bob Hope to help him along the way to success. It is interesting to note that neither Ardell nor Alan noted the pun in the name *Hope*. Though the Bob Hope figure did bring hope to each dreamer, this was not the major impact of the dream figure.

Put Your Dreams to Work.   Never forget that your dream producer is trying to touch your life in a meaningful way. He or she will help you solve problems and will try, bit by bit, to renew and transform your life. But your dream producer needs your help to do a good and rewarding job.

Dreams do not take the place of conscious effort. You must deliberately grapple with the contents of your conscious mind. You must know and recognize your thoughts, beliefs, and feelings and use them to try to unravel the questions and conflicts in your life. Your dreams will help you. You will not "become lost in your dreams" to the detriment of your conscious life if you honestly seek to understand your dreams. You will not go off into some nebulous "dream world," because the meaning of your dreams is so intimately related to and made up of your daily experience. Your dreams will urge you to use even the most "far-out" mystical experience to change your life as you live it today and tomorrow. You can, of course, ignore such impulses. Your dreams will just keep trying to get the message through for as long as it takes. You can speed up the process of growth by learning how to use your dreams. In learning, you will also sharpen your critical conscious decision-making faculties as you see how different dream interpretations make good sense or not. If you decide while wide awake that a given dream message could lead you to change your life for the better, it is then up to you to decide to *use the dream*. Only you can put your dreams into action. The best interpretations and understanding of your dreams will not do much for you if you cannot put them into action in your daily life. To some extent, you will dream dreams that will change you, for the very experience behind and in dreams will affect you as any life experience does. However, you have the power to vastly increase the impact of your sleep experience if you choose to use it.

Nina was a member of one of the Dream Meetings, She incubated a dream, asking, "Where is my relationship with Scott going?" She had lived with Scott for almost a year and loved him, but the relationship was a turbulent one full of tears and fights and good times. The dream response came in the following form:

I was somewhere, not sure where. Scott came up to me and said, "Nina, would you like to go on a voyage with me?" "What is the name of the ship?" I asked. "It's the Titanic," said he. "Oh, my!" said I, "that ship is going to sink!" "No it's not," said Scott. "Oh, yes it is, I know it. Don't you realize that?" I said. He persisted, "Well, at least come to the bon voyage party with me." I agreed. We arrived on the ship, and I found the whole scene just appalling. Everyone was wasting their time and energy. They were drinking too much and eating too much, wasting their bodies. They were gambling, wasting their money. It was very depressing. I decided to leave.

The next thing I knew, I was walking down a road. Coming up the road on a tricycle was an infant. The infant was really a skeleton pedaling the bike. It had a heart which I could see. The heart had a skull and crossbones on it. It was awful. ("The Titanic")

It was clear that Nina the dream producer was telling Nina the dreamer that her relation-"ship" was not going anywhere now, and when it did go somewhere, it would go down! Nina recognized this but couldn't accept it. Still, she knew it was true.

Soon after this dream, she suddenly left for the East Coast to work in her parents' business and see if she could forget Scott. She had not made a definite break with Scott; she just delayed the decision of whether or not to marry him. She spent a year trying to forget instead of trying to understand. Then one day I telephoned another Dream Meeting member whose name was also Nina. Somehow I dialed the first Nina's old number at Scott's house. I had assumed that she was still in the East. What a surprise to hear her gentle voice at the end of the line! She had been living with Scott again for a couple of months. I said, "But Nina, what about your Titanic dream? How is it going?" She said that things hadn't changed; that they were still at the bon voyage party. "It's funny that you should call this afternoon," she said. "Do you remember the second part of that dream?" I had forgotten it, so she reminded me of the infant with the skull and crossbones on his heart. Then she said, "I've just returned from the doctor's, and I'm pregnant. I have made an appointment to have an abortion on Tuesday. I am really upset because I very much want to have a child. But I know that Scott could never be a good father for my child, and I don't want to have one on my own. Oh, Gayle, I guess it took this to make me face up to the fact that I could never marry Scott."

If Nina had taken the time to study herself a year ago, she would not have had to act out the tragedy which her dream had pictured as a possible outcome. She dreamt dreams that were trying to help her see why she had such a hard time letting go of a relationship that wasn't right. But she wouldn't look. She ran home. Then she found herself in the same old boat again.

As you read the examples of dream interpretation included in the first two chapters, you will begin to get a feeling for dream interviewing. By the time you read the specific instructions, you will have already acquired the sense of how to use them.

Before you learn how to interpret your dreams, it is helpful to learn how to incubate them. Though we shall study the interpretation of both spontaneous and incubated dreams, we shall begin with the incubated ones because they are more easily interpreted. The first-hand realization that you can cause yourself to have a dream on almost any issue that concerns you, when you ask for it, will increase your sense of conscious participation in your dream life.

☆ 2 ☆

Dream Incubation

Have you ever awakened in the morning with the answer to a problem that had been troubling you before you went to sleep? Sooner or later, people who pay attention to their dreams will find that sometimes when they sleep on a difficult problem, they receive good advice or new ideas in a dream that helps to resolve the problem. For most people, dream resolutions are a rare and lucky phenomenon, but you can learn to make them a regular part of your dream life by learning to incubate your dreams.

Incubating Your Dreams Using the Phrase-Focusing Technique. Because incubated dreams are generally easier to understand than others, it will help if you have a few of your own to work with as you practice the art of interpreting your dreams.

My goal to render dreamers more self-sufficient in their dream work and thus in their growth process led me to the development of what I call *phrase focusing* or *secular dream incubation*.[1] The method is relatively brief, requires no therapist or guide, and quite consistently results in useful dream responses. I tested this method in a study of fifteen dreamers who learned and practiced phrase-focusing incubation over a period ranging from one to fifteen months. The average dreamer in this study who recalled a dream on the morning after an incubation was successful in obtaining a relevant and helpful dream eight times out of ten.

Phrase-focusing dream incubation is secular in that it is meant to be part of the normal, everyday life of the dreamer. Incubants may ask for and feel they receive dream answers from a divine power separate from themselves. Incubants may direct their petitions to their inner, higher, or unconscious selves. The resulting dream responses are sometimes experienced as coming from the dreamer's personal unconscious. Sometimes they are experienced as coming from what Jung called the *collective unconscious,* the area of awareness that unites the individual with the creative forces of humanity and the universe.[2]

The phrase-focusing technique of dream incubation will enable you to find new resources in the development of your strengths, talents, and inner life on your own, without a priest, therapist, or hypnotist.[3] You will need to learn the technique, practice it, and learn to interpret the resulting dreams. There will be occasions when your incubated dreams answer your questions in very literal terms that will need no interpretation. Sometimes, these dreams will provide you with an experience of insight or understanding that in itself will give you your answer or aid in the resolution of your problem. The rest of your incubated dreams and most of your spontaneous ones will need interpretation if you are to benefit fully from their meaning. Learning the art of interpreting your dreams takes more practice than does the art of incubating them. Easiest of all is remembering your dreams. If you simply take a notebook consecrated to the recording of dreams, write the date on a new page each night, and place the notebook beside your bed before going to sleep, you will soon recall many of your dreams. If you record your dreams immediately upon awakening, you will maximize your recall. A complete discussion on how to recall and record your dreams will be found in the Part V.

You can incubate a dream on any problem or question that concerns you. In choosing your incubation issue, be careful that it is one you are really willing to explore, because if it isn't, you will be likely to forget any dreams you may have about it. If you choose too trivial a problem, you will have little incentive to produce a dream on it. Your best chance of successfully incubating a helpful dream will be to ask for aid in dealing with a problem that is close to your heart and which you are determined to resolve. What area of your life is giving you trouble? Your job? Your health? Your relationship with a relative or friend? Is there an area of experience you would like to explore, such as psychic perception? You can ask your dreams to help you explore any of these areas. Here's how.

Step 1: Choose the Right Night. First, choose a night when you are not overly tired. In order to work with your dream self rather than against it, it is imperative that you be free of intoxicants like alcohol or drugs.

Valium and sleeping pills cloud the mind, and most users who take an active interest in their dream life find they no longer need them. Be sure you will be able to spend ten to twenty uninterrupted minutes just before sleeping working with your dream journal. You will need at least ten minutes the following morning to record your incubated dream, unless you awake and record it in the middle of the night, so be sure to leave time for this.

Step 2: Day Notes. Before going to sleep, record your day notes as described in Part V. Getting the thoughts and feelings of the day down on paper will clear your mind, relax you, and orient you to your journal. A few lines about what you did and felt during the day will do.

Step 3: Lights! (Incubation Discussion). If you were directing a movie, you would call for lights to illuminate and highlight the set. In this step, called *incubation discussion,* you use your conscious mind (and heart) to take a close look at the various aspects of your situation. Direct your attention to areas which have previously been insufficiently illuminated. Ask yourself if you are really ready to examine the problem, called the *incubation issue,* and do something about it. Discuss the matter thoroughly with yourself, writing down as much of the discussion as possible. You might consider such questions as the following:

What do you see as the *causes* of the problem?

What are the alternative solutions you now recognize, and why won't one of them do?

How are you feeling as you write this?

What "secondary gains" or benefits might you be receiving from perpetuating this conflict?

Does living with the problem feel safer than resolving it?

What would you have to give up (e.g., sympathy, martyrdom) if the problem were solved?

How would things be different if the problem were resolved?

You may not be asking about a problem but rather seeking information or advice related to various life interests. In this case, ask yourself why you want or need the information and what you plan to do with it when you receive it.

Go as far as you can with the incubation issue while you are awake.

Churn up your feelings. Get the thoughts out of your mind and on to the paper.

It can be very tempting to skip this step entirely. However, this has proven to be one of the most important steps in the process. The more completely you use your conscious mind to grapple with the issue and actually write out the discussion, the more positive you can be of getting an answer to your question in the morning. Sometimes a brief discussion will suffice. Later, as you become familiar with the process, the written form of the incubation discussion can frequently be partly or entirely eliminated. More difficult and confusing issues, however, will require a written discussion. Remember, if you want to insure that dream incubation will work for you on your first try, your incubation discussion will be a crucial factor in your success. Place the letters *ID* in the margin at the beginning of your discussion for later reference.

Step 4: Incubation Phrase. On the next line in your journal, write down a one-line question or request that expresses your deepest and clearest desire to understand the dynamics of your predicament. This will be your *incubation phrase*. Make it simple. You may want to play around with several phrases until you find the one that feels best. Your incubation phrase might be, "Help me understand why I am afraid of heights and what I can do about it," or "What are the dynamics of our relationship; what's *really* going on between X and me?" If you were hoping to discover new ideas for a project, you would clearly state your request, asking, for example, "Please give me an idea for my next painting." Whatever your question or request, find a phrase that expresses it as briefly and as clearly as possible. The more specific your incubation phrase, the more specific will be the resulting dream. Write your incubation phrase in bold letters and place a big star (★) in the margin to the left of it.

Step 5: Focus! Camera! Now you are ready to place your journal beside your bed, turn off the lamp, and close your eyes. Having done this, focus all your attention on your incubation phrase. Imagine that you are about to begin production of a dream scene that will answer your question. You direct the camera to zero in on a closeup of your main point of interest, your incubation phrase. You take control of the camera, your consciousness. It is focused exclusively upon the image of your incubation phrase. As you lie in bed, repeat the phrase over and over to yourself. As you fall asleep, forget about the written ruminations of your incubation discussion. Concentrate on your question. If distracting thoughts occur, such as, "Will this work?" or "Tomorrow I must remember to . . . ," let them go. Keep bringing your focus back to the incubation phrase, which is the distillation of your query. Let all your feelings focus on this phrase. Keep it in your mind up to the very last second when you fall alseep.[4] If you do this, sleep assured that you will dream about your problem the first time you try. This is the most important part of the incubation procedure, so be sure your camera is focused well.

Step 6: Action! This step is the easiest. Just sleep. In ways we do not understand, a portion of our consciousness which usually appears *un*conscious from the point of view of the waking self will make contact with sources of experience and wisdom most often available only in the sleeping state. As we quiet the daytime barrage of sense perceptions and fall asleep, we tune into a subtler order of reality and experience.

In our sleep states, we can contact higher centers of our inner selves which apparently have access to the great storehouse of all our personal history (deeds, attitudes, memories, impressions) as well as to information concerning our future. As many psychologists, psychiatrists, and countless students of dreaming have found, our inner self sees our life and problems more clearly, more objectively, and from a far broader perspective than we usually do while awake.

On rare occasions, you may even become aware enough or conscious enough to witness your dream producer at work. You can become aware of a part of yourself who's busily choosing just the right cast of characters and associations from your personal memories in an effort to translate your experience with the non-three-dimensionally oriented parts of your inner self into terms that will make sense to your conscious mind. This encounter with your inner self apparently takes place in highly symbolic form. The dream-maker self has the task of breaking down these very powerful symbols into more specific guises that we can relate to our daily experience. The dreams we remember are like the tail end of the sleep process. In Chapter 9 we shall discuss ways we can increase awareness of the various levels at which we operate while our body sleeps.

Your incubated dreams will usually come the same night you ask for them. The dreams may redefine your problem, translating it from the way you consciously see it into the way your inner self sees it. The discrepancy can be very enlightening. The dreams may present alternatives to your dilemma which you've not considered. They might introduce you to whole new areas of psychological awareness and understanding. Finally, some incubated dreams will seem to have a resolving, soothing, healing effect in themselves. The very experience of a dream may change your mind, or feelings, in a way that resolves your conflict. Trust your dream producer to do the job well. This creative part of you is aware of your incubation concerns and quite capable of responding to them with skillfully directed dreams.

Step 7: Record. Record in detail all your dream memories *as soon as you awake with them,* whether it is in the middle of the night or in the morning. Include any feelings, thoughts, songs, or fantasies that come to mind. *Try to reexperience the dream.*

If you have time, jot down any associations that come to mind regarding different dream elements and sketch unusual images in the margin. In the commentary section of your journal, keeping your incubation phrase in mind, make an attempt to draw meaning from your dream in any way that seems appropriate. In the next chapter, you will discover guidelines to help you develop your interpretive skills. As you come to understand your dream language better, you may find that incubation efforts you thought had failed were, in fact, quite successful. Give your dreams the benefit of the doubt. Until you can understand what issues they *do* concern, suspend your judgment as to whether certain difficult dreams do or do not deal with your question.

The Effects of Dream Incubation.

The first time my students receive a dream answering a question they posed the night before, they experience a new sense of excitement, prowess, and achievement as they realize a new partnership with their dreams. Incubated dreams tend to be easier to remember and more vivid than most spontaneous ones, probably because of the heightened degree of conscious participation in the dream process.

You may be surprised at the number of dreams you incubate that provide almost literal responses to your requests. William, a struggling artist who had many other talents, was constantly tempted to give up serious painting and take a regular job that would provide him with prestige and a regular income. He incubated a dream, asking, "Should I get a job to earn money, or is there a better way for me?" He dreamed:

I see a twenty dollar admission ticket to financial well-being. I somehow understand that this will hold me over until bigger things come my way. In the dream, I think this means I should continue to teach my drawing classes even though the going will not be easy. ("Drawing Classes")

In a way typical of many incubated dreams, William seemed to understand his dream as he was dreaming it. Upon awakening, he recognized that twenty dollars was the fee he charged students for a month of weekly drawing lessons. He had considered giving up these classes in order to take a regular job because they provided only erratic income. He took the dream to mean that he could count on earning an income at least sufficient to live on through his teaching. He further interpreted the dream as an encouragement that bigger and better opportunities would come his way if he chose to continue his art work. A year and a half after this dream, William was still teaching his classes, which had become more popular and thus more profitable. And his art was beginning to appear in a few good galleries.

Some of your incubated dreams will take some interpretive effort, but even then, knowing that you asked for the dream, you will be more motivated than usual to understand and use it.

There will probably be occasions when you will not remember a dream after an incubation. This happened to me a few months ago. I had just determined most of the chapter titles for this book, but for several weeks I couldn't find the right title for the first chapter nor could I decide how I would begin the chapter. It occurred to me to ask my dreams for some help. My incubation phrase was, "How shall I start my first chapter and under what title?"

The next morning I awoke with a total blank on my mind, or so it seemed. While I stood in a hot shower, I found myself singing a simple song:

Come study your dreams
Come study your dreams
Come study your dreams and you will find them your friends.

Then suddenly it struck me that I should title the first chapter "You Were Born to Be a Star," open with my Otto Preminger dream, and carefully develop the idea that we are the producer-directors of our own dream scenes. I recalled no specific dream, but the idea filled my consciousness as if the entire chapter outline had already been planned in detail.

Insights and solutions you receive in both incubated and spontaneous dreams may not be recalled in dream form. They may come to you later as hunches or urges to take specific actions or make decisions in ways that help to resolve your difficulties. In cases where you ask questions to which you are not truly ready to hear answers, you may repress the recall of dreams providing them. If you are patient with yourself, you will be more open to intuitions that may come to you in the days following an incubation effort. Whether these intuitions arise from a specific, though forgotten incubated dream or whether they result from other unconscious, problem-solving processes is impossible to determine. Of course such intuitions and urges to take certain action should be reviewed in light of your conscious judgment and good sense before being acted upon.

It seems clear that at least some dreams in themselves can significantly influence the course of the dreamer's life. The insights gained from these and other dreams certainly provide many opportunities for growth and change. The degree to which our dream life influences our daily life is, to some extent determined by how we use our dreams. Learning to incubate dreams is a step in the direction of using them to enrich our lives and often drastically shortens the time it would normally take to resolve certain conflicts or to explore new areas of understanding. Asking our dreams for inspiration will also help to open doors to greater creativity in both our day and our night life.

In the dream state, we seem to be more exploratory, more playful. We seem to allow ourselves more freedom to experiment with different solutions to problems and to try out different creative responses to our questions. In the dream state, we are freed from the constant distractions of sense data and daily concern. We are able to focus intently and seem to have recourse to all the history of our feelings, actions, and life experience. Some dreamers feel strongly that in sleep we can even have experiences in other planes of existence, contact spiritual guides, as well as glimpse the nature of the universe.

Is Dream Incubation Dangerous? Might dream incubation be a vehicle to repress certain spontaneous dream content that should be dreamed? Might not the temptation to incubate on only acceptable issues be very strong? Dare we tamper with an apparently autonomic process which comes to us in the night and plays such an important role in the balancing of our psychological and perhaps even physical health? Most experts believe that dreams serve the function of bringing to our attention attitudes and behaviors that we do not sufficiently recognize and deal with in our conscious life. If this is true, who are we to tell our wise, balancing unconscious forces what to do?

Those who have never tried dream incubation but have extensive knowledge in other areas of dream study often ask these questions. They tend to divide into two groups with different opinions. One group believes that the unconscious dream world is charged with forces of such enormous power that there is ever the danger of consciousness being flooded and innundated if dream explorers are not very cautious and accompanied in their explorations by an analyst. These people, who believe in the relative fragility of the conscious mind in the face of unconscious forces, feel that using the conscious mind to incubate dreams might lead to a breakdown in the natural, balancing function of the dream process. Although this group is likely to hold fast to their opinions and generally do not experiment with incubation, therapists with such an orientation often suggest to their clients that they dream on specific issues by saying something like, "Let's hope you have a dream on it this week." As I discovered in my own Jungian analysis, dream incubation was more effective than hoping, and very useful.

The second group is distinguished by their attitudes regarding the role and strength of the conscious mind relative to those of the unconscious mind. They tend to have a greater respect for, and confidence in, the ability of the conscious mind to deal with the contents of the unconscious. They see psychotic breaks as a result not of interested, purposeful investigations of the unconscious but of a long history of purposeful avoidance of a serious examination of the contents of the conscious and unconscious mind. Those who fall into this group tend to be much more open than those in the first to exploring ways of using the conscious mind to actively participate in processes that are normally considered unconscious. They are more likely to experiment with techniques such as dream incubation because they trust that the normal unconscious mind has sufficient defenses to protect its integrity if it finds itself inadvertently in hot water. They also believe that the unconscious is wise enough in its function of balancing the psyche that it will let the conscious mind know if it gets too pushy, either by providing messages in dreams or by simply frustrating the dreamers efforts in incubation.

Those who do have some experience in dream incubation tend to have formed similar opinions based upon that experience. What they report are not tales of frightful encounters with unconscious forces that have weakened the stability of their conscious minds but, instead, new experiences of fruitful partnership between their inner and outer lives. What might have once seemed a mysterious, perplexing dream life is recognized as an ally that can both give to and take direction from the conscious mind. Instead of losing control, these dreamers feel that they gain a new awareness of their own power, initiative, and ability to influence their dream and their day life. The dreamers in the Dream Meetings and incubation studies I have conducted over the last five years have neither fallen prey to unconscious powers beyond their control nor become dictators trying to program their dream life in the service of repressive conscious desires to avoid the spontaneous nature of conscious or unconscious life. These dreamers have instead discovered new respect for both the directive and the receptive functions of the conscious mind. None of them has, nor have any of my collegues to my knowledge, overdosed on incubation. While a few students have incubated as many as six dreams in one week, most dreamers find the time, inclination, and energy to incubate dreams once or twice a week. From these efforts usually only two or three dreams on the incubation issue are recalled. Since we have approximately twenty-eight to thirty-five dreams a week, this leaves plenty of time for spontaneous dream processes. The unconscious seems quite capable of defending itself from an escapist or misguided incubation request. In the rare cases in which incubations are followed by dreams that are remembered but which apparently do not deal with the incubation issue, it often turns out that an incubant's effort to avoid something important has been aborted by spontaneous dream processes. These spontaneous dreams usually deal with the issue the dreamer was trying to avoid by incubating escapist dreams.

One dreamer, named Maria, knows this well. She has been studying her dreams and incubating them for four years now. Once before she had asked her dreams simply to cheer her up. She had recently broken up with her sweetheart and had confronted both him and her feelings of loss, anger, and resentment very courageously. She wanted and received a dream that would help her out of the heartache blues. However, about a year later, when she tried to incubate a pleasant dream in an effort to escape from a difficulty she had failed to confront for quite a while, she was in for a surprise. Maria had survived a harrowing day at work. She incubated for a dream that would provide her with some peaceful fun. However, Maria dreamed that she went to a faculty meeting peopled by teachers she found dull at best. These people would not let her into the meeting, saying she did not have the proper pass. She was very distressed and searched all through the school building for the pass or someone who would give her one. She found the whole building to be a very depressing place. She tried several times to enter the meeting, each time being turned away. The last time she tried to gain entry, the most likeable, though rather dull, teacher said to her, "But you don't belong here." Maria commented that this dream was "just hideous, and enormously upsetting," but that it was very important.

After this dream, Maria finally began to ask herself if she really needed the frustration of her job as a public school teacher. She was, of course, concerned with her needs of financial and job security, and worried that she could not find a new job if she left her present one. Maria was exceedingly unhappy with her job. For some years she had been assigned to a depressing and frightening school, where she had to step over drunks to get into the building, withstand physical threats and attempted assault from the students, and confront staunch resistance to her innovative programs from the administration and staff. In the school system there was one school which was worse. If she insisted on a transfer, she was told, she could go there or quit. She incubated a dream on "where and what next, jobwise?" She dreamed:

A friend who teaches rather happily in another school district goes with me in the car after having visited somewhere else down south of Market Street. It gets late, and for some reason I have the feeling that George, her husband, has come to get us in her car (a Fiat, rather new). There is a man in the front seat, but it is not George. I feel a little afraid of him, as if he can change our course, but I have faith in Judy's getting us to where we are going. It is late at night. We drive down to where we see the #22 bus. When I notice the bus going that way, I tell Judy I don't want that. So we drive into an abandoned parking lot, where there is a car that belongs to me. It is white and shiny. I get the feeling it is new. Judy tells me that I can go in my own car, or she'll drive me home. The guy in the front seat disappears. There are a couple of men in the parking lot looking on, minding their own business. I am a little afraid, because it's dark and they are standing there, even though they pose no threat to me. She says, "Maybe I could help you with the clutch." I say "Maybe. . . ." I woke up. ("Shiny White Car")

Maria felt her incubation had failed. So two nights later she incubated with the same question one more time. To her surprise, she had the exact same dream again! Before this, Maria had not recalled any recurring dreams since childhood.

She brought her screenplay to a Dream Meeting, and after our discussion she interpreted her dream as follows:

My dream presents the alternatives I now see facing me in my career life. I could accept the transfer offered me to a school which seems even worse than the one I now teach in. The #22 bus goes there. In the dream, I reject this. I could let my friend drive me home. She is also a teacher in the city school system, and she's fairly happy. In other words,

I could stay in the school system as a teacher and be content and safe. Or I could work independently as a school system resource person (if I could get such a job), or even start a school myself, since I do know some wealthy people who are interested in helping me. I think the shiny white car represents this. And it is true that I have often abandoned this alternative out of fear (the men loitering) of failure. The dream suggests that the fear is unnecessary. Judy offers to help me get the car started—to get me into gear. I am going to give a good deal of consideration to the possibility of working independently—it turns me on, and it scares me.

This dream experience prompted Maria to create an image of an ideal job in her own mind. She began to concentrate upon this fantasy image and pretend that it was a possibility for her. Her fantasized ideal job was one in which she would teach at a public school within walking distance of her apartment. She visualized the school as a peaceful one, run by people who could appreciate and encourage her innovations. For at least a few minutes a day, Maria stopped focusing on the worst that could happen to her. She let herself try believing that she *did* have the "Judy alternative" to her predicament presented in the dream. She could not believe that she really had the shiny car alternative. So she chose to focus her energy on the one she felt most comfortable with.

Maria was trying out the hypothesis that "you get what you concentrate on." After a few weeks of fantasizing the possibility of the "Judy alternative," it was almost miraculously offered to her. She was transferred to a school ten walking minutes from her apartment that is peaceful and where the administration is extraordinarily supportive of her innovative programs. She is rather happy there, as her dream suggested she would be. Her shiny white car is still in the abandoned parking lot, and at some future date she may or may not get it into gear. For now she is safe and content.

As I was writing out this dream story, Maria telephoned. She told me that her friend Judy had been notified that she was to be transferred to the same school where Maria now taught, although Judy had made no request for this. Three years after Maria's dream, it looks as if she and Judy will, in fact, be in the same boat—or car. Maria's dream had presented her with three alternatives for her consideration. She used her dream in the way she felt was best for her.

There is always the question of whether or not an incubant would have dreamed the incubated dream sooner or later without ever engaging in an incubation process. Perhaps, perhaps not. The repeat of Maria's white car dream in the second incubation, two nights after the first run, suggests that there is more than coincidence involved. When dreams are remembered after an incubation night, they so consistently deal with the incubation issue that it is hard to believe any dreamer could so accurately and consistently anticipate what issues are already on the agenda of the spontaneous dream mind on a given incubation night.

The question has been raised as to whether someone with a very self-destructive bent might incubate dreams that steer him in the wrong direction? I have yet to see anyone who has recalled an incubated dream (or any dream) that, accurately interpreted, misdirects the dreamer, no matter how negative his mind-set. We do not fool ourselves in dreams, although we can and often do interpret dreams in ways that perpetuate a given cherished position or point of view. When a dream is well interpreted, its appropriateness and good sense will usually be apparent.

What is significant is that dreamers who have used incubation credit it with making them aware of new issues and experiences in their dream lives. Incubated dreams have triggered important developments in their lives. Some, like Maria, have found better jobs. Some have lost weight. Others, who have come to understand the dynamics of difficult relationships, have chosen to end or modify them.

Dream incubation will become more and more rewarding as you discover new and creative ways to use it. You have already read how a few dream producers have put it to use. You will find many more ideas as you read the stories of dreamers you will meet in later chapters.

3

If You Want to Know What the Show Was All About

Ask the Producer

Dream Interviewing. Your dreams are not senseless blitherings of the night. They come to enlighten you, to inspire and guide you. They do not parrot what you already understand. They come to show you something you have not yet fully grasped. They serve a purpose and have a message. It is up to you to understand it.

Your dreams spring from your psyche. You produce them. The part of you that creates them knows what each dream means. As you study your dreams, as you learn to participate more consciously in the process of their production, their meaning will become increasingly clear to you. More and more of your dreams will seem to interpret themselves as you dream them; you will perceive the significance of the symbols in the process of the dream itself.

As a novice dream watcher, you will find that most of your dreams need interpretation. Even after years of dream study, you will sometimes awaken with dreams you do not understand at all. What you need to do is contact the dream producer in you and ask what he or she is trying to express with the dream show. Sometimes your dream producer will be very open to discussing the work with you, sometimes not. On other occasions, your dream-maker self will seem tongue-tied, and you will swear that in no part of you could there exist a producer who knows anything at all about your dream. Whenever it is unclear just what your dream writer is up to, you can find out by asking. At times, when your producer is being obscure, you will need to conduct the interview with special tact and patience. But if you develop good interviewing skills, your producer won't be able to resist telling you all you need to know.

This thinking has led me to develop the method I call *dream interviewing*. The principal idea is that the dreamer interview the part of herself which has produced the dream and thus has direct access to its meaning. This is a process of eliciting *relevant* associations and intuitive linkings until the dream elements click into place and the dreamer realizes the meaning of her production.

Only you, the dream's creator, know what you wanted to communicate to yourself via the various elements and events in your dream. A part of you produces it in order to tell your waking self something important. You, better than anyone else, have access to the richness of associations that make up the pictorial language of your dreams. Awake, you are a somewhat absentminded producer, at times quite unclear about your sleep activities. Yet your dreams, once understood and appreciated, are striking evidence that, in the sleep state, you are very clearheaded and creative. A skillful interview can draw out the knowledge of your dream producer's intentions and goals even when your waking self seems to have quite forgotten them. You can interview the dream producer aspect of yourself, playing both the role of the dream producer and that of the interviewer. This is most practical when you work with your daily dreams in your journal. Now and then it may be easier and more amusing to invite a friend or dream specialist to play the role of interviewer. When your dream producer is least communicative and most obscure, you may discover that externalizing the role of interviewer in the person of an informed friend or therapist will greatly facilitate finding out what you need to know. Learning good interviewing skills is very important if you are to do a good job interviewing yourself and other absentminded dream producers.

To begin with, a good interviewer knows how to create a relaxed atmosphere in which the dream producer feels comfortable. The interviewer wants the artist to feel free to express herself without fear of being judged or laughed at. For best results, the atmosphere should be one of acceptance, interest, and joint adventure, so that the producer will be more likely to experience and express important feelings. The producer's associations will flow more freely and fall into a meaningful configuration more quickly. Both the interviewer and the producer should enjoy their discussion and not fall into "working at it" too hard; an attitude of playful, Sherlock Holmes–like adventure will stimulate a far more rewarding exchange.

As a dream interviewer, you will need to know the tools of the trade. Following is an outline of the skills and knowledge that will allow you to interpret almost any dream.

The Interviewer's Tools. The basic tools you will need include, above all, an inquisitive style. You will need to know what basic questions are most useful in opening up the producer. You will also need to gain experience in asking appropriate questions which follow up on the producer's responses or lack of them. A knowledge of the basic structural tendencies in the dream world will help to orient you and the producer to dream reality, which follows its own set of laws. Finally, an appreciation for dream puns and metaphor along with a sense of creative play in piecing together the dream puzzle will heighten your appreciation for the expressive skills of your dream producer.

Style. The ability to tune into or reexperience the feeling tone of your dream (or to encourage another producer to do so) is particularly important. It is through reliving the way we felt at different points in a dream that we are led to recognize areas in our present life that give rise to similar emotions. The interviewer and the producer should remember (and remind each other) to keep in touch with the feelings experienced in the dream. This will facilitate the questioning later, as the interviewer searches for associations and thoughts that are relevant to the dream.

If you as the interviewer can let yourself be fascinated by the dream, you will see it much more clearly, and your waking self will follow your lead in appreciation of the dream, whether it is a pleasant one or not. The original and the unusual in dreams is interesting in itself, be it frightening, surprising, or beautiful.

As you explore dream scenes with this attitude, you will at times receive flashes of intuition regarding part of its meaning. These hunches may help the dreamer to make fitting intuitive linkings, or they may not. Your hunches may be wrong, or the dreamer may be resisting the obvious. In either case, a good interviewer knows better than to push an interpretation, for this will only lead the producer-dreamer to withdraw from you. The best an interviewer can do if he feels strongly about some dream meaning is to present it as a hypothesis. If it fits for the producer, hopefully it will be used sooner or later to trigger an intuitive, first-hand understanding.

If you are interviewing yourself, be patient, exploratory, accepting, and humorous. If you are interviewing another dream maker, do unto him as you would do unto yourself.

Preparedness. All good interviewers have at their disposal cue cards listing the initial questions they want to ask their guests. These questions get things going and are designed to cover the essential areas of interest. A list of such basic questions for you to ask the producer will be provided below. These questions are very effective in getting your dream writer-producer to tell you what you need to know in order to understand the dream.

Experience in Interviewing. Knowing how and when to ask further questions suggested by the producer's response, or lack of it, will distinguish the novices from the experts in dream interpretation. As you develop the skill of follow-up questioning, you will learn to follow the producer's lead. You will usually disorient the dreamer by asking questions suggested by your reading of some patriarch's pet dream theory rather than those suggested by the dream or its producer.

For instance, consider Nicholas's dream about the intake notes described in the Appendix. Suppose I had told him that the black couple who asked him to make the notes or pay twenty cents represented his shadow or his repressed instinctual side. Psychological terms, even when accurately used, distract the dreamer from the immediacy of his dream feelings. A statement about his shadow would have given Nicholas less freedom than the question, "Why did you cast the couple as black?" In response to such a question, Nicholas relived the dream scene and told us something more specific and meaningful to him than any acceptance or denial of a general psychological term could convey. He responded, "That would signify part of me and my lady that is better connected to the earth, more natural and easygoing." This response sheds more light on the meaning of the couple than could any labels.

It is risky to assume anything in your questioning. Though you may love German shepherd dogs and see in them love and loyalty, another dream producer may use them to represent vicious, untrustworthy, and overly aggressive characteristics of a dream figure. Keep in mind whose dream you are exploring. When it is your own, your associations are the last word. When it is someone else's dream, his associations will tell the tale. When you interview another dreamer, you are dreaming about his dream, letting your own associations and hunches flow. This can provide you with hypotheses as to the meaning of the other's dream that may trigger the dreamer's own ability to relate the dream to his life. But you must remember which is the producer's dream and which is your own fantasy about that dream. One example of the helpfulness of an interviewer involves Nicholas, who dreamed that he was one of several soldiers who were about to be executed. His interviewer, who was his girlfriend, let her own imagination picture the scene. Then she asked, "What were the soldiers wearing?" Nicholas laughed and replied, "Fatigues. We were all in fatigues!" The meaning was clear to him: Nicholas was working himself to death lately, but he had made valiant efforts to deny the fact. Had it not been for his girlfriend's effort to picture the dream herself, Nicholas probably would have missed the important pun.

An Appreciation for Metaphoric Expressions. Most dreams use symbolic metaphor to refer to, describe, and illuminate certain characteristics of the dreamer's life and relationships. As we have just seen, the visual pun in Nicholas's execution dream was the key to its message. Some puns and metaphors take more questioning to uncover.

Virginia Jack, an operating-room nurse, brought us a difficult dream. The starring character in her drama was Dr. James, whom she had described as a "pretty good surgeon" at the hospital where she worked. He remined her of no one and of no event in her life. When her interviewer asked if the doctor was at all like her father, she replied "no," but she did say he was older than her father. The discussion was stalled. The interviewer persisted and said, "Is that *all* that comes to mind about Old Doc James?" Virginia laughed. "Well, his nickname is Jack-the-Ripper if that's of any interest." When asked why he had that nickname, she explained, "When he is operating, he has a habit of carelessly handing the cutting instruments back to the nurses. He frequently cuts their fingers or hands, so we call him Jack-the-Ripper." The interviewer followed the lead, asking, "When have you felt cut, in the way you feel cut by Jack-the-Ripper?" "Hmmm . . . I feel cut by my brother's lack of interest in relating to me. This hurt cuts, and I feel cut off from him. And you know, I usually think of my brother as older than my father because he is so conservative." Virginia was tuning in to her dream producer's intent as she saw the verbal pun relating Jack-the-Ripper to her brother, who also had the name Jack. This dream was one in a series which began to show Virginia how many of her attitudes and actions had been molded by her exaggerated need to win approval from her distant, older brother.

Metaphorical thinking is crucial to the understanding of dreams. If you can truly appreciate metaphor as a style of expression, you will be less likely to get bogged down by translating dream images into words that make sense. The pleasure you take in the wit displayed by your dream puns and metaphor will lead you back to the fullness of the dream itself. After discovering the meaning of the puns, metaphors, and symbolic action of a dream, you will be led back to a new experience of the dream in its own language. When you do this, you will see how much better the dream "says it" than any interpretation into words ever could.

Familiarity with Basic Structural Tendencies of Dreams and Dream Imagery. The structure of dream language is usually quite different from the structures by which we understand our waking reality. When you interview yourself or a fellow dreamer, it will help if you know the ropes in the dream world. You can familiarize yourself with the general mechanics of this world by studying your own dreams, by reading and working with the dreams of others, and by studying what dream explorers have written.

Following is a list of the basic structural tendencies I have found most frequently in dreams.

1. *Almost all dreams directly concern the dreamer.* Except in very rare instances when we dream about future events somewhat removed from us, we dream about people, places, things, and events that portray some aspect of ourselves or represent our feelings about important people and issues in our daily lives. Even the most bizarre dreams of psychic perceptions or of dream journeys into other dimensions of reality often serve to enhance our perception of our daily existence.

Dreams can be interpreted on the *subjective* level, where each figure is seen as an aspect of the dreamer's personality, hopes and fears, struggles and achievements. In interpreting a dream on the *objective* level, you treat the figures in it as who and what they seem to be. When you dream about a friend you have not seen in years, you have probably used his or her image to represent some part of yourself which is like that friend. If you dream of family members with whom you share an active relationship, you may well be dreaming about the dynamics of your relationship with them. It is generally agreed that dreams are often best interpreted on both levels. When you dream about your husband, you may be dreaming about your feelings toward him, about the way you relate to each other, or about that part of yourself he represents for you. You may, on the other hand, be perceiving some personality pattern or future event which actually pertains to him.

In Alan Vaughan's "Looking for Crosby" dream (Chapter 1), it made sense for him to consider Frank Sinatra, Bing Crosby, and Hope as different aspects of himself. Sinatra and Hope represented some of his professional personality characteristics, and Crosby represented his professional goal. A few determined souls have tried to interpret all the people and objects in a dream as a part of the dreamer. We could think of the sports arena in Alan's dream as a part of him, inasmuch as his professional life is a part of him; other dreams may be more profitably interpreted on the objective level. For example, in considering Scott, in Nina's "Titanic" dream (Chapter 1), it is more useful to interpret Scott as Scott rather than as a part of Nina's personality. A case can be made for considering all dream figures on the subjective level, but I think it an extremist position. However, it is very easy to fall into the trap of seeing most of your dream people on the objective level and thereby miss out, often entirely, on the message of your dream show. You really are the star behind most of the actors in your dreams. With practice, you will learn to recognize the appropriateness of either or both levels of interpretation for a given dream image.

If you dream about someone with whom you have a rather intimate, current relationship, an objective interpretation will often be the most plausible. But a subjective interpretation of his role will sometimes be the most telling. Someone as close to you as your husband might represent not himself but some strength or weakness in you that you consciously think is in him. For instance, when a woman dreams about her husband's having an affair, it may be that she has unconsciously picked up subtle, telltale signs in day life and only in the dream state realizes what is happening. Perhaps she perceived the truth in a psychic fashion via her dream. But it might be the case that her husband represents *her* wishes to have an affair—wishes she does not care to recognize as her own and so projects onto her innocent husband. This is an example of the phenomenon called *projection.* We frequently see in others characteristics we do not realize are our own. It is often easier to project our own unacceptable feelings onto others rather than recognize them in ourselves.

Projection is a defense mechanism we all use at times to ward off anxiety that would come if we allowed ourselves to experience certain unacceptable (positive or negative) emotions or thoughts as coming from ourselves. Part of maturing is the reclaiming and "owning" of our projections. Projections are the major building blocks of dreams. Interpreting and understanding dreams is a process of reclaiming or recognizing as parts of ourselves the characteristics, thoughts, and feelings that we have projected onto other characters on our dream screen.

Negative dream figures tend to represent conflicts in the dreamer's life.

They are personifications of attitudes, beliefs, and habits that are causing the dreamer difficulty in understanding and enjoying life. Benevolent dream figures tend to represent the dreamer's strengths and achievements. While both positive and negative images can represent the dream producer's appraisal of the character of intimate friends and family, most often they represent an aspect of the dreamer's personality. You will find many examples of objective and subjective interpretations in later chapters.

2. *The action in our dreams describes the dynamics of conditions in our lives.* The hopes, fears, questions, and conflicts of our lives are the stuff dreams are made of. By understanding our dreams, we can better understand the experience of our lives. Often, though not always, a dream concerning a particular conflict will not only describe its dynamics but go on to point to a way out of the difficulty. Dreams seem most of all interested in promoting our personal growth. Our dream producer uses the events and experience of our days to illustrate where and how in our lives we need to mature and gain insight.

Dreams will often compensate for a lack of insight into ourselves, our relationships, or our daily experiences. They do this by presenting us with scenes that emphasize and often exaggerate the aspects of a situation which we have neglected to consider while awake. As Jung pointed out, the compensatory nature of dreams functions to help us recognize and integrate the various aspects of our personality by helping us to see more clearly dimensions of our personal reality which we otherwise would not know. Thus, by understanding our life experience more completely, we move toward wholeness and balance.

Dreams also seem to serve the important function of giving us "a safe space" to express feelings which we do not usually allow ourselves to express. We may be too proud to cry at a very upsetting moment. In our dreams we can cry the deepest tears, tears we need never admit to. We can let out anger we dared not express or perhaps even consciously experience while awake. Besides helping us to let off steam, these dreams warn us to reconsider the attitudes that repress the emotions which characterize our humanity. It takes energy to dam up our emotions. And it is quite impossible to repress certain feelings without inhibiting the flow of those we cherish as distinguishing us from automatons. Dreams help us to see how we block the flow of our life energy, why, and what we can reasonably do about it in our lives.

3. *Dreams offer us new insights.* An experienced interviewer will persist until he discovers something the producer did not fully realize or appreciate before the dream occurred. The interviewer or the interviewer-producer tries to find out just what the producer wanted to say through the dream.

While you may dream about familiar events and even replays of past experiences, there is always something there for you to understand within the context of the dream.

4. *Dream producers often use images collected from the experiences of the day or two preceding the dream.* Dream images that remind the dreamer of an experience still easily remembered increase the probability of easy, vivid associations, which can translate the dream into familiar terms.

Suppose you dreamt of John X strangling your boss. You didn't dream this *because* you received a letter from John the day earlier or *because* you saw a show on the Boston strangler the night before. It is much more likely that your producer used the image of John because his recent letter brought to your mind what an assertive, no-nonsense fellow John is. And as your producer looked about to find an image that would express how you really felt that day when your boss gave you extra work to take home, what did he choose? He chose last night's television show because its motif was a perfect expression of how you felt when your boss saddled you with the extra work.

5. *Some common dream images tend to have similar general meanings in many people's dreams.* The images in your dreams are highly personal in that they almost always mean something to you if you allow your personal associations to relate to them. Dream imagery is quite idiosyncratic, yet at the same time it is culturally molded. I once dreamt of an enormous, powerful snake that had the beautiful colors of a luminous goldfish. I knew it was my spirit and guide, and I loved it very deeply. This image, and the intensity of the dream feelings it evoked, were peculiar to me, yet the snake is a common image that tends to represent similar issues in many people's dreams. An interviewer would do well to keep in mind the various general meanings snakes are likely to express. For example, Freud pointed out that snakes often represent the dreamer's phallic, sexual concerns, conflicts, and attitudes. And Jung noticed that snakes often represent the spiritual, or integrative, forces in the personality. Knowing this may help in triggering other more specific associations in the dreamer's mind. However, such general interpretations usually should be rendered more specific in order for the dreamer to draw from them insights directly related to her present life. This can be done by taking into consideration the context of the dream in which the common symbols appear, and by being tentative about the general meaning of your ideas until one leads the dreamer to other more specific and meaningful associations. Further, if the interpreter looks only for the ways that snakes represent common themes, he could obscure and miss what might be a far more idiosyncratic use of the symbol. A college student who dreams of five snakes that threaten to attack and kill her may well be dreaming about the five exams for which she has been studying. After a week of about two hours sleep a night, little substantial food, no exercise, and a great deal of anxiety, she might well picture her exams, and not her sex or spiritual life, as five very threatening snakes.

As you continue your study of dreams, you will come across an increasing number of images which can be clarified by a skillful, nondogmatic reference to their common, if very general, meanings. It might be helpful to discuss a few common images to orient you toward their use.

Often, when people dream of being in a Victorian house, they are dreaming about Victorian attitudes they hold and which are usually causing them some trouble. Just what attitudes are being explored will be defined by the action and context of the dream as well as by the associations related to them. This is generally true even in the dreams of people who live in or are surrounded by Victorian architecture. Of course, in some cases the Victorian style of a dream friend's house may be quite coincidental to the major emphasis in the dream. The house might represent the attitudes of its owner. There are rules of thumb to assist you here. If the dreamer notes the architectural style of a dream house, it is probable that the style is a significant feature of the dream. If so, the interviewer might ask the producer if the particular architectural style suggests something useful in the interpretation of the dream.

Rooms often suggest certain areas of concern to the dreamer. Living rooms may point to daily living conditions or recent conscious family concerns. Bedrooms may refer to sex, private issues, or sleeping activities such as dreaming, refreshment, or tranquility. Dormitories are common in dreams of people who are studying their dreams in groups. Basements can contain unconscious, forgotten, and rejected parts of the dreamer's life, as can attics. Most people look down on *base*ment concerns but are more aware of the possible value of things found in an attic. However, sometimes there are treasures buried in the dreamer's basement just as there might be valuable things stored away in attics. Patti, a very progressive woman, once dreamed that she found a priceless painting in her mother's attic, which she had thought was filled with junk that needed to be cleared out. Her producer-self was trying to show her that, while many of the rigid, reactionary attitudes she inherited from her mother indeed needed to be discarded, she had also inherited some valuable characteristics from her. The dream encouraged Patti to appreciate the beneficial aspects of her similarities to her mother rather than throw the baby out with the bath water in her efforts to "develop" her personality.

Water frequently represents the spirit of life. Oceans, rivers, or bays may suggest the unconscious turbulent or calm emotions, or perhaps— in the case of bays—closed in or protected feelings. Shoes many times are images of the dreamer's footing or various qualities of comprehension or under*standing*.

When figures die or are dead in a dream, this may mean that the part of the dreamer represented by the dying person is losing its influence in the dreamer's life. This may or may not be desirable, according to the context of the dream. On very rare occasions, a dream can forecast the death of the dead dream person. President Lincoln, shortly before his assassination, dreamed that he saw the coffin of someone lying in state, surrounded by military guards. When he asked one of the soldiers who was in the coffin, he was told that it was President Lincoln. This is a most unusual case. When you dream of someone's death, you will probably learn most by asking what it might mean that the father, or Frank Sinatra, or Rita Hayworth in you is dying. How do you feel about this event?

A dream producer will often use cars to represent the dreamer's physical body, or perhaps her way of getting around in life—the personality. One producer used the image of a rootbeer-colored Cadillac to symbolize a lighthearted, sturdy, yet easily maneuverable and fun part of herself which she seldom drove, or expressed in life. Her style was more practical and work oriented, like the small and practical truck she owned in day life. Her dream producer was encouraging her to make room for a rootbeer-colored Cadillac in her garage.

Suggesting to the absentminded, waking producer that cars can symbolize one's way of getting around in the world is at times very catalytic in helping the dreamer to tune into the appropriate wavelength of the dream; however, it is not always so. The other night I dreamt that I was repairing and polishing my car so that I could sell it at a good price. When I interviewed my dream self, suggesting this general meaning, there was no response. I had to let go of my first guess before the obvious image of polishing reminded me of the work I was doing on my book. I was being encouraged to polish and repair certain parts of it before giving it to an agent. When I understood this, the details of the dream fell into place, and the dream had the effect of revitalizing my flagging efforts to polish my writing.

The above examples are only a few common dream images. You will naturally learn more about common dream images and dream themes as you discover them in your own and others' dreams, and you will become less likely to use their common meanings in a restrictive, dictionary fashion. You will probably be more impressed by the contexts in which they appear and thereby be more likely to use them in a suggestive, exploratory manner.

6. *Just as dreams usually express themselves through metaphor and symbols, they often use sequence and juxtaposition as an expression of cause and effect. Dream action is neither accidental nor simply coincidental.* When you are working with a dream which portrays a conflict and feel puzzled about what one dream scene has to do with another, consider the following hypothesis. The first scene describes the conflict or issue being examined. The action in the first scene "causes" or results in the action of the second scene. The second scene results in the third and so on, until the last scene, which usually points to a possible direction toward the resolution of the conflict portrayed in the earlier scenes. This progression of scenes can also be reviewed in terms of where the dreamer now stands with the problem. The first scene, or scenes, may illuminate the dynamics and development of the problem in the dreamer's life. The middle scenes might pinpoint just where the dreamer is now in relation to the problem, and the last scene might indicate possible future resolutions or ways of dealing with the issue.

This tendency of dreams to use sequence and juxtaposition as if *therefore* and *because* could be written on our mental screens between scenes has occurred to me often as I have worked with small groups. Suggesting such relationships between scenes has clarified many difficult dreams.

In Alan Vaughan's "Looking for Crosby" dream, when we put a mental *therefore* between the scenes, the dream clicked into place. *Because* Alan was acting or moving from his Frank Sinatra attitudes, he (therefore) could not make contact with his very successful yet humble Bing Crosby professional goals. The third scene was the suggested resolution to the problem, that Alan use his Bob Hope ability to laugh at himself and enjoy a light and easy 1940s humor about life to get him in touch with his Crosby self.

In Nina's "Titanic" dream, there were three major scenes. The first, in which Scott asked her to go on a voyage with him aboard the Titanic, gave her a rather pointed dream appraisal of where their relationship was headed. The dream had responded to her incubation question with a clear statement but also with an examination of where she was now with the matter—at the bon voyage party, going nowhere and wasting herself and her energy. The dream then cut to the skeleton-infant with the skull and crossbones on his heart to indicate one possible result of attending and of abruptly leaving the bon voyage party. She had heard part of the dream message. She left Scott because she could no longer deny her own better judgment. However, she did not say her adieus to him, neither explaining nor understanding herself the unresolved conflicts she felt in leaving. In order for her to have said "good-bye," rather than to flee saying "I'm going away for awhile," she would have been obliged to study the dynamics of her relationship more fully a bit sooner than she finally did.

Patrick dreamt that he and some good friends were sailing peacefully down a lovely river. In the boat with him were Werner Erhard, the founder of Erhard Seminar Trainings (est), whom Patrick considered to be a brilliantly skilled but overbearing, loud, self-centered self-development expert who seemed to have difficulty in forming a lasting love relationship of the sort Patrick was searching for. Also in the boat was James, an est trainer or teacher whom Patrick admired, and who seemed to know how to use his est experience with self-growth in forming a warm and lasting love relationship with his wife. In the first scene, Patrick remarked that, for once, Werner was not stealing the show and was in his place as a welcome sailing companion. On the boat, Patrick was given a test of some sort, which he passed with flying colors. He felt happy, competent, and supported by James, the est trainer. Then, gazing at the magnificent scenery, Patrick saw one of his favorite mountains, which was part of a state park. It was now crowded by modern housing developments. In the next scene, still in the boat, he was given the same test again, but this time he was finding it terribly difficult, and Werner Erhard was very displeased with him for his poor performance. Patrick ended the dream feeling unsure of himself, insecure, and unhappy.

Without knowing more than this, what might you guess the sequence of scenes would indicate?

What occurred to us was that Patrick was content with his performance in a general test of his competence in living and growing when he focused on attitudes and people whom he saw as in harmony with nature and capable of strong, enduring love relationships (represented by James). When he was distracted by or focused on whatever he represented by this defaced mountain, he ended up feeling unsure of himself and distressed at his performance.

Hearing this structural sketch, Patrick suddenly said, "O.K., you don't have to say any more. I've got it." What he "got" was that the defaced mountain represented his attraction to people who were very achievement oriented, wealthy, and successful. He hoped that through such people he might find security and ease. In fact, the night before he had been out with such a person, who was an architect. The dream logic of these juxtaposed scenes triggered a realization in Patrick that, whenever he focused on his own extremely goal-oriented attitudes or surrounded himself with people who exemplify them, he felt rather inferior and insecure. He compared himself to a standard that he honestly did not admire, for he felt that such extreme concentration on financial or personal-growth success defaced the landscape and his own nature. When he nevertheless focused on this standard, he felt unsure of himself and failed the test that was so easy before. In the person of Werner Erhard, he criticized himself for not measuring up. After understanding the dream, Patrick still had to ask himself what sort of attitudes, goals, and people would harmonize with his nature instead of defacing it. The James figure was a good hint.

7. *The concepts of underdogs, topdogs, and secret saboteurs can be very useful in working with some dreams.* Fritz Perls,[1] the founder of Gestalt psychotherapy, first developed the concept of topdog versus underdog. Ann Faraday has elaborated these concepts and that of the secret saboteur in work with dream interpretation.[2]

Briefly, Perls has labeled the "shoulds" and internal authority voices in us as *topdogs*—relentless perfectionists, always telling us that, if we give in to our impulses instead of doing what we "ought" to do, something terrible will surely happen. In the section on journal reviews in Part V I relate my dream of losing precious time not ice skating. At the time of the dream, I was in a painful conflict with my "study and be serious" topdog, who threatened that, if I dared skate at all, my plans for a career in psychology would go out the window. I believed my topdog's dictate that nothing less than perfection and total application of my energies to skating would do. I feared that, if I tempted myself with even a little skating, I would fall into the trap of perfectionism, abandon my studies, and become a skater with little intellectual development. The important needs of my personality for a creative and physical outlet were being largely denied. This other part of my personality crystallized into the *underdog,* who planted in my mind voices saying, "I want to go skating," which would occur at frequent intervals and haunt my days that were then so far removed from the sport. At night, underdog would taunt me with dreams of the joy of gliding and dancing on the ice. Underdogs that represent the basic needs which topdog's strictures frustrate will fight to get their way even if they have to content themselves with simply frustrating topdog's goals.

This would seem to be the case in Patrick's dream described above. One of his topdogs insisted that he constantly "work" at personal growth and development, and that this growth should bring with it financial rewards. In his dream, Werner Erhard represented topdog's growth-work ethic. The housing developments represented Patrick's "success at all costs" topdog. While the Erhard topdog is in his place as a companion, it's smooth sailing. But as soon as Patrick focuses on his goal-oriented success and security topdog feelings, Erhard is there criticizing him for the fact that he doesn't measure up to the success standards of either topdog. Underdog's revenge is to sabotage the second test, making it a miserable experience for Patrick, who is trying to please topdog.

Secret saboteurs, as Faraday calls them, can be topdogs or underdogs who manage mysteriously to frustrate us in our dreams. When events seem to conspire to frustrate you in your dreams, you might try personifying the sabotaging event and asking it why it is out to defeat you. For instance, you could ask the saboteur why he has arranged the storm that blew your car off the road. If you miss a plane, find your wallet missing, or try to reach out to people you can't quite touch, a secret saboteur is at work in your dream. Personify him, and ask him why he is frustrating you. If his response comes in strong, judgmental tones, full of shoulds and warnings of disaster if you do not do as he says, then you can be fairly sure that a topdog who is made up of these exaggerated and often worn-out beliefs is causing your dream and corresponding life problem. If, instead, your dialogue with the secret saboteur reveals him to be a complaining victim, pleading for forgiveness from topdog, then an underdog is resentfully sabotaging your conscious intents to live up to topdog's unrealistic demands.

Many of the most dutiful, docile, and charming wives of the world are living under the spell of a topdog belief system which decrees that one of woman's roles in life is to obey and defer to her husband. As family therapists know only too well, these same sweet, nondemanding, women may make their men pay for their deference as the underdogs, crying out for a sense of individual identity, personal achievement, and autonomy, sabotage their marriages. This kind of underdog often gets revenge by riddling the environment with oppressive undercurrents of resentment and nagging. These are the wives who seem to whine even when they are not complaining. The underdog part of a personality *will* express itself, even if it must do so in distorted, destructive ways.

The resolution, however, is not usually as simple as telling topdog to get out of your life as some Gestalt therapists suggest. Kow-towing to topdog has its attractions. The wives who give up all their decision-making power and live in a subordinate relationship to their husbands are freed of the adult responsibilities that come from making decisions. They are free to let their husbands take both the responsibility and the blame for decisions, especially those which don't work out to their satisfaction.

8. *Dreams of the same night often treat the same issue.* When you are working with a dream, other dreams and dream fragments of the same night can often provide clues to its meaning. Even apparently coincidental events in the days following the dream can sometimes trigger an understanding of obscure dream elements.

9. *Images that transform themselves in dreams tend to represent past, present, or future transformations in the dreamer's life, attitudes, or feelings.* Transformation of dream images can reflect psychological growth or regression. In other cases, dream images can transform themselves in immediate response to the dreamer's expectations. Fear often distorts the apparent nature of dream images. As we shall see, if the dreamer can overcome his fear of terrifying dream figures, they almost always transform into friendly figures or disappear from the dream action. When you are confused as to the exact nature of a dream element, experiment with the idea that the confusion itself suggests a past or future transformation of the symbols and thus of your attitudes and feelings which they represent. For example, one dreamer was confused as to the nature of the insects in a dream. Were they praying mantises, which serve the important function of eating many other insects harmful to growing crops, or were they locusts, a deadly threat to crops (personal maturation)? In this case, the dreamer, who had participated in countless growth groups and classes, was beginning to wonder if his efforts to clear the bugs out of his personality were, at this point beneficial to his development or crops. Was he overdoing it, studying, examining, and analyzing the spontaneity out of his life? Was he treating his crops with praying mantises, or was he subjecting them to a plague of locusts?

10. *Recurring dreams and nightmares are the dream producer's method of last resort to try to impress upon the dreamer something he or she* *needs to understand but has not recognized.* A skillful interviewer, sensing that the dreamer is frightened and averse to exploring recurring, unpleasant dreams, might suggest to the waking producer that he recount the dream with the relish of a child enjoying a horror movie. Laughter can result from telling a dream story in this manner, and the humor can effectively free the dreamer to explore the dream with interest.

An unusual recurring dream was recounted to us by Si. For twenty years he had repeatedly dreamed of a tornado headed toward his house. Invariably the tornado would change course at the last minute and do him no harm, leaving him much relieved. With questioning, it appeared that this dream seemed to come to Si toward the end of a period of significant stress at work. Si was the principal at a public high school, where he had worked for twenty years, the same period as the dream's recurrence. In this case, the repeating dream acted as a signal that all was or would be well and that Si would survive. The dream came in times of stress to reassure the dreamer. Most recurring dreams however, are trying to tell us something we are trying not to acknowledge.

11. *The dreamer's mood, feelings, and reflections on the dream, as he or she dreams it, are as important as the dream action itself.* How the dreamer feels about the people and events in the dream, both during and after it, reveals a good deal about his or her inner feelings about the life situation portrayed in the dream. Henri, a Frenchman who lived with his lively wife in a luxurious house on the Riviera, told me of a very vivid dream. He dreamt that the gardener had dug up the grounds around the house. There were tunnels and dirt mounds so high that it was hard to see the house at all. The gardener had apparently begun many different landscaping projects at once. It seemed as if the gardener had gone berserk, digging everywhere and planting nowhere.

I asked Henri what part of his life was like the grounds in his dream. He laughed, and replied that his own work was like the gardener's. He had recently begun many different projects in different parts of the world and was wondering if he had been overly ambitious. He hoped, of course, that, like the gardener, he would be able to plant seeds that would lead to a blossoming of his business interests. Since Henri had presented me with this dream at a dinner table, I was reluctant to pursue it, but he insisted, not believing that the dream could tell him anything important anyway. I asked him how he felt about the state of his (dream) grounds. He repeated that one could hardly see the house. Then he said that he was actually very upset, and inappropriately saddened by the dream. I finally asked him if his many business interests and the travel they entailed might have the effect of preventing him from seeing much of the home he so loved, and of his life with his wife in it. He simply said, "Yes, that is true. I miss my home very much." At this point, Henri's wife said, "You'd never know it the way you travel and work so much!" In fact, Henri had begun the dinner telling us how much he liked his business and the travel he was doing to expand it. Both he and his wife had made a point of saying how much they valued their independence from each other and what a wonderful marriage they had. If Henri, in the dream, had felt happy or glad, or even hopeful that the gardener's work would sooner or later result in lovely grounds, we could have interpreted the dream as showing that Henri's ambitious work had cut him off from his home life, but, as soon as the groundwork was laid in his business affairs, he would be able to "see" his home again, beautified by his effort.

Henri recognized that, though he would like to think so, this was not the case. His dream feelings of distress at seeing his grounds torn up and ransacked told him that things on the homefront were not as gay as he and his wife had led themselves to think. Henri's reaction to this dream scene opened an important avenue of neglected communication between him and his wife.

12. *Dreams that can be interpreted literally can also be true symbolically.* All dreams should be briefly examined to see if they might contain a literal message or warning. A few dreams, acting on unconscious or psychic cues, can give us obvious suggestions for action in a matter we need to attend to but have overlooked in our day lives. Dreams in which we are extremely fatigued may be giving us good advice to catch up on our rest. In dreams where you notice that some part of your body is not functioning properly, you may be telling yourself to take care of a problem you had not noticed or admitted existed. Sometimes dreams give us literal warnings about being prepared for upcoming opportunities, challenges, and personal and social disaster.

Some dream researchers stop here. They suggest that the dreamer should try to interpret her dream only if a literal understanding does not apply. There are two major disadvantages to this approach. First, by interpreting a dream literally and letting it go at that, it is easy to mistake a symbolic warning of, say, a decaying tooth for the physical event. Thus the dreamer might make an appointment with a dentist for the following week while the real ache may be occurring within her psyche, work, or marriage right now. It seems very important to consider each dream from both a literal and a symbolic standpoint.

Even dreams that do prove to be literally true may well be just as true symbolically. In fact, the symbolic meaning of these dreams may be the more enduring one. Some sources[3] have even suggested that the psychological conditions represented in these dreams are the cause of the literal, physical manifestation of the dream event in day life.

Dreams may come before or after the actual events they literally portray. Many consider the actual events to be a synchronistic, or meaningfully coincidental, underlining of an important psychological issue, which is thus emphasized by its representation in day life. The universe seems to be saying, "Take a closer look at this. It is important."

13. *The dream itself says it best.* Of all the structural tendencies a good interviewer should know about dreams, this is the most important. Whatever the meaning of your dream, or that of your friend, efforts at understanding it should lead you to an appreciation for the unique and skillful expression of that meaning in the dream itself. An interpretation should lead you back to the dream not away from it. Once understood, a dream will have the greatest impact on the dreamer if it is relived and remembered in its own pictorial-feeling language. Once you have translated a dream and can then easily understand its language, you will be able to realize the richness of its symbolism, which cannot be captured in words.

The Interview.

How to Begin. Now that you have been briefed on how to approach your dream producer and know something about the general nature of his kind of work, it will help if you have some specific questions to ask him so that the interview will get off to a good start. Remember that whether you play both the role of producer and that of interviewer or whether you take only one role and assign the other to a friend, the procedure will follow the same lines. In conducting many dream interviews with my students' dream producers, I have found certain questions to be consistently the most effective in revealing the meaning of a dream. For the most part, these questions ask the producer to simply *define* and *describe* the dream imagery. Asking dream producers to give their associations to a particular dream element often results in vague and tangential responses. By defining and describing the images and events in the dream, the producer will keep to his dream and be less likely to free associate according to patterns suggested by vague and perhaps unconcious recollections of dream theories. Usually relevant associations will make up or accompany definitions and descriptions of dream images. These tend to be the least contrived, most spontaneous associations a producer will offer, so be a gentle interviewer and give the producer time to expand on his responses. You can use the list of initial questions presented here as a cue card. Not all questions will apply to all dreams. Not all dreams will require a full-length interview before the producer suddenly realizes what his dream-show is all about; these questions might trigger an intuitive understanding of the dream at any point of the interview. You may or may not wish to proceed further after the dream meaning has become clear. However, further exploration of the dream might modify the meaning taken from it; at the very least, it usually clarifies and confirms the dreamer's understanding of the dream.

You may find the producer more willing to answer your questions if you first ask him to pretend that you come from another planet. This way, when you ask him, "Who is Bob Hope?" he won't simply answer, "You know who Bob Hope is!" and miss the opportunity of discovering his associations to the man. So often what a dreamer assumes to be general knowledge or fact about a given figure or event is really a very personal web of attitudes, beliefs, and associations. Ask the producer to be as patient with you as you will be with him. Use the interviewer's cue card only after the producer has reread and then told you his dream in the *first person* and *present tense,* as if he were reliving it.

Initial Questions.

1. When you reexperience the feelings you had in the dream, what do they remind you of in your current life?

2. What would you guess the dream is about?

3. What literal meaning might the dream have?

4. Would you please describe the setting(s) of the dream?

5. If, as the producer, you were using the setting to express a certain mood and indicate the nature of the dream action to follow, what would these be? What areas of your life do they remind you of?

6. Who is X? *Ask the dreamer-producer to tell you who each person in the dream is. He will respond best if you remind him that you come from another planet and do not know a thing about Earth life.*

7. What is X like? *This will encourage the producer to tell you what he thinks of X, and he will usually supply associations automatically. Another way to phrase this question is to ask what kind of person X is. Encourage* *the dreamer to give you his impressions of the dream person and not to worry about being accurate or objective. If X is a person unknown to the dreamer, ask "What kind of person would you* imagine *X might be like?"*

8. Can you recognize and feel that part of you which is like X? *You may meet with a lot of resistance here, especially if the dreamer has just described someone he strongly dislikes. While you may see some of X's characteristics in the dreamer, it is risky to mention it. An offended producer won't talk much. You can always return to this or any question later when the interview has warmed up a bit.*

9. What is your waking relationship with X like? *With this question you are trying to discover the nature of the relationship—intimate, casual, troublesome, enriching, etc. The dreamer will often supply revealing anecdotes of the history of the relationship if given the chance or the encouragement.*

10. What is a Y? *Ask the producer to define each of the major objects in the dream and tell you what it is used for and how it works. Reassure him that you are interested not in scientific accuracy but in his ideas or understanding of what a Y is and how it works.*

11. What is the Y in your dream like, and what does it remind you of? *When the producer describes his dream objects, he may also add some associations, which you may or may not want to explore further.*

12. Would you please describe the major action or events in the dream and tell me what they remind you of in your waking life?

These questions need not be used in this exact order, and follow-up questions may be appropriate after any response or lack of response. As you continue to read examples of dream interviews in this book, and as you work with your own dreams, you will develop an intuitive sense for asking good follow-up questions. A flexible use of the cue card will be the most rewarding.

The answers to the initial questions will sometimes provide enough information or elaborative material to make an intuitive understanding of the dream possible. However, if it is the interviewer and not the producer who feels she has understood the dream, it is very important that the initial responses be followed up by other questions which will clarify the significance of each dream element and of the entire dream for the producer. It is appallingly easy to misinterpret another's dream. Even if her hypothesis is correct, the interviewer is better advised to keep it to herself for a while. She should ask more follow-up questions to see if (1) her hypothesis is borne out by further information and (2) she can trigger the producer's own intuitive piecing together of the dream.

Making the Most of the Interview. Usually, just below the surface of awareness, the dreamer has access to the associations needed to make sense out of the dream. Keep in mind that each dreamer produces her own dreams and, at some level, knows what the dream producer was trying to express. Good dream interpretation is, more than anything else, a matter of asking the right questions. The "right" questions are those which facilitate the dreamer's relevant associations and her ability to understand their relationship to the dream. It will help if, as you continue the interview, you ask questions using the words and images of the dream whenever possible. Asking effective follow-up questions is an intuitive art best learned by example and practice in working with your own and others' dreams.

It is often easier at first to understand the obvious metaphors of another person's dream, because waking dream producers are often quite concrete in their thinking, whereas in sleep they are masters of symbolic expression. Therefore, the interviewer working with another producer's dream will sometimes spot the metaphoric or symbolic meaning of a dream well before the producer does. When the interviewer has formulated a possible interpretation, he will be tempted to ask rather leading questions in the hope of verifying his hypothesis and of getting the dreamer to see the dream as the interviewer does. This may or may not be helpful. The interviewer must have as his goal facilitating the dreamer to find the meaning in her own dream. If he tries to prove his own ideas and hypotheses about the interpretation correct, he is likely to forget to listen to and take the dreamer's lead. His questions may become directions, and he will be less likely to encourage and receive feedback from the dream producer.

If the interviewer and producer are pressed for time, suggestions from the interviewer can greatly speed up progress. The interviewer can suggest that the dreamer consider her dream scene in light of certain relevant structural tendencies in dreams. The interviewer might also ask very leading questions and even suggest possible meanings of interpretations of the whole dream or of parts of it. These suggestions should be worded in the dream imagery as far as possible. You must be very careful when being such an active interviewer. Constantly asking for feedback, or the dreamer's opinion about your suggestions, is very, very important. Whenever you make a suggestion be sure to ask such questions as: "Does that fit?" or "Does that make sense?" or "What do you think about that?"

Asking how a proposed interpretation does not fit also can be very useful in getting onto the right track.

There will be times while working with another producer's dream when you will feel sure that she is resisting or avoiding admitting your hypothesis. This may be true. However, you could be wrong and only stubbornly attached to your hypothesis. Whichever is the case, it is almost always unwise to insist upon a given interpretation. If you are incorrect you will mislead the dreamer or distract her from the accurate appraisal of her dream. If you are correct, and the dreamer is resisting, you will be wasting your breath. If the dreamer-producer does not care to recognize a dream insight, she will not hear it no matter how loudly you shout it. Your insistence will only increase her defensiveness and make further dialogue unlikely, or at best guarded. You can always ask more questions to ease your idea across. If the producer entirely misses the message in this dream, she will be presented with the same issue in later dreams until she "gets" it.

Throughout the interview, allow silent moments. The dreamer may be linking things together just below conscious awareness. She may add important associations just after you thought that she had nothing more to say. Sometimes the dreamer will say, "I don't know why this occurs to me now but. . . ." Such apparently unrelated thoughts are often very relevant to the dream, and the interviewer should take note of them and encourage their expression. Experience will be your best guide in distinguishing what is relevant from what is not in both the interviewer's questions and the producer's responses. In order to encourage immediately relevant dialogue, remember to keep bringing attention back to the dream and to use the language and images of the dream wherever possible in the interview.

As you engage the producer, encourage her sense of play and intuitive piecing together of the dream. "Dream" the dream yourself, and enjoy its uniqueness and its imagery. These interviews can be very amusing if you allow the dreams to strike you funny.

Winding It Up. Encourage the producer (or yourself, if you are taking both roles) to play around with the pieces of the dreams you have explored. Suggest that he make a hypothesis about how they fit together. Of course, this may not be necessary if, as often happens, the dreamer has already realized what the dream means during the earlier part of the interview. If it seems appropriate, tell the dreamer how you would put the pieces together, and ask if he thinks your interpretation is appropriate. If the answer is "Ah yes, that's it!" or something of that nature, you can probably believe him. If, on the other hand, his response is something like, "Well, sort of," you can be quite sure that you've not hit home. Either your hypothesis is not quite correct or he is resisting. Dream interviews rarely end up this way, but if they do, do not force an interpretation, which should spring to life with a bit of surprise and a great deal of satisfaction. You will both have learned much through the dialogue, and this knowledge will not be wasted. The clarification and elaboration of the dream images and action will be useful in working with similar dreams that follow this one. Furthermore, the images explored in the dream often click into place a few hours or days after the interview, when the dreamer has had time to integrate the ideas and mine insights gained from the interview.

Most dreams will yield their messages to a skillful interviewer with surprisingly little effort. In the last few minutes of the interview, the producer should be encouraged to relive his dream in the light of the insights gained through the interview. However far you take the dialogue, and however clear the dream's meaning has become, the producer in you or in your friend will best appreciate that meaning by reexperiencing the dream in its own terms. Knowing the structural tendencies of a dream and translating its images into meaningful, comprehensive words is a good start in understanding it. But having a dictionary in one hand and a Berlitz phrase book in the other is hardly the way to experience the uniqueness of another language. It is by learning to think in, or live in, the picture language of your dreams that you will most vividly taste their richest meaning. When you can truly feel the emotional reality of your dream, you will be able to hold it in your heart and mind during the day. This will help you to understand your dream better as you become more familiar with the dream's imagery, and as certain daytime events trigger insights into how the dream relates to your waking life.

Most importantly, keeping the dream in mind during the day will encourage you to try out the insights you have gained from it. This may mean recognizing the dynamics of a problem in your life, and testing the dream's suggested solution. The solution may be as simple as just seeing the issue from another perspective, or it may involve taking a definite action to change the difficult situation. Sometimes living with your dream in the daytime will mean remembering that the hero or heroine of your night's drama is within you, and that you can draw upon his or her strength to deal with the problem you explored in the dream.

Recording the Interview. If, in the interview, you play the roles of both the producer and the interviewer, you will probably find that writing out the interview in your journal will be more effective than simply thinking it out in your mind. In Part V you can see how Ginger used her journal to interview herself about her dream of "Keeping the Proselytizer Out." As you continue, you will read other examples of journal interviews which the dreamers adapted to their specific dreams and tastes. It is surprising how much of a dream becomes clear by just writing out a few questions and answers. For more difficult dreams, like Ginger's, you may need to conduct a more lengthy interview, but it will be worth your while to do so. Interviewing the part of yourself that created a dream and writing down the highlights of your dialogue is the most practical and effective approach to daily dream interpretation that my students and I have found.

Asking a friend or someone with experience in dream interpretation to play the part of interviewer will usually render the dialogue more engaging. Especially with difficult or long dreams, a good interviewer will help you stay focused on the dream. The interviewer might also be able to see certain aspects of your dream more clearly than you do and thus ask questions or make suggestions that can hasten your understanding. You will also learn a great deal by playing the part of interviewer for other dreamers. It is much easier to concentrate on the process of dream interpretation when you must find the questions that best elicit revealing responses. Working with dreams in small groups will multiply the benefits of your dream explorations. By listening to different styles of interviewing, you will learn very quickly which approaches work best. A group meeting also provides a forum for pooling each member's talents in dream interpretation. What is more, the humor generated by a group of friends sharing dream stories is a tremendous boon to the free flow of associations and ideas so necessary to the interpretation process. In the Chapter 12, you will find suggestions for conducting your own dream groups.

After exploring your dreams with a friend or a group of friends, it is a good idea to write out as much of the interview as you can remember. A record of these dialogues will help you in working with the dream at home as well as in working with future dreams of a similar nature. Tape recordings of your shared dream interviews can be amazingly instructive to both the interviewer and the producer. They permit both a detailed review of the issues discussed and an opportunity for a more objective appraisal of both the interviewer's skill and the producer's facility for exploring his or her own dream shows.

Taking Your Dreams to Heart.   The final step in understanding a dream is to let its meaning affect your life. You will not learn very much from your dreams if you keep them filed away in a notebook. Carry your dreams in your heart as you go through the day. Test the insights and ideas you gain from your dream study in the light of day. Do they deepen your understanding of yourself and your relationships? Do the solutions and ideas you found in your incubated dreams work out well in waking life? When you imagine that you have the qualities of a dream heroine who knew how to get along well with her son, do you find it easier in fact to relate to him? If, like Ginger, you keep in your heart what it felt like to cut yourself off from someone because of stereotyped assumptions, can you catch yourself when you are about to do the same thing in your life?

It is important to test your dream insights and interpretations in your waking life. If they make your life better for you, then use them. Remember the dream images which remind you of personality quirks that get you into trouble. And remember how your dreams suggested you might deal with them. This will help you to accept your own weaknesses and those you find in others with greater compassion and understanding and, sometimes, humor. It will also assist you in overcoming some of your more troublesome characteristics and habits.

Many of your dreams will present you with positive, helpful images. Ardell dreamt of Bob Hope and shipments of gold; Alan dreamt of Bob Hope and Bing Crosby; Ginger dreamt of the born-again Christian. By keeping these images alive in their hearts, these dreamers were inspired to feel, act, and live better. Even your most troubled dreams often include a positive, beneficent figure. The good guys may not win in every dream, but if you try to concentrate on their characteristics during the day, they will help you out. If you recognize that the strong, brave, wise, beautiful, and talented figures in your dreams are as much a part of you as the demons and villains, you will begin to understand your dreams and yourself better.

Just how far you go in using the dream interpretation technique described above will depend on how long it takes you to understand what your dream producer is trying to express and on how interested you are in pursuing the meaning of a given dream and each of its images. Some dreams are easy to understand, and some are very difficult. This is a function of the relatedness you feel to the dream images, the vividness with which you recall them, your awareness of their metaphoric nature, and the degree of resistance or eagerness you feel in dealing with them.

When you start to consider the meaning of an incubated dream, one advantage is that you will have a good hunch as to the meaning right from the start, because you have asked for the dream. You can then proceed with the interview to see if your incubation was indeed successful. My "Otto Preminger" dream (Chapter 1) was easy to interpret, in part at least because I had incubated it and knew what it was likely to be about. Ginger's dream of "Keeping the Proselytizer Out" was easier to work with because it was extremely vivid and had an obvious relation to her incubation question of the night before. It was nevertheless a rather difficult dream to interpret because, as is often the case where the dreamer is trying to keep someone or something out of her private space, there was a certain degree of resistance to overcome. However, having incubated the dream, Ginger was determined to figure it out even though it took a bit of time.

Some dreams which preview future events in our lives are often almost impossible to interpret, especially if we have no idea that they are showing us a picture from our future. If you review your dream journal monthly for a year or so, you will probably discover that a few of your most perplexing dreams were of this nature. We shall discuss this sort of dream more fully in the chapter on ESP in dreams.

The majority of your dreams will probably be neither very easy nor very difficult to interpret, but the real bread and butter of almost everyone's dream life is made up of the dreams that need interpretation. Dream interviewing is a sleuth's sport. There is a bit of Sherlock Holmes in every one of us. Following are two interviews between myself and two members of a Dream Meeting composed of people who were exploring dreams for the first time in their lives.

In the second meeting, Rachael, a social worker, began the interview by saying that she had incubated a dream with the phrase, "Why have I been so depressed lately?" Then she told us what she dreamed that night.

I am outdoors, and the world looks green and beautiful. Amid trees and plants, I see Barbra Streisand, lying dead in an open coffin. I feel very sad that she has died. Then I wonder if she might not be dead, but in a very deep sleep. ("Streisand's Coffin")

Gayle. What do you think the dream might be about?

Rachael. I don't have any idea. It is so odd.

G. Who is Barbra Streisand? Pretend I've never heard of her.

R. Well, she's a very creative and successful actress.

G. What is she like? What do you know and think about her?

R. Every artistic career she has tried she has been a success in. She is very talented and can sing, act, compose, design, and who knows what else. I like her. I hear she is very good to the people she likes. I admire her art, and I've always felt I would meet her one day.

G. Can you picture Barbra Streisand as a part of you?

R. No. You mean she might represent a part of *me?* I don't think so. I think I was dreaming about Barbra Streisand not myself.

G. What else comes to your mind when you think of her?

R. Well, she comes from Brooklyn; so do I. And just after I moved to California, so did she.

G. Rachael, in our first meeting, didn't you say that you are really an artist, and that you have a job as a social worker mainly to earn money?

R. Yes. What I really like to do is write poetry and fiction, and paint and sculpt.

G. If you were producing a movie about the different parts of yourself, whom would you cast in the role of your creative, artistic self?

R. I guess Barbra. She would fit, in that her art is varied like mine, and I've always identified with her in an odd way. Still, she's far more talented than I.

G. So, what is the action in the dream?

R. I see that Barbra is dead.

G. What would it mean that the Barbra Streisand in you is dead?

R. That my artistic, creative self is dead, or at least in a very deep sleep.

G. Have you been doing much art work lately?

R. None! . . . I've got it. I asked why I've been depressed for the last two weeks. The dream is showing me that at least part of the problem is that I have let my creative self die, or nearly. For the last few months, I've been very disparaging of my artistic talents and have not been using them at all; that has a depressing effect on my whole life. The dream setting is beautiful when I really look at it. When I write or paint of sculpt, I see the world more clearly, more vividly, and it looks beautiful. If I had more faith in my talent, or if I could accept my artistic work as a wonderful part of my life, without demanding excellence, I would do more of it. My life seems drab because I haven't been letting my creative self live. That is obvious to me now. I can only lose by disparaging my talents. I need to resurrect whatever there is of Barbra Streisand in me and let her express herself.

G. I remember a dream you told us last week where you saw fantastic, clear, ceiling-to-floor panels with transparency designs in them. When one of the class members asked you if it would be possible to create ones like them, you said yes. But even though you thought the panels would be a great idea, you kept thinking of reasons not to actually make them. Has that sort of dream come up before?

R. Oh yes. I've gotten several good ideas for my art work from my dreams. I've thrown them all away because I just don't think of myself as talented enough to make the effort worthwhile.

G. What happens inside you as you relive the dream now?

R. Wow! I am aware of how sad it would be to let Barbra Streisand die when there is so much beauty around her. I am inspired at the thought that there is a Barbra Streisand in me. Reliving the dream makes me want to go home and start a new art project.

As so often when someone dies in a dream, a part of Rachael was dead, or at least quite unconscious. Dreams often exaggerate to get their point across. Death in dreams rarely signifies a psychic warning of a real person's death.

A more complicated dream was presented by an engaging fifty-year-old school teacher from Pennsylvania. Joe had taken a year off from his work and his marriage and come to California to immerse himself in some of the self-development programs which abound there in an effort to get to know himself better. He had become fed up with his life in the East. Joe, like the other dreamers in this meeting, had been working with his dreams for only two weeks when he told us of a dream where he was trying to find the pet tiger that was hiding from him. When, at the end of the dream, he finally found the tiger, he was dressed in women's clothes. One week later, Joe told us the following dream:

I was driving in a car at night and I saw a group of people ahead. I didn't like their looks, so I made sure the doors were locked and the high-beam lights on. I drove straight ahead. The people weren't there. Next, I was in a building and walking my pet lion. He was on a leash. I gave him a lot of leash. He would trot ahead of me and stop, crouch down, wait for me, then he would spring ahead. I was giving him a little exercise; it was fun.

Then I was sitting next to some guy named Bill. We were at a national teachers' convention. He was smooth, handsome, a good talker, and powerful. He wanted to talk about Fred, a friend of mine, who is active in my field.

Bill said I should call Fred and have him call Bill back. I figured that was strange, but since it was a local call, maybe I should humor him. I realized it was really a long-distance call and said that I would have to be reimbursed $1.11. Bill regarded this as a smear, saying, "If you think I'm going to my room at this time of night for $1.11, you're mistaken."

Then we were in front of the room. There was a meeting of the California State Branch of teachers who were going to recite the Pledge of Allegiance and give a weather report. We went back to our seats, and I said to Bill, "I don't need to have the money in advance, but I certainly expect to be repaid." He replied, "You know what? You're going to do it because I know you. At bottom you know you're not worth much." I was astounded. Then he said, "In the future, whenever people run for office in the organization, the resumes should carry a psychological evaluation. If we know what they're like, we'll pick the right people."

An out-of-state guest, sitting in Bill's place, asked, "Where are the little ones?" meaning the little women or girls. Someone said they were still on the second floor at their meeting. You see, the hosts, who were the California contingent, were all female, and the newcomers from out of state were males. The guest was frustrated because he was not able to find the pretty young women or, as he called them, "some sweet young things." The chairperson started to call off the names of the members of the Pennsylvania delegation. She skipped over my city. I jumped up and said, "I'm from Pittsburgh."

I suddenly realized that a good friend had been sitting next to me all this time. I told him I doubted that any of the Erie County delegates would come. ("Pet Lion")

Thus the dream ended. Here is the verbatim account of the dialogue that followed:

Gayle. Joe, have you any ideas as to what this is all about?

Joe. Well, during the day following the dream, I realized that there is a prototype for Bill. I think his nickname is Bill. I met him at a convention once and got on with him fairly well. He ran for national president of our organization. He is smooth and a good talker. He probably could have acted the way this guy acted in the dream. The other connection that I have is that often I speak of myself as being powerful. And I think people see me as powerful. But many times I see myself as powerless, particularly dealing with a guy like Bill. That's because I like to compromise and do nice things for people. When someone says something like, "Please make this call for me," I'd probably do it even if it's the responsibility of the other guy. Although, in the dream, it seemed just too much for this Bill to ask me to place a call for him when he should have done so directly and transacted his own business. I felt good to have stood up to him.

G. Is he the one who said, "At bottom you don't think you are worth much anyway?"

J. Ah, yes, but I think *he* didn't think I was worth much.

G. Oh.

J. No, I'm sorry, you're right. No. He said, "At bottom you know you're not worth much." This really meant that was what *he* thought.

G. O.K. Could you fill me in on this professional organization? Do you in fact belong to it?

J. Yes.

G. Why?

J. I was involved in the politics.

G. Why would one get involved in the politics?

J. For power, prestige, and for the feeling of being somebody.

G. So it is a front organization for various peoples' movement toward power, prestige, and being somebody in the field.

J. Right.

G. And what do these "politicians" do for the members?

J. Well, in theory they are supposed to be representing the people in the field, providing power for them to get their needs taken care of, providing resources and information for them.

G. Like a union?

J. Well, the distinction between a union and a professional organization is that a union is mostly concerned with material benefits and working conditions. A professional organization is more likely to concentrate on professional development benefits—which is where I differ with the organization.

G. Why?

J. Because I think they should function more like a union and concentrate on material benefits as well.

G. So you see them wasting some time on professional development benefits?

J. I see them wasting a lot of time, and I'm just about to cop out.

G. What are they wasting time on?

J. Conventions, journals, commissions that study *and study* problems. They spend their time on national study groups rather than local action groups.

G. So you think there are a lot of people in the organization who are mostly seeking prestige. . . .

J. There are a lot of people there in the dream, and *in fact,* who are there (1) to booze it up and have a good time, and (2) for politicking—internal politics, prestige, position, etc.

G. So in the dream are you dealing with that part of yourself which, at least in the past and probably now (since you've just dreamt this), has gone to those meetings for these very same purposes?

J. That's right.

G. And you are beginning to feel that this front organization should shape up and start to fill the needs it was supposedly created to meet, as well as those more material needs regarding pay and working conditions. It seems that your dream is reminding you that your California year has not cleared you of all your political front needs. And that you still need to deal with the parts of yourself that push you around for their own "Bill" purposes. What do you have to say about this business of the California delegates being all female and the others being male?

J. The only thing I could think of was the pure sex basis. That if this represents portions of me, I'm still looking for women.

G. Hmm. What do you think about that?

J. I'd rather not let it be known. I don't mind it internally, except that after next week, when I plan to go back to Pennsylvania to resume my marriage, I'm going to meet the restraints of the marriage. I will act in a proper manner and do not intend to seek out other women.

G. How about the guy who wants to find the girls?

J. Well, that's natural, given the circumstances.

G. Why wasn't he satisfied with the women downstairs?

J. They weren't good looking enough. They weren't up to his lecherous standards. The young and pretty ones were still at a meeting upstairs.

G. So the young ones are upstairs! Any association?

J. Well, if I'm that man, the only association I can get is that there aren't enough women around at this time to make out with.

G. It could be that part of this dream represents some feelings about your last fling in California.

J. Could be.

G. Would that fit?

J. I don't think so, because my behavior doesn't go along with it. In other words, if I'm regretful, if I feel this is my last fling, you'd think I'd go out and have it. But I don't.

G. Why not?

J. Too much of the old me is still there.

G. Which is the old you?

J. Well, I think of all the reasons why I shouldn't. . . . O.K., the other night I went to a meeting and a fairly attractive young woman sat beside me. We were instructed to pair off for a communications exercise, and we got friendly. I think she wanted me to invite her for coffee, but I didn't. I thought it would be unfair to start anything when I'd be leaving in two weeks. Besides, I have several friends to say good-bye to and I wanted to leave time for them. Then, driving home, I thought, "What a jerk." I always think in terms of sex and, damn it all, there are a lot of nice people I could talk to! I might have got a lot out of a relationship with her, without any sex! I really have missed out on a lot of good people (who happen to be women) by thinking that way. I cut myself off from all sorts of good people because I immediately start thinking that, if I can't develop a sexual relationship, I'm not going to start anything.

G. I'm thinking of Sally's dream now [one the group had just discussed]— of Arlene and all the limiting "shoulds" and "should nots" she represents for Sally. It seems that one of your shoulds, Joe, is that your relationships with women *should* be sexual. And this belief limits you, prevents you from seeing rewarding alternatives.

J. Right!

G. Does anyone have any questions or comments for Joe at this point?

Sally. The lion part is interesting; anything more on it?

J. We were playing together, and it was fun. There was more to that part of the dream, but I can't remember it.

G. What's the difference between a tiger and a lion?

J. In dreams or realistically? In reality I'd say none. A tiger's slightly more powerful than a lion. Otherwise, I'd say none.

G. O.K. In the dream, what is the difference?

J. In my other dream, the tiger was a big animal. He was a pet. He was a tame but a wild animal. The lion was a playful little animal that might have weighed 500 pounds! The lion was like a dog my daughter has, full of playful energy.

G. And how was the tiger?

J. Quiet, peaceful, a cat, not withdrawn, as I usually think of a cat, but not as playful as a dog.

G. Might the lion and the tiger represent different aspects of your aggressive, strong, powerful self?

J. I feel that the lion is a development of the tiger self. He is more out in the open, more playful. I like the lion better, too. Actually I've just seen some friends whom I've not seen for a while. They commented on how I seem different. One said, "You're more mellow," and the other said, "No, you're firmer." I said, "Thanks, I'll take them both!"

G. Congratulations. I find your pet tiger and pet lion images appealing. You commented earlier that at times you feel powerless. Let's pretend that what you remember of the dream is all there was. The first part sets a scene for the rest of the dream. I don't know, but I imagine that in the history of theatre there was a style of presenting a short scene or skit that served as a sort of keynote address which one was meant to remember throughout the play. Say, the part from driving through the threatening characters with your bright lights on through the point where you were exercising your lion. This would be the keynote scene. O.K.?

J. Go ahead.

G. No, *you* go ahead and tell us what you think is going on in the keynote address.

J. Let's see. I'm about to drive right through a part of my life that I experience as threatening. I could have gone around another way to avoid the threatening characters, or I could have called the police. I didn't. With the car doors locked and my brights on, I feel safe enough to go straight on through with it.

G. Why do you choose to put on the bright lights?

J. Well, the brights would elucidate the frightening figures and show them up for what they are. But when I get there, they've disappeared. When I decide, even in a "safe" way, to confront or look at the fear, represented by the frightening figures, it just sort of evaporates. So, if this introduces the dream, I guess I am about to confront something frightening in my path that will lose its fearful quality if I take a good look at it. Then I'll be able to move right along.

G. Joe, remember last week we talked about how you need to see yourself as always the nice guy? You said, too, that you were getting tired of such a constraining life role, but aggressiveness seemed so unenlightened. Might these threatening figures represent your aggressive tendencies which from your present viewpoint (in the locked car) look to be loitering, waiting to be destructive and violent.

J. That fits.

G. When you take a good look into this exaggerated fear you have of your potentially destructive aggressiveness, you see there's nothing to fear. And what do you get out of this confrontation?

J. My pet lion! He's on a leash, under my control. He is playful and energetic, and I get a lot of pleasure from our relationship! I really like that.

G. So your aggressive self is your friend. I've often thought that aggression and assertiveness have a lot to do with playfulness. After all, feeling timid, who feels playful? "Nice Joe," always giving in, gets resentful and feels less and less powerful. Exuberance requires a sense of your own strength. The lion in you, Joe, is fun, playful, strong, and content to be on a loose leash—he's not wild and ferocious if you don't tie him up in your backyard and ignore him. What do you think about that?

J. I like it, and that makes a lot of sense when I think of the other self-exploration I've been doing this year.

G. What a great image your lion is! Who is Fred?

J. He's a good guy, honest, puts a lot of energy into his work, generally sees no evil, is successful because of the amount of work he does and because his interest really is in helping other people.

G. Is he a winner?

J. Up to a point. He couldn't deal with a Bill on a negotiation basis. Bill is too smooth, too two-faced for him.

G. What would happen if Fred were to deal with Bill?

J. Fred would deal with him on an open basis, but Bill would hold things back, twist things around. Finally Fred would be swindled.

G. And Bill is an ambitious manipulator?

J. Bill is out for Bill.

G. And Bill is in the organization for his own power purposes. Can you see Bill as that part of you (in caricature) which uses your aggression in ways you don't like, in a manipulative, power-seeking way?

J. Who me? [General laughter]

G. Well?

J. Yes that fits, or did fit. I don't do that any more.

G. You know, Joe, since you just dreamed this last week, I would guess that Bill is still a living part of your psyche that you are learning to deal with now.

J. I'd rather not think that, but it may be so. I *am* learning to stand up to him.

G. Right. Fred represents what part of you?

J. A part I admire, honest, principled, successful. But I would say that the Fred in me is a bit too naïve. He needs some of the shrewdness that Bill has.

G. So it's just as well that all the Bill in you isn't dead?

J. Right, I can use him if I don't let him use me. [At this point, Joe reread his whole dream in order to refresh our memories and to try to reexperience the dream in light of our discussion so far. You, too, may want to read it again before continuing.]

G. So your complaint is that Bill should contact Fred directly and not use you as a middleman. It seems that, if Bill wants to contact the Fred in you, he can use you, or your sense of worthlessness, to get you to call Fred for Bill's purposes not for yours. In other words, your Fred self, the good guy in you, is bound to be dominated by Bill when he returns the call. If you were to refuse to place the call for Bill, he could not use or dominate you, because you would be aware of your worth and not feel obliged to play the nice-guy role. The Fred, Joe, and Bill parts of you would have to come to terms on a more equitable basis. You begin to stand up to the Bill in you, your topdog, who puts you down and calls you worthless. However, you still give in and say you'll place the call even though you say he'll have to reimburse you. This seems to reflect some of your current struggles that you've been having regarding this vacation-self-development year you've taken in California. I have the impression that you've come a long way from your old feelings of worthlessness in the last few years. Do you?

J. Gayle, I'm a very specific person. I would say that I've developed the feeling part of myself especially this year. Yoga, meditation, dream work, and the general California experience have helped me to feel more satisfied with myself. But I can't put it in terms of self-worth.

G. O.K. But now I'm wondering why you used the terms of self-worth in the dream when you wrote the screenplay.

J. Well, in the dream I had the feeling that Bill was relating to me the way a fellow had related to me about three years ago. This guy was saying to me, "You know, *I* really know you better than you know yourself." I felt that he was implying that at bottom there's not much there.

G. How did that make you feel?

J. I had the sickening feeling that he might be right, although I tried to deny it.

G. If he were to say the same thing to you today, how would you react?

J. I don't know. I guess that would depend on how I was feeling. But if he said that now, today, I wouldn't even take him seriously. That's today. Tomorrow, I don't know. I guess feelings of worthlessness and powerlessness really are the issue after all.

G. I think so. I would guess that the feelings of worthlessness you experience lead to your need to be liked. This need leads to your being a nice, nonaggressive, nonthreatening guy who ends up feeling powerless at times.

J. I'm afraid that's pretty accurate. But doesn't everybody feel worthless at times?

G. Maybe some more often than others, and you less often now than a few years ago, no?

J. True. I give Bill a harder time than I would have a while ago.

G. Bill's type tends to have to be domineering and manipulative because they feel they need to get power from the outside since they don't feel it inside themselves.

J. Yes, it's a sense of powerlessness that motivates the Bill-type power mongers. That really fits. If I can give my lion free reign, more leash, my Bill self will not feel so powerless. Then I could use Bill's assertiveness and shrewdness in a healthier way. I could get Fred and Bill together in myself.

G. What about the scene where Bill tells you that from now on the organization should give psychological tests to candidates for office or positions of power?

J. I had the feeling that he was saying that, if they had done that all along, I would never have been allowed to run for office. That it's people like me they want to be rid of.

G. So he's continuing his topdog put-down?

J. Yes, but here I don't believe his line—that tests would be useful. He sounds foolish to me at this point, not threatening.

G. What happens to Bill in the next scene?

J. [Laughter] He disappears!

G. So you are free of him, at least for now, having seen through him!

J. We forgot the scene where Bill and I were at the front of the room for the Pledge of Allegiance and the weather report. That scene came just after I had insisted that Bill reimburse me. He responded that I was crazy if I thought he'd go all the way to his room to get the money. The scene that followed the weather report was the one where I said he could pay me back later.

G. What does being at the front of the room, pledging allegiance and hearing a weather report, make you think of?

J. The Boy Scouts! [Laughter from all of us]

G. So you are reminded of your pledge to be a good boy, nice guy, and the next thing you know, you are saying you'll call Fred and Bill *doesn't* have to pay you now.

J. Yeah, I give in, but not all the way. This dream is getting to look a lot like the organization of my life. Even the fellow who is frustrated because he can't find the easy young women he expected fits. He's missing out on them entirely because he's looking for them on the wrong level. The ones who meet his standards are more than sex objects and are upstairs organizing new materials (feelings?). They exist on an emotional, almost spiritual level. Next, the chairperson skips over my town, and I jump up and let her know it. I feel good about having done that, even though I'm not an official delegate to the convention and had no business being there.

G. Really?

J. Yes, and as I sat back down I suddenly realized that a fellow whom I don't know now, but who in the dream was a friend, had been beside me throughout the dream. He was a friend, and I was glad and proud that he had heard everything that had transpired between Bill and me. I told him I didn't think that the Erie County delegation was going to come. Oh, I forgot to mention that the chairperson who had called off the roll call named people from counties near Erie County then went on to call names from Philadelphia. Then she said, "I guess there's no one here from in between." It was at that point that I jumped up and said I was from Pittsburgh.

G. What is the difference between the people from Erie County and those from Philadelphia?

J. Off the top of my head? The Erie County people think of the Philadelphia people as unthinking, uncaring, aggressive people. The Philadelphia people think of the north county people as sort of country bumpkins and innocuous. They don't understand them at all, they think they're very shallow.

G. What would be the positive aspect of the rural county people?

J. Good human people.

G. Sort of like Fred?

J. Like Fred. Erie County would be a real extreme of Fred's naïveté.

G. And the Philadelphians would be sort of like who?

J. Well, I guess [laughs] sort of like Bill. [General laughter now as the class catches on]

G. Wouldn't it be nice to find a delegate from somewhere in between?

J. You bet!

G. Well?

J. [Pause, questioning look]

G. Joe, that's you! You stood up to let the chairperson know that you come from Pittsburgh even though you used to work in Philadelphia. And geographically your home town is between Erie County and Philadelphia. You needn't worry that any terribly naïve parts of you will even get into the picture, since the Erie County people probably won't arrive.

J. That's beautiful! I never would have put that together. My home town is right in the middle of that psychological continuum. No wonder I felt so good after this dream!

G. Your dream seems to be reminding you to remember who you are and where you come from, whenever you start feeling like Bill or Fred. When you identify yourself, you won't identify with either extreme—and you are the guy with the pet lion.

J. I'm going to try to remember that.

Actually, Joe probably would have been able to put together the last dream scene if I had asked a few more questions or just given him more time. I took a somewhat more active and directive role than I usually would, because Joe was a beginner in dream work and interpretive suggestions speeded up our interview about a long dream in a class of four other producers who wanted to discuss their dreams in the same meeting. It would have been better if I had let Joe make more of the connections himself by asking more questions at different points. However, this interview worked out well in the end, and Joe did get the "aha!" experience as the dream elements began to make sense to him.

The Esthetic Experience. A strong indication that Joe's dream was both interpreted adequately and well understood is that he and I both felt what has been called the *esthetic experience* of the dream. This is another term for what is commonly known as the "aha!" experience, but it expresses the feeling better. Two psychoanalysts, Erika Fromm and Thomas French,[4] have proposed the term to describe what the interpreter or the dreamer feels when the clues derived from a discussion of dream elements suddenly fall into place and the dream watcher has an intuitive, artistic insight into the meaning of the dream. The person (ideally the dreamer) who has the insight feels exhilarated and triumphant; he or she can see how almost all the pieces of the puzzle fit perfectly and beautifully together. The experience is one of esthetic pleasure.

The esthetic experience, especially when the dreamer has it, is an almost positive confirmation that the significance of the dream has been discovered. A dream is not interpreted until either the interviewer or the producer has this feeling, and it is important to pursue dream interviews until the dreamer has this experience, because only then will he or she really appreciate the meaning of a dream in an immediate way. Once this occurs, all or almost all of the dream elements will be seen to add to or clarify the meaning of the dream. Further interviewing will demonstrate that dreams can be understood in extraordinary detail; this may take quite a while or almost no time at all, depending upon the dream. Many dream researchers insist that in every dream there will always be a number of elements which can not be interpreted. Some even hypothesize that the significance of some elements *must* remain unconscious in order for the major thrust of the dream message to have a significant impact on the dreamer, without distracting details. I strongly disagree. It seems much better to assume that every detail in your dream was carefully chosen by your dream producer to express something of significance in the dream show. If you are so inclined, it is often possible to discover just what you wanted to express by each dream element, and you will find that these details clarify your understanding of the dream. When you then reexperience your production in light of your esthetic experience and your appreciation of its exquisite detail, you will marvel at the creativity you display as a dream producer.

You Can Do It!   There are many theories on dreams. Freud believed that dreams expressed repressed sexual desires and fears disguised in less offensive images. The role of the interpreter was to use the dreamer's free associations to uncover the sexual conflict or infantile desires.

Jung saw dreams as the expression of the psyche's urge toward wholeness, or psychological integration, rather than as an expression of only the individual's conflicts in coping with a storehouse of socially unacceptable instinctual drives. Jung emphasized the compensatory nature of dreams, which tend to show us parts of ourselves and our behavior that we do not accept consciously. He was a master at illuminating the integrative, sometimes almost mystical, beauty of dreams and of the process of growth they encourage.

Alfred Adler saw in dreams the individual's aggressive urges and attempts to deal with them in a socially acceptable way.

The difficulty with adhering too enthusiastically to any one dream theory is that, one then tends to use dreams to reconfirm one's theory about how the human psyche works and thus the interviewer's and the dreamer's freedom to see each dream anew are inhibited. The real meaning of a dream can easily be distorted to fit one's preconceptions about what dreams can mean.

Though sometimes useful in long-term psychoanalysis, psychological theories dogmatically applied to dream lives have a constricting effect upon the understanding of them. For example, a few dogmatic practitioners of the Freudian school of dream interpretation get lost in a quagmire of past events and voluminous free-associative material. Those who practice Jungian dream interpretation with less than consummate skill tend to lose the immediate impact and meaning of the dream in their feverish search for archetypes and numinosity.

Of course, both Freud and Jung had their favorite ways of dealing with issues concerning maleness and femaleness. Their interpretation of dreams followed their personal beliefs about the psychological natures of males and females as well as about the male part of the female personality and vice-versa. While Freud was clearly a product of the Victorian era, let us not forget that Jung, brilliant as he was, was a product of Switzerland, which allowed all its female citizens of majority age to vote only in 1971, a decade after Jung's death. It is my opinion that fixed ideas as to the psychological nature of men and women distort far more than they elucidate. These qualifications considered, the books of the great pioneers in the field of dream interpretation are highly recommended because they can sensitize one to many aspects of dreaming. Although they have their limitations, it is well to remember that the life work of these geniuses is not to be taken lightly and does have much to offer anyone desirous of understanding dreams.

Some dream analysts insist that one must be an expert to interpret dreams. Jung went so far as to write that he considered it "impossible for anyone without knowledge of mythology and folklore, and without some understanding of the psychology of primitives and of comparative religion to grasp the essence of the individuation process, which according to all we know, lies at the base of psychological compensation" found in dreams.[5] Jung admitted that an intelligent layperson could "diagnose" the compensatory elements in dreams, but he held that a great deal of specialized knowledge was required before one could interpret the direction and essence of the dream in the context of the dreamer's personal growth. He felt that a dreamer could not interpret his own dreams because they dealt with parts of the dreamer that were unconscious.

If you experiment with your own and others' dreams, you will soon discover that, although specialized knowledge can be helpful in interpreting dreams, it is not necessary. Knowledge of the religious, anthropological, psychological, and mythological history of humanity can indeed enrich your appreciation of certain aspects of dreams. It can also be used to obscure a very practical dream message in the search for archetypes and universal symbolism.

As you get to know more about dreams and different ways of looking at them, you will find it is not too difficult to sift out what is of use to you from what is not. For now, assume that you have all the information and psychological knowledge you need to understand your dreams.

Why not conduct a dream interview right now? This will help you to review this chapter and begin to increase your interpretive abilities. Be your own interpreter or ask a friend to play that part for you.

Choose any dream that you have recently dreamed and clearly remember. Shorter dreams will be easier to work with in the beginning. Review the dream by reading or telling it, and then conduct your interview as described above.

Keep in mind an outline of the questions you or your friend will want to ask:

1. What do you feel the dream is about?

2. Describe and relate the setting to day life.

3. Who is each dream person and what is he or she like?

4. What is each dream object and what is it like?

5. How does each feeling, person, or object relate to day life?

6. Describe the dream events. What do they remind you of in your present life?

If you are conducting the interview with a friend, be sure to exchange roles so that you will play both producer and interviewer. The interviewer should be careful not to push his hypotheses about the meaning of the dream. After every suggestion he makes, the interviewer should elicit either confirmation or correction from the producer. The producer will profit most from the interview by remembering that he produced the dream show and has access to the memories, thoughts, attitudes, and feelings that will make its meaning clear.

You will know that you have succeeded in interpreting your dream when:

1. it tells you something you did not realize before.

2. you have the esthetic experience, or at least a sense of "Oh, so that's it."

3. a clear idea of what you might do about the situation explored in the dream emerges.

It is up to you to use the insights you take from dreams in living your life. A dream can, and usually will, point you in the direction of a resolution to a conflict or of a new discovery about yourself or your world. It is your responsibility to put your new understanding into action if you want to experience the best part of dreaming.

Enjoy the interview. Play with your dream images. Record the results of your first efforts; they will be fun to compare with notes made from later interviews after you have practiced the art for a while.

In the meantime, talk about your dreams with your friends, practice interviewing yourself and other dream producers, and keep reading. In the following chapters, you will find ideas on how to use dream incubation creatively, and you will have the opportunity to sharpen your interpretive skills as you read how other dreamers have used theirs.

PART TWO

Screenplays

How to Choose and Use Them, or Notes on the Direction and Interpretation of Your Dream Scenes

4

What's Really Going On in
Your Relationships?

Our Own Soap Operas. We all need to be loved. Most of us know that. But being loved will not bring us happiness if we don't know how to recognize, accept, and return the love we receive.

Of course, if we do not think ourselves worthy of love, we will see those who offer it to us as fools who don't know any better. However, even those of us who know ourselves and our world well enough to appreciate our own lovable qualities often become tangled up in a knotty web of difficult and sometimes destructive relationships. Much like the characters in a soap opera, we may struggle through our relationships, stumbling from one conflict to another and back again because of a lack of insight into the ways we relate to the people in our lives.

As observers, it is easy for us to see what is going on in soap operas. We can identify without much trouble the personality quirks and the lack of communication or miscommunication that gets the characters into their painful and conflict-ridden relationships.

In our own lives, we tend to be almost as unaware of some of our faults and unproductive or hurtful styles of communicating as are the mothers and fathers, daughters and sons, friends and lovers in the soap operas. Often an outside observer can see more clearly what is really going on in our relationships.

A perceptive friend or psychotherapist can see some of our attitudes and behavior patterns which we do not recognize but which consistently cause us both internal conflict and problems in relating harmoniously with others. A good family therapist can point to patterns of communication and behavior in a marriage or a family that may have caused years of unnecessary suffering, resentment, and unhappiness. A skilled family therapist can help a couple or a family to see how each partner or member cooperates to maintain a system of communication that will perpetuate unhappy situations.[1] In order to relate in an honest way to those we love, it is important to know how we feel inside, what we need and can give in a relationship, *and* how to express it all in a way that others can understand. If we are out of touch with our basic needs, we will not know how to express them and will usually feel a growing resentment toward our loved ones for not giving us what we need. It is easy to fall into seeing ourselves as victims of a world that denies us the gentleness, love, freedom, and respect we require when we fail to see how we frustrate those needs within ourselves and when we fail to communicate them to others who might satisfy them.

An observer more objective than ourselves, who knows us well and can skillfully show us what is going on behind the scenes of our relationships, can initiate dramatic changes in the way we experience our relationship to the world and the people we meet in it. A good therapist can do this. So can our dream producers.

You can ask for dreams that will help you to understand why a given relationship is not working out well. You needn't be a victim of all the awful men in the world, you can instead ask why you keep choosing men who are unkind to you. Rather than suffer indefinitely wondering why you and your wife can't survive a day without a fight yet can't survive apart, you could ask your dream producer to show you how and why you both cooperate to create this situation. Your dreams will respond to your requests with compassion, humor, and wisdom. They will help you to understand your interpersonal conflicts and the personal ones that are usually behind them. Your dream producer who knows you so well, who in fact *is* you, will give you the insights you need to change unhappy relationships into rewarding ones, or, if that is not possible, will show you your neurotic attachments to destructive relationships and help to free you from them.

When Nina incubated a dream about her relationship with Scott, she didn't like the response she got ("Titanic," Chapter 1). So a week later she incubated a dream about why she was so attached to Scott that, even though she knew the relationship was likely to continue to be a painful one, she was unwilling and unable to end it. She received the following response:

I went to a house near my parents' home. An old ladyfriend and some of my family are inside. I am anxious to move in. Scott sits behind me and is very upset because the dress I am wearing is too sheer. Father is sitting behind Scott. Then I am outside in a dry, overcast field. ("Sheer Dress")

In the commentary section of her dream journal, Nina wrote out a modified interview between herself and her dream producer:

Feeling—I felt a tie between Scott and Father, both being somewhat stuffy about my "lovey-doveness." I never achieved the warm, loving relationship I wanted with Father and now am experiencing similar difficulties with Scott.

How are Scott and Father alike? Both are distant. Neither can express feelings or emotions comfortably. I always try to elicit the warmth from them that I need and almost always feel that I fail.

Sheer dress—Exposes my naked feelings.

Action—Father and Scott disapprove of my dress and of showing my feelings so freely in life.

Old ladyfriend—Lois, who is kind and warm. I'd like to be like her and have a family in a cozy house at her age or even right now.

Action and setting—I am anxious to have or to move into the love and warmth of a family. Aha! I seem determined to get blood from a stone. I never gave up trying to get tenderness from Father. I just found another man like him and tried to teach Scott the joy of letting love show. I thought I was saving Scott from his inability to let love in or out. But really I am trying to get the loving I never feel I received from my father. Neither of them can help, but judge my "lovey-doveness" as foolish. I need a man who wants to share a warm, cozy house, not one with whom I feel as if I am in a cold, dry, overcast field. But Scott is still young. Maybe as he matures. . . .

It was another year before Nina gave up her need to be Scott's wise mother, who would teach him, as she never could her father, how to feel the joy of love openly and happily shared. She had hoped that Scott would stop gambling and drinking and magically "grow up" under the spell of her love. She finally had to live out her "Titanic" dream in order to realize that she had not chosen the kind of man she could ever be happy with.

Jan, a young married sculptor, was quicker to listen to the message of her dreams. In the first year of her marriage, she and her husband had numerous struggles around the issue of who should do what in their household. Jan was not about to slip into the role of housewife. She would be a wife as Anthony would be a husband. But she was determined to see that the housework be divided equally between them and that her husband modify his ideas of what constituted "woman's work" or "a man's job." This is a struggle going on in countless homes today as male-female roles are being redefined. Often the question of who does the dishes is just a concrete manifestation of deeper concerns in a relationship between a man and a woman.

One evening, Jan and Anthony had a row over who should do the vacuuming. Jan felt that her husband was being very sexist and that he expected her to do an unfair share of the housework. She felt she was already doing more than half of it, whereas Anthony felt that he was doing seventy percent of it. Jan believed that her husband honestly felt that he was doing seventy percent of the work, but she thought that his estimate was so grossly exaggerated because he had been accustomed to a mother who did all the housework. Now the forty percent or so he did do seemed like seventy percent to him. Anthony felt that Jan was taking unfair advantage of his willingness to share the duties. He felt unappreciated and unfairly accused of being a male chauvinist. The matter was unresolved at bedtime, so Jan incubated a dream on it. Her incubation phrase was, "What are the dynamics behind this fight over little things?" She produced the following drama:

I was looking at my foot and saw that the second toe was just enormous, with an ugly mushroomlike growth on it. I wondered if I should have the growth removed. I looked again and saw that several of my toes as well as the growth had been amputated! I panicked. How would I ever dance or even walk again? ("Big Toe")

Her interpretation went like this: Her mother was fond of saying that the woman whose second toe is her longest one rules the roost. In the dream, Jan's second toe was not only long, it was grossly oversized and deformed. She saw clearly that her need to control her husband and home had gotten out of hand. Jan also saw how part of her need to control was motivated by the fear that, if she did not do so with vigor, she might lose all control or power. She feared giving up her excess control (her ugly growth) for fear of losing all her influence (all her toes). Jan noticed how this black-and-white thinking colored many of her attitudes. As a result of the dream, she began to modify some of her positions and thereby promote a finer harmony in her marriage without feeling she was giving in to unfair pressure from her husband. She was also able to see how much work Anthony was indeed doing and apologized to him for not fully appreciating it. In later days, whenever she would make excessive demands of him in the name of defending herself from his "sexism," both she and Anthony could laugh that her big toe was hanging out. Then they could look at the situation again from a less defensive standpoint and discuss the matter more objectively, with fewer accusations. This doesn't mean that Anthony didn't have to admit to a few sexist attitudes now and then!

A young lawyer also decided to incubate a dream after a fight with her sweetheart. They had been discussing their religious and spiritual lives, and Alyse had taken offense at a few remarks Tim had made regarding her relative immaturity in this area. She was furious and felt that he had been quite unfairly condescending toward her. Yet she wondered if she was not in fact closing out some good counsel from Tim. In her incubation discussion, she explored her feelings and doubts. She came up with this incubation request: "Is Tim wiser than I? If so, show me how; help me to accept his counsel." She dreamed:

Tim and I are on our way to a vacation house owned by an eccentric uncle, who has built it on a hill of sand without an elevator so that only the fittest will be able to enjoy the house, which is somehow like the top floor of my family's home. Tim holds on to a great book (like the Lord of the Rings *by Tolkein, which he has been reading to me lately). The book is like a motorcycle or is also a motorcycle. As Tim holds on to the handlebars, I hold on to his waist. He speeds up the sand hill over what is at first a road with double yellow lines. I tell Tim he is going too fast at times. We cross over the lines. I am frightened. He tells me not to fret. I finally bother him so much about his speed that he turns the book-motorcycle over to me, saying, "You'll see that you have to go up fast or you will slide back." I try it alone. He is right. I begin to slip. I wish he had a rope to pull me up. (He is already on top of the hill.) But he has no rope. So I go up my own way to the right (more conservative way?) of his straight route. I am on foot. I arrive. Whew! We made it. ("The Motorcycle-Book")*

Alyse had an immediate sense of what the dream was saying:

I take the dream to say that Tim has a lot of wisdom to offer me regarding the spiritual life. The setting reminds me of my picture of spiritual development's rewards and a good image of how I see God. God is like an eccentric uncle who offers us a relaxed, harmonious, happy life if only we can make it up to his place (the highest level, my true home) through a steady application of our energy (motorcycle). He has ordered the world so that we have to learn and grow to arrive at his resort (enlightenment). Tim has been lovingly reading me all the Tolkein books, which symbolize for me a new understanding of the world, brought into my life via Tim. Last night Tim was offering to ride with me straight up to the resort. He was trying to show me how he thinks it should be done. But his way scares me. In life, sometimes I feel he is overdoing his spiritual development "program." The dream makes me think that I will probably take my own less steep, if longer, route to enlightenment. I'll make it on foot, the motocycle, in book form, in my hand.

As I relive the dream, I am struck by Tim's patience and by my inability to trust him. That's too bad. I can feel that my natural way is a more gradual development toward spiritual wisdom. Motorbike enlightenment scares me. Yet I feel a new openness to learning from Tim, because in a way he is already where I want to go. He is very much in touch with the God within. I'll tell Tim all this at lunch.

As Alyse was writing these comments in her journal, Tim was recording a dream in his. At lunch that day, he told Alyse that he had had a very vivid dream compensating for his condescension to her the preceding evening. He dreamt of a very wise old woman who showed him in nonverbal, non-three-dimensional ways how much he had yet to learn. As the dream became more realistic and specific, she gave him a test, which he failed because of his overbearing pride.

Tim and Alyse's dreams were showing them things about themselves which were causing some friction in their relationship. Tim's pride and Alyse's lack of trust were easier to deal with after they had shared their dreams. Their dreams were bringing them closer together.

Ned, a jealous husband, went to bed one night very angry because his wife was out late having dinner with a male graduate student, helping him with a paper. The student was writing a thesis on medical ethics and had telephoned her because he had heard that she was a journalist who had been particularly interested in the subject. Although Ned rationally knew his wife was just enjoying an innocent dinner with a bright and probably flattering student, he was very jealous. He felt that late dinners with students were hardly the best way to further their education. He wrote out much of his anger in his journal. He paced the floor and finally went to sleep alone. He had a startling dream that came without any specific invitation beyond his extensive venting of his anger in his day notes. He dreamed:

I think I've had an operation. In any case, part of my spleen is out of me, and the doctors are experimenting with it to bring to it a life consciousness of its own. Now it hates me and is out to get me. You can't stop science from experimentation, even if it is dangerous. I start to awaken in fright, trying to forget the dream. ("My Spleen Is Out to Do Me In.")

Ned interviewed himself in his journal commentary as follows:

It seems that my jealousy, the externalized portion of my spleen, is out to do me in.

Spleen—Organ that breaks down old red blood cells and may produce *antibodies!*

Showing my spleen—Venting my jealousy and anger. Only part of my spleen was out to get me.

The relentless march of scientific experimentation—It's true that scientists have unwisely created Frankensteins.

The doctors—Represent my belief that all feelings should be vented, expressed, and not hidden. Yet the dream tells me that last night I was not just expressing my anger, I was actually fanning its flames by concentrating on it so much. I really worked myself up and intensified my anger, feeding it with jealous fantasies. The spleen I let out boomerangs. It wants to destroy me. Sounds like my jealousy could harm my marriage and myself. This dream is so frightening, I think I had better see what is at the bottom of the destructive part of my jealousy.

The morning after the dream, Ned was a little less self-righteous in his expression of his anger and began to explore with his wife the possible reasons behind his intense jealousy.

Dreams like these can make important changes in a relationship if the dreamers care to explore them and put their insights to work. Imagine having nightly access to a very wise observer who can give you counsel on the relationships that make all the difference in your experience of life. Your dream producer is waiting to be of service to you.

Virginia asked for a dream that would give her a clue as to the future of her relationship with her boyfriend Bob. Her incubation resulted in the following dream show:

Bob and I go to see our prospective apartment. The landlady has papers for the rental, which are all in Bob's name. Bob, not wanting to make a fuss, signs the rental agreement without seeing the apartment. I think this hasty, but I do not stop him because I, too, want to get this over with. We then enter the apartment. Everything is very vivid. The first room is tiled in beautiful blue tile (like Bob's eyes), but the higher part of the walls and ceiling are in dirty white plaster. Next, through a half constructed doorway to the second room, is a bed all in grey, dingy, blah, icky, colorlessness. There is construction material strewn all over the floors in this and other rooms. There are several sinks about. The place is a great disappointment. I wonder if Bob is right, that we should ask if we ourselves could paint it. I had thought it would take too much effort, but the apartment really needs some attention. It is a noisy, awful apartment. We'll do what we can with it since we've contracted for it. I say, "We shall stay the required time, then leave." ("Our Apartment Needs Work")

Actually, this is just what happened in their relationship. It was a drab one from many perspectives. Yet both learned a great deal and washed away (the sinks in the apartment) a lot of troublesome old preconceptions and rigid attitudes in the process of finishing the constructive work of their relationship. After Virginia and Bob had learned some important things from each other, they naturally moved away from each other. Both were glad for the insights their relationship had brought to them, and both were glad to discover that their lease was up. After they went their own ways, both found partners that suited them better. It seemed that a prerequisite to more lively and enjoyable relationships was understanding the one they had created together.

Getting the Message Let's look now at a series of six dreams which span a two-year period in the marriage of a young couple. These dreams, in sequence, will illustrate several important points regarding the continuity of dream life. We will see how dream producers try again and again to get their message across to us until we hear it. And we will see how intimately related to our everyday life are the most bizarre of night shows.

I met Tanya in a woman's consciousness-raising group, where we discovered our common interest in recording our dreams. We shared dreams with each other for the next two years, and the dreams described below come from Tanya's journal. She had married Ian immediately after she graduated from college in 1970. After six months of marriage, Tanya had the following nightmare:

My hair has been cut upon my request. It is set. I am uneasy about how it will look. It looks quite nice set; it has a good shape! Then I say to Ian, "How about if I comb it out before we go to bed just to see how it looks?" I take the rollers out and brush my hair. It looks horrible, hanging around my neck like a limp, unexciting pageboy. I decide it looks better in rollers. The feelings of distress at cutting my hair were very intense and awoke me with a start. My beautiful hair, why did I cut it off? ("Hair")

Tanya told me this dream as she might have recounted any distressing daytime event. She felt somewhat victimized by it and was seeking the comfort a friend could offer by saying, "Oh yes, that *was* a bad dream." I asked her what she thought it might mean, and she replied that it was just a nonsense dream. "Doesn't it remind you of anything?" I asked. "Just of Samson and Delilah; only I'm Samson," she answered. Because she was not interested in pursuing the dream further, we dropped the subject. Yet I was wondering what was amiss in her marriage (the bedroom setting with Ian). What was happening in it that she was cutting herself off from her strength and crowning glory? Whatever it was seemed very important, judging from the intensity of distress she felt in the dream. Part of the reason for the vivid nightmare quality of it, I reasoned, was probably the fact that her dream producer was having a hard time getting her to look at something in her relationship with Ian and so resorted to a mini–shock treatment.

A little over a year later, Tanya told me another more exotic dream:

An Egyptian Pharoah (of pre–high civilization Egypt) is about to be executed by the new, more developed people now in power. He is lying on his back in the desert under a bright afternoon sun. His chest is bare, sweaty, and golden-toned as he is being prepared for the execution. I kneel beside him to the right of his feet. I am his partner or co-leader in the spiritual and political life of the people. My loyalties are with him not the new rulers; therefore I, too, must be beheaded. An unseen narrator says, "It's too bad. She was their last hope as a leader." My skin is the color of Egyptian gold, and, as I kneel, a beautiful white dress flows about me. A pillow of many fascinating colors is placed before me. I am to place my head on it to have it cut off. The time has come. I look to the king, then to God and place my head upon the pillow. ("Egyptian Executions")

At the time of this dream, Tanya was experiencing considerable conflict in her relationship with Ian. He was a very success-oriented lawyer who spent his free time relaxing with a law book. He was almost completely uninterested in physical sports and preferred to be alone with his wife and reading more than anything else. Tanya admired his intellectual pursuits and used them to encourage her own. But she was getting tired of such a sedentary life. She loved meeting people, running, playing tennis, and traveling. She also liked to read, but enough was enough.

As an outside observer, I found it clear that Tanya felt that she had to give up much of what she loved in life, including her own style of interacting with the world, in order to maintain her marriage. I asked her if she was not executing the liveliest and most natural part of herself in the name of loyalty to a rigidly defined idea of a divine partnership. She said that she had changed her lifestyle to accommodate the man she loved because, whereas he did not feel comfortable living in her more extroverted style, she was glad for the occasion to force herself to "grow up" and to turn inward more than she had before marriage. She also thought that the dream might be a review of an earlier reincarnation as an Egyptian woman because the dream and her different skin color seemed so real.

Tanya was ready to change the subject, and I did not pursue it. She obviously was not ready to question her rigid conception of what was required of her if she wanted to continue her marriage with Ian. Again, I was left wondering. The motifs in this dream suggested in a general way that something was very wrong in Tanya, in her marriage, or both. Without being able to interview her, but knowing her well and being familiar with the basic tendencies of the dream world, I formed this hypothesis:

She is in a desert setting, and while it is very romantic and exotic, there is no (personality) growth there. Both she and her partner (Ian?) were going to be killed in this emotional environment. Because she felt that their partnership was divinely ordained (marriage), she was ready to give up the life in herself and die with him. The narrator provides a clue to the nature of the king and the problem with Tanya's readiness to die just because tradition decrees it. If we are not the rulers of our own dream dynasties, empires, or groups, then the ruler we obey in the dream represents some (usually unconscious) part of ourselves or some other person's or group's attitudes that we have internalized and have accepted as our own. We should each be the leader of our own dream and daytime worlds. The narrator (almost always a wise figure in dreams) expresses his regret that the people's last hope for a leader was allowing herself to be executed. The setting in Egypt prior to its period of highest cultural and political achievements suggests that "the people" represented the aspects of Tanya's personality which needed good leadership to realize its greatest potential. The old king must die before the new king can use his power to revitalize the kingdom. This is a common theme throughout world literature. In dreams, it often symbolizes the fact that old belief structures and attitudes must die before new ones can revitalize the personality. Perhaps Tanya dreamed of a young king who reminded her of Ian because Ian represents for her some old restrictive beliefs and attitudes which have determined the nature of the way she relates to herself and how she feels she should relate as a wife to her husband.

I was puzzled by the image of the vividly colored pillow. A few months after she had this dream, Tanya told me that the fascinating pillow of many colors was her dreams, or rather her attitude toward dreams. At the time of the dream, as she later realized, she seemed easily distracted by the sumptuousness and fascination of dream imagery. Though she loved to discuss the exotic, mythological, and archetypal elements of dreams, she failed to recognize the fact that most of her dreams were dealing with very concrete issues. In this case they were signaling her self-imposed execution.

The night after Tanya's "Egyptian Executions" dream, she dreamt that Ian momentarily had control of a geyser which she herself owned. It seemed to the public that Ian owned it. An entrepreneur offered Ian a great deal of money for it. Ian wanted Tanya to sell her geyser to him so that he could sell it and make a good profit. Tanya was angered and told Ian that she would not sell it to him, that it belonged to her, as would any profit derived from its sale. As the dream ended, she felt very guilty for being so selfish toward her husband. Tanya was beginning to catch on. When she asked herself what a geyser was, she saw it as a symbol of endless energy and creativity. She was beginning to feel that, by not living a more active, extroverted life, she was stifling her creative energies. Yet it was such a struggle for her to involve Ian in what she thought was exciting that she usually gave in and participated in his enjoyments instead of doing what she enjoyed apart from him. They had grown accustomed to being together in almost all their free time and were jealous of any time one spent away from the other.

Approximately three weeks after the "Geyser" dream, Tanya dreamt that Isadora Duncan was telling her that Ian was the wrong man for her and that her husband was just too different from her for them ever to find a compromise in lifestyle that would satisfy both their needs. Isadora then took Tanya to Carl Jung himself and said, "Carl, will you please make her understand that these two personalities will always be in opposition?" Tanya kept refusing to accept either's prognosis of her marriage. She insisted that their love would overcome their differences, and besides, she only needed to grow up a bit to recognize how superficial most of her extroversion was. Tanya awoke very troubled from this drama. She had incubated this dream, asking for guidance in overcoming her discontent with her marriage. She deeply loved much about her husband and felt a profound spiritual link with him, but she had a very difficult time living with him day to day. Now two people she respected most highly, one for her creativity, energy, and courage, the other for his insight into people, were insisting that her struggle to adapt herself to life with someone as introverted as Ian was hopeless!

Tanya responded to this dream by redoubling her efforts to find some way she could feel free to do the things she loved without feeling she was abandoning her husband. She also decided to come to grips with her jealousy, which made it hard to let Ian spend an afternoon or evening alone, doing what he enjoyed most. She had become very aware that, since she and Ian were of two such contrasting temperaments, it would be necessary to make room in their relationship for both partners to feel free to express and enjoy themselves in their own styles. Otherwise their relationship would become an unbearable pressure cooker for both of them. This would not be easy, because they were both very dependent upon each other and very afraid of losing one another. Their relationship began to change, if just a little bit.

As in the soap operas, Ian and Tanya had their good days and their bad days. But as they became a little freer from the idea that they always had to be together doing the same things, their good days were more exciting and their bad days less frustrating than before. Ian and Tanya were becoming a little more independent, a little more like the individuals they each were. They were growing up. They were becoming more aware of the necessity of satisfying their own individual needs without demanding that the other be a constant companion in that endeavor. Nevertheless, this was rather disrupting in a marriage where the husband and wife were still extremely dependent for their emotional security upon the other's almost total devotion and attention. Perhaps the fact that Tanya was finally finding the courage to assert her needs for greater freedom within the marriage and was more willing to grant the same freedoms to Ian indicated that she had become somewhat less dependent upon Ian than he was upon her. Ian had not felt the same need to change the expectations of a marriage which had suited his needs quite well. He had not bargained for a very independent wife, and now he was faced with having to give her more freedom or risk losing her. He had always recognized how very different they were, and he both loved and feared his wife's growing independence.

Tanya wanted very much to make her marriage with Ian work, but she was less and less willing to live a life without running and dancing and exciting people in it. She recognized how much Ian had tried to accommodate her needs, and she felt guilty for the pain this sometimes caused him. Tanya knew how he hurt inside when she would go off without him for a day of tennis and folk dancing. She said she felt stifled and selfish. Tanya was confused. She appreciated Ian more than ever, yet had never been more miserably conflicted in her life.

Two months after the Isadora Duncan dream she incubated another, this time asking for a progress report on the work she and Ian had done to make their marriage a more mature one. This is her dream producer's response, followed by Tanya's commentary:

I am walking down a path in the desert. Ian is a small boy whose hand I hold. There is a breeze, and suddenly the gods come down to me in a whirlwind and say in many echoing voices, "If you do not separate from Ian, you will die." I tell the gods to stop trying to push me around and that I am going to stay with Ian forever, no matter what. We'll manage.

The next thing I know, I am in a sort of hospital-jail, awaiting my execution. Ian visits and brings me flowers, but he cannot help me. At dawn, I know I must walk outside again to my execution. There is no way out. The gods have won. ("The Gods in a Whirlwind")

This dream was unbelievably vivid. It tells me that things have not changed that much after all. I am heading for a DEAD end. *Ian as a small boy?* How much of my love for Ian is a desire to mother him, to give him the confidence he lacks that he is O.K. just as he is? Maybe I see him that way because I need so badly to feel needed and loved myself. A child will never walk out on me as a grown, confident man might. Ian was not in prison; I was. I was the sick one in the hospital, not he. Oh my. So that's why I refuse to listen to the gods. I am so afraid of being alone that I've chosen a man I feel safe and secure with and who would never leave me, as my father divorced my mother. I chose a good man, a wonderful man, but one I was bound to have a very difficult time living with. I have criticized him for just being the way he is. I tell myself that he is shy and introverted because he is emotionally immature or because he doesn't know any better so that I can mother him. I feel ashamed that I have not realized earlier how much my need for emotional security motivated me to marry Ian. But I also love him; even when I realize all that, I love him. He is such a fine person. What now?

A few weeks passed. Ian was invited to Europe for a very important series of conferences on international law. Tanya decided not to leave her work to accompany him on the six-week tour. She wanted to see what it would be like to live alone for awhile. As Ian's departure date approached, Tanya would burst into tears at the thought of the upcoming separation. Ian encouraged her to accompany him, but she refused, saying that she knew she had to convince herself that she could survive on her own for at least six weeks. The morning he left, Ian was very sad to be going without his wife, but Tanya was far more upset. She later wrote in her journal, "It felt as though my heart had been torn out of my chest and that all that would remain after Ian was gone would be an unbearably heavy black hole. Even as I felt this, I told myself how foolish I was being to make so much of a six-week separation. But that didn't diminish the real anguish in my whole being."

After what was a very painful early morning parting, Tanya went back to bed and prayed for a dream that would help her understand why she was so terribly upset, as if she might never see Ian again. This was her dream:

A group of us are having lunch in a lovely garden outdoors. Someone tells me that the "cowhorse" behind me is suffering terribly because he is having to eat a lamb. Without turning to look at the cowhorse, I say, "But he must eat lamb to survive. There is nothing intrinsically terrible about that. Though I guess it must be hard to actually do. Yet don't forget, the cowhorse must have been doing it all its life." I then turn around to look at the part cow, part horse, animal which is in anguish at having to kill and eat a lamb that lies, nearly all eaten, on the ground. Someone says, "Yes, but this is the first time it has had to do it consciously" (i.e., kill and skin the lamb instead of receiving it in a bowl from a can). Then the cowhorse and I tune into each other, recognizing that we share the same suffering—I from Ian's and my separation, and the cowhorse from its having to eat a little lamb to survive. The cowhorse, mostly horse now, snuggles up to me and comforts me. The anguish leaves my heart completely. I begin to feel a new energy and sense of well-being. How wonderful! I awake, feeling healed of my sadness and with a sense of strength and energy I

only now realize I have been missing for the past two years of my life.
("The Cowhorse")

Tanya felt no need to interview her dream producer about this dream. Its meaning and its effect were obvious to her. She entered in her dream journal the following dream commentary:

By following through with my determination to survive without Ian for six weeks, I am eating the sheepish, overly dependent part of myself. It is hard, but if I am to survive as a whole person, there is no choice. Even the confusion about the cowhorse makes sense. It is both a cow and a horse. The cow represents a gentle, receptive female; the horse an energetic male. I haven't been expressing both these sides of my being, because I didn't dare sacrifice the security of a sheeplike need to be secure and dependent. Life should be more exciting than that. My cowhorse has tremendous energy, because it went ahead and ate the lamb. I am filled with that energy and realize that the last time I felt this way was before I became very attached to Ian. I feel really alive after not even realizing I have been giving up my sense of strength and independence for one of security. I could not bear ever to give up so much of myself again. Now I see how I was executing myself. What a price I've been willing to pay for security! I feel like a very different person this morning. Will Ian and I stay together? I don't know, but if not, I know we will both survive. I wasn't at all sure of that before now.

As things turned out, not only did Tanya find new strength and happiness during those six weeks apart, but Ian, to his great surprise, felt a great surge of strength and independence as well. When he returned from his trip, Ian and Tanya compared notes and discovered that they had been playing the same security-at-any-cost game, which had been draining them both of a lot of energy. They tried to re-create their marriage on a new basis. Yet now more than ever, their temperamental differences were so marked that it soon became clear they were mismatched. They divorced, and eventually each remarried. Ian found a partner who was more like him and who enjoyed the things he did without feeling she was giving up the chance to do something else more exciting in the name of compromise. Tanya married a man who enthusiastically shared many of her interests. Their relationship felt more like a merger than a compromise to her. She had taken her dreams to heart and participated in some workshops in family therapy to explore the dynamics of relationships to which those involved can be so blind. Her dream producer had to work to get the message across to her, but when she finally got it, she knew what to do with it. As we consider all Tanya's dreams together and in the context of her life, each one makes more sense than if it were considered alone.

You will find that your dreams, too, will be easier to understand if you review them regularly and examine series of dreams which treat the same issue. By discussing dreams with friends and perhaps by exchanging journals, as Tanya and I did, you will discover that it is often easier to notice and study structural tendencies in dreams and dream series which are not your own. You might want to review Tanya's dreams and practice spotting some of the basic structural tendencies illustrated in them. For instance, notice how the images of the hospital-jail and the cowhorse are not confusing when they are accepted as being both a hospital and a jail, a cow and a horse. Examine the juxtaposition of scenes within a dream and see if it is useful to consider a causal relationship between some of them. For example, in Tanya's "Gods in a Whirlwind" dream, it makes sense to think that the gods tell her she will die because she walks with Ian as if he were a child. Because she ignores the gods' warning, she finds herself in a hospital-jail awaiting execution. Notice also the role of the narrator in Tanya's dream of the Egyptian king. Now and then your dreams will provide very distinct verbal clues to their meaning, especially those dreams you have incubated. Sometimes these interpretive commentaries will seem to come from an unseen narrator; at other times, they come from a seen or unseen actor in the dream, as they did Tanya's cowhorse dream, where someone at the picnic table tells her about the activities of the cowhorse. As you reread this dream series, ask yourself how Tanya might have understood her dreams differently if she had interpreted them all, expecially the figure of Ian, on a subjective level. What questions would you like to ask Tanya if you could interview her about these dreams?

Answering the Questions   There are many other ways to use dream incubation to increase your understanding of the relationships in your life. Suppose you are lonely and have very few friends. If you were to ask your dreams why and what you could do about it, you might receive some very surprising answers. Often people who are lonely feel there is nothing they can do about it. Yet there is almost always an alternative to loneliness, and dreams can show it to you. They can also help you to see how and why you have been unable to recognize and accept these alternatives, which have always been available to you.

Members of our Dream Meetings have received helpful dream answers to quite a variety of questions about relationships. One member incubated a dream asking for aid in understanding and dealing with his son, who was getting involved with dangerous drugs. Another asked why her friends always took advantage of her. A mother's dream incubation helped her see what was behind her son's stealing money from her purse and suggested how she deal with it. A loving but very strict father was warned that, if he didn't moderate his excessive scolding of his young son and praise him and play with him more, he would soon have a very insecure and rebellious teenager on his hands. His dream also made it clear that the father's own self-critical and perfectionistic attitudes, inherited from *his* father, were being unfairly visited upon his son.

Kay, who had begun to fall in love was troubled by what she thought might be unfinished business with an old flame. She wanted to be free of the "what if" syndrome and her lack of commitment resulting from it. She incubated a dream, asking, "Am I free yet of my attachments to old boyfriends, especially Bret?" She dreamed:

I am on a beach; it is "the meeting place." All my old boyfriends are coming here. I am to meet with each one, review my relationship with him, and see if I am free of a desire to reanimate it. If I am truly unencumbered by "what if" fantasies, then I will be free to commit myself to a relationship with Michael. Then every boyfriend of my life comes before me; even ones I had crushes on in grammar school! I review our relationships, one at a time, thank each man for his contribution to my life, and move on to the next, feeling free and glad for the one before. But where was Bret? I looked for him all over the beach, hoping to find him and afraid of finding him. What if I see him again and can't resist loving him? That would ruin my relationship with Michael, and yet things could never work our well for Bret and me. I meet a sixteen-year-old girl who says she was with Bret on the boat coming here, which apparently carried my other old flames. She tells me that Bret had introduced her to the joys of sex and that she was very lucky to have met him, but she had no idea where he was now. I am continuing my search when a kind old man approaches and says, "You have just received a letter that will answer your question." ("Where Is Bret?")

When Kay awoke, she was relieved and felt that she had actually worked through some old resentments, hurts, and hopes she had not even realized she was still carrying around inside herself. But what about Bret? She incubated a dream three nights in a row, trying to discover what was in the letter that was supposed to explain it all. Kay suggested to herself that she would find the letter and understand it easily. No response. She found it very maddening that a dream would tease her like this. When she brought her dream to the Dream Meeting, another member asked her if the recorded copy of her dream on the paper in her journal might not be the letter to which the dream referred. It dawned on Kay that the dream itself was the letter. She then asked another member to interview her about the sixteen-year-old who had seen Bret. She discovered that her dream producer was pointing out that Bret had been the perfect man for her at one point in her life. He had introduced her to a new, more adult level of love between a man and a woman, but, as the sixteen-year-old implied, the voyage together was over. This is the sort of dream which seems to consolidate past experience and open the way for new development.

Do you recall any dreams in which you were told that you have received a letter or will see a picture or film regarding a troublesome matter? Try looking at the dream itself or your recording of it as the letter, photograph, or film referred to. If you dream of being photographed in a situation which would embarrass you if other people saw the pictures, you can bet that one of the "other people" is you, and the picture is your dream. The embarrassing situation will probably give you a clue to attitudes or behaviors which, when acknowledged, may embarrass you. However, if you do acknowledge them, you will able to deal with things that are probably causing you difficulties in your day life.

In one of our Dream Meetings, a student suggested that each member choose the most frustrating or painful relationship of his or her present life and incubate a dream for guidance in improving it. Three students decided to try it. A young woman who strongly resented and perhaps hated her alcoholic father asked for a dream that would liberate her from the weight of her hatred by helping her better understand both her father and her feelings toward him. She awoke from a nightmare in which a deep-sea monster was attacking her. She found the dream so frightening that she refused to look into it. She decided that her feelings toward her father were just too much to handle, so she contented herself with continuing to hate him until some later date when she felt up to dealing with it. Was it her deep hatred that was attacking her in the dream and in her life?

Another member, the weary husband of an alcoholic wife, incubated a dream asking for strength to cope with his wife or to leave her. John had one of those dreams in which everything seemed more real than in waking life. Colors were more vivid, and the meaning of everything in the dream was profoundly and instantaneously understood. This is how he told us his dream:

I saw two beautiful flames of light, one green, one blue. They represented and were the divine essence of my self and of my wife (she, the blue one, and myself, the green one). I became aware of actually being these flames whose colors blended exquisitely. As the flames, we looked up and saw whiteness like an angel or god passing over us. We were blessed by this loving, peaceful presence, and it filled us both with vibrant energy. ("Flames")

John told us that he awoke feeling revitalized and full of hope and love for his wife. He asked for and received dreams like this two more times when he was feeling discouraged and almost hopeless about his marriage. Each time the dreams reanimated his hope. About eight months later, his wife stopped drinking, and she has not returned to it in the five years since. John's dreams helped him when he needed it most.

The third member used an incubation of rapprochement. In *rapprochement* incubations, the dreamer asks for help in dealing with particularly difficult relationships that have come to an impasse. The dreamer may have tried many approaches to harmonizing a relationship with unsatisfactory results and finds herself with no clear alternative but to suffer the relationship. At this point, when there seems nothing more to be done in the waking state, the dreamer can ask for a dream experience of "coming together" or rapprochement with the person in question. The goal is to come to some understanding with the other person while in the sleep state, when one is apparently more objective and open to new and different perceptions. Whether the dreamer actually somehow meets the "adversary" in the sleep state or whether the dreamer simply dreams a normal dream about the other person is not clear. What one can say is that people who have incubated rapprochement dreams report having "been with" their adversaries in the dreams and having come to a new understanding, compassion, or peace with that adversary. The result of most rapprochement dreams is a marked improvement in the problematic relationships.

Lynn was a young feminist whose mother was unable to accept the fact that her daughter's values and morals were not in line with the dictates of her church. This had resulted in the mother's judging her daughter as sinful and almost entirely immoral. And, of course, her daughter judged her as rigid, naïve, and reactionary. Lynn was saddened by the emotional distance she and her mother suffered. She wanted to share more of her life with her mother, but she wasn't able to pierce through the Mormon armor. The mother, meanwhile, felt she had failed as a mother and didn't know what to do. Lynn incubated a request that she and her mother meet in the dream state, if that was possible, and talk with each other at a level where their hearts could speak and understand without the noise of reciprocal judgments and criticisms based on conscious opinions.

Lynn told us that she dreamed of meeting with her mother in what seemed to be an out-of-body state of awareness. She and her mother had a long talk, in which each listened to the other with interest and love. They found a way of understanding and accepting each other and were rejoicing in their new closeness when the dreamlike experience ended. Lynn awoke feeling as if she had actually been talking unguardedly to her mother for the first time in years. She had wanted to telephone her mother in Salt Lake City to see if she had had the same dream but hesitated, knowing what her mother thought about "dreams and all that nonsense." A few hours later, her mother telephoned, and they had one of the most intimate and pleasurable conversations they had shared in several years. Lynn cast about to see if her mother had shared her dream experience of the night before but discovered no indication of it. Lynn decided to be grateful for the experience of accord with her mother, whether it had actually happened between the two of them or whether it occurred just within herself. She, at any rate, felt less condemning of her mother's lifestyle and more accepting of her as a lovable person in spite of her opinions!

Nan asked for a rapprochement dream that would help her resolve a very awkward situation. She was on a two-week cruise, during which she was obliged to dine with the same group of people each night. Nan found one member of the group, Bill, to be an extremely unpleasant dinner companion. She felt that he tried his best to control all conversation, that he was loud, and that he lapsed into an irritated silence whenever the direction of the conversation was wrested from him. Nan chose not to confront Bill, who seemed not to like her at all and who might somehow embarrass her. Yet she resented having her vacation marred by the dread of dinner time. After a week of dismal dinning, she decided to ask for a rapprochement dream. Her hope was that in the dream state they would both be more objective and perceptive and would be better able to understand each other. In the vivid dream she had,

I found myself knocking at Bill's bedroom door. He appeared, and we talked in the hallway. I was pretty sure that I was out of my body in a dream state, but not positive. I told Bill why I didn't like him and how I

had been hurt by his inconsiderateness. Whereas in day life I would never have thought that he would understand my feelings, in our present reality he did. He thanked me for telling him how I felt and apologized for having hurt my feelings, explaining that he had thought I "had no time for him." He added that he hoped we could become friends in waking reality. I was glad, for I really liked him now. Then I seemed to go home, but I can't remember how. ("Dinner Companion")

Nan had this to say about the experience:

The next day I told Bill that I had dreamed about him. He was very curious to know what I had dreamed, but he had remembered no dreams himself. When I told him the dream, he responded much as he had in the dream. We related to each other with the same interest and spirit as in the dream and only a little more defensiveness. We became friends after this. Had the dream portrayed an actual event, or did it simply give me the courage to confront Bill, who would have reacted in the way he did even if I had not had the dream?

A son who hated his alcoholic father for all the pain he had experienced in living with him incubated a dream as a last resort. Phil asked for a dream experience that would help to free him from his heavy burden of resentment and anger. He dreamed that he was holding an ugly frog with bumps all over it. Phil worried that the frog would give him warts. Then the realization dawned upon him that he should love the poor, lonely, ugly frog, and so he kissed it. At that point the frog turned into the dreamer's neurotic, lonely, and very grateful father. The dream had the effect of showing the son that at this late stage of the game, compassion and love were the best means by which he could free himself from his own hatred. Perhaps the father was unable to change, but the son was not. The experience of loving, repugnant frog-father was vivid and profound enough to teach Phil to let go of some of his resentments and experience the loving, compassionate feelings they had been hiding. The pathetic frog remained a potent image in Phil's memory, one which he conjured up each time his resentments began to overcome him in his relations with his father.

Dreams can also be used as a form of direct interpersonal communications. Frequently clients in psychotherapy will dream dreams which inform their therapists of their clients' hidden thoughts and feelings. Dreams can provide that extra push many of us need to say things we find awkward or embarassing.

Barbara had the following dream:

I was in a pool swimming with my eight-year-old son on my back. I would swim under the water while my son's head would stay above it. I did this in several short bursts, while my husband was supposed to take a picture of us in this position. But somehow he wasn't getting the picture taken. I was beginning to feel as if I was going to drown if he didn't get it soon. Each time I surfaced, I asked him, "Did you get the picture?" Each time his answer was, "Not yet." ("Get the Picture?")

It was immediately clear to the other members of the Dream Meeting that Barbara was trying to get her husband to see that she felt she was being submerged by her solo child-rearing duties and that she wanted some acknowledgement and relief. Barbara herself took quite a while to recognize the obvious play on words in her only line in the dream scene: "Did you get the picture?" When she finally got it after hearing another dreamer repeat the words, she laughed, then decided to take the message home to her husband.

A year after meeting Steve, my fiancé, I began to worry that my relationship with him was going too smoothly. Was I just fooling myself or was our love as wonderful as it seemed? I asked my dream producer, "Can a relationship this happy last?" She responded with this dream:

I saw in a beautiful, sunny, redwood forest two magnificent redwood trees dancing in the wind. They were young, graceful, and majestic. I realized that the taller tree symbolized Steve, the smaller beside it, myself. Then I was aware of our having become these trees. We were at peace with the world and would grow in the forest for centuries to come. ("Dancing Redwoods")

5

Your Dreams and Your Body

The ancient Greeks and Romans believed that dreams come from the gods and could both diagnose and, at times, precipitate the healing of physical infirmity and disease. Many cultures, both primitive and highly developed, have shared this belief. Freud, who has influenced our contemporary beliefs about dreams profoundly, hypothesized that the purpose of dreaming is to cope with emotional problems stemming from repressed instinctual drives. He believed that dreams, properly interpreted, lead to the diagnosis and at times the resolution of sexual conflicts. Although both ancient and Freudian dream theories today seem somewhat limited in their descriptions of the origin and purpose of dreams, they nevertheless emphasize at least two important functions of dreaming. In this chapter we shall look into ways we can use dreams to improve both our physical and our psychosexual health.

Coping with Illness, Accidents, Bad Habits, Insomnia, and Old Age. The ancient Greeks built sacred temples to the god Aesculapius and conducted elaborate dream incubation rituals designed to elicit divine assistance in combating physical illness.[1] The Romans and some Hebrews, who shared with the Greeks the belief that dreams come from supernatural powers, also visited Aesculapian temples, where they incubated dreams to obtain cures for (usually physical) illness. Although the Talmudic sages discouraged such Graeco-Roman practices of appealing to dream oracles through incubation rituals, they nevertheless believed that dreams often shed light upon the dreamer's state of sickness or health.[2] Galen,[3] the second-century Greek physician and founder of the science of experimental physiology, and Aristotle,[4] founder of the science of logic, both held that dreams reflect bodily states and that they could profitably be used to diagnose and treat illness.

Later Western philosophical and scientific developments led to the belief that physical illness had physical causes which, when scientifically and logically studied, could eventually be cured by physical treatments. The fundamental concept that illness is caused by germs or chemical imbalances in the body has left the theory that dreams reflect or influence physical illness without many admirers. Some medical researchers, encouraged by the fact that some mental illnesses have been found to respond to certain drugs, hope one day to identify the physiological or biochemical basis of all illnesses, and to develop chemical treatments which will cure them.

However, a growing number of researchers in the fields of psychology and medicine feel that the causes of physical and mental illness should be sought not only in laboratories but also, and perhaps more importantly, in the hearts and minds of those who are ill. The discovery of the role played by emotional tension in precipitating and exacerbating problems such as headaches, ulcers, asthma, and intestinal dysfunction has resulted in a greater respect for the theory that many physical illnesses have at least some psychological determinants. Dr. O. Carl Simonton,[5] a radiologist in Texas, has gone so far as to propose that physical maladies, even life-threatening illnesses such as cancer, are associated with certain mental attitudes and beliefs in the mind of the sick person. He is experimenting with the use of psychotherapeutic techniques as an adjunct to the traditional radiation and chemotherapy treatments received by his cancer patients. It will be some time before there is sufficient data to define to what extent and in what circumstances attitudes and emotions influence or perhaps even cause physical illness. However, it is already obvious that, in many illnesses, there is a psychological component which, when understood, can lead to a lessening of the severity of troublesome symptoms or, at the very least, to an improvement in the sick person's attitude toward the illness.

Several members of our Dream Meetings have used dream incubation to investigate the possible influence of psychological factors in their physical illnesses.

Ann, who had recently moved to California from Florida, became ill with swollen ovaries, which caused her such pain that even walking was difficult. She was seen every few days by a gynecologist, who could find no cause for the condition. After two months, the gynecologist suggested exploratory surgery to see what the problem might be. Ann decided to obtain another medical opinion before proceeding with the surgery and flew back to Florida to see her former gynecologist. On the cross-country flight, Ann decided that she would try to incubate a dream which might heal her or at least show her if she was somehow psychologically causing this illness. That night she incubated a dream with this long phrase: "O.K. This is your last chance to save me from the doctor's knife. Why am I sick, and what can be done about it?"

Ann had a long dream in which she was constantly reminded through voices and images that "there is time, there is plenty of time for all of this." There unfolded before her dreaming eyes several scenes in which she bathed peacefully in a river; gave easy birth to an infant; with effort climbed a ladder, at the top of which she found her law degree; and sat peacefully in meditation beside the river. All these scenes seemed to occur simultaneously, and in all of them she was in or beside the river. She felt a sense of triumph in the ladder scene, one of surprised pleasure in the easy birth scene, and one of pleasure and tranquility in the scenes where she washed her hair in and meditated beside the river. She awoke feeling extraordinarily refreshed and peaceful after this dream. Then she noticed that she felt no pain in her abdomen for the first time in two months! She saw her doctor that day. He could find nothing abnormal about her ovaries. Another doctor who examined her could find nothing unusual either. When Ann suggested that her dream might have healed her, the doctors said, "That's impossible." They decided that the most likely explanation was that the letter describing Ann's symptoms while in California must have been written by an incompetent gynecologist, and that Ann's experience of pain must have been all in her mind.

Ann had another explanation. She felt the dream had relieved her of a great deal of partly unconscious conflict she had felt about having children. She had felt that having a child would rob her of her private time, of her tranquility, and of her chance to be a success in her career. In fact, as she realized after this dream, she had begun to feel that her determination to finish law school would evaporate if she gave in to her more "feminine" desires simply to enjoy life and let in all the gentle, pleasure-oriented feelings she had put aside as she applied herself to her studies. Now her dream was telling her that she could relax. There would be enough time for her to experience both sides of her nature, the achievement-oriented side and the feeling-oriented one. There need be no life-and-death opposition between them. Ann hypothesized that her swollen ovaries were a symbolic representation of her psychological efforts to reject her pleasure-oriented, "feminine" self for fear that they might sabotage her career plans. She interpreted the birth scene as symbolic of the fact that what she thought of as her feminine nature would enrich her life with a greater sensitivity to her feelings without disrupting her privacy or her work. Ann's dream had made a big impact on her. Whether or not it actually healed her is impossible to prove, but as far as she was concerned, she had realized in her dream something very important for the happiness and enjoyment of her life. The fact that Ann awoke feeling fine for the first time in two months led her to believe that there was more than coincidence involved.

A less dramatic but more common dream response to incubation questions about psychological factors influencing illnesses such as viruses, headaches, and arthritis suggests that the dreamer needs to resolve some tension-producing conflicts in his or her life. The illness is usually seen in the dream as an escape from dealing with such issues. When you are ill, you might ask your dreams, "What am I trying to avoid or get out of?" You may be surprised to find that, if this is the case, your illness will quickly clear up as soon as you have confronted the problem your illness helped you to avoid. Of course, illness can also be used in order to elicit sympathy and extract extra attention. Such "secondary gains" are often easy to see in minor illnesses such as colds and headaches; they may also operate in injuries sustained in "accidents."

A student whose favorite pastime was playing tennis sprained his back one day when he was lifting something heavy out of the trunk of his car. There was some question as to whether he might have slipped a disc, as he complained of pain radiating down into his legs, a common symptom of a pinched nerve. He knew that a common treatment for pinched nerves (or slipped discs, as they are popularly referred to) was to immobilize the patient in a hospital bed for six weeks. He found this an unpleasant prospect, especially as it offered no promise of alleviating the pain. He and his doctor decided to wait and see if the pain would subside. Five weeks later, Peter was still spending most of his time in bed, because the pain was least severe when he was lying down. It occurred to him that he might try to incubate a dream to see if he was amplifying or mentally exaggerating his pain for some psychological reason. He also wondered if his "accident" had occurred at this particular time by something more meaningful than coincidence. He incubated his dream, asking,

"Why is my back malfunctioning, and what can I do about it?" Here is his dream response:

The Communist Party is going to have me executed for not toeing the party line. I accept my fate, because I feel their power is too great to resist. Dean, who is a fervent party member and yet my friend, is also to be executed as a warning to the rest that "the party" can kill anyone, that no one is safe. Dean is ironing the shirt he will wear for his execution, because he feels this is part of his duty to "the party." If they say he must do it, then he will. I am furious that he is willing to help dig his own grave and tell him so. Then I see myself doing an exercise that is good for my back, and the dream ends. ("Commie Execution")

Here is the dream interview Peter conducted in his journal:

The Feeling? The dream reminds me of how I felt yesterday when I was telling my classmate Dean that he was going to kill himself working so hard. He is trying to run a business and be a full-time student at the same time, and the wear is beginning to show.

The Setting? The Communist Worker's State! I am under their control. Am I, in fact? I see myself as relatively free of the work ethic most males in our society are burdened with.

The Action? I am to be killed because I rebel; Dean will be killed as part of "the party's" terror tactics. I've got it.

Aha! Both Dean and I live under the oppression of a system of beliefs called the work ethic, or the Worker's State. Even though I rebel against my own work ethic (by putting off writing my master's thesis for six months, for example), I still operate under its basic assumptions. Who rebels against something that doesn't affect them? Dean also lives under this system of thought, but he follows the rules. By being such a good worker, he is killing himself. I've been using my back pain as an excuse to continue putting off starting my thesis. The dream suggests that, as long as I remain locked in this authority conflict, I will suffer my self-execution: spending most of my time in bed. Dean may be willing to accept his fate, but not I. If I could realize that I'm doing the paper for myself because I want the degree, I would probably get to it sooner. Besides, if it is true that I'm perpetuating this back pain to avoid the paper, I'd better get it done, or it could keep me out of commission forever! I'll ask the doctor if the exercise in the dream would be safe to try, and

I am going to prop myself up and write that thesis no matter how much it hurts.

Peter did just this. In two weeks his thesis was finished and his back pain gone. Had he been amplifying the pain of the injury as an escape? Or might he have unconsciously arranged the "accident" to provide himself with a good excuse for putting off his thesis for a few more months? Either or both hypotheses might be true, but in any case Peter's work with his incubated dream seemed to put him back on the tennis courts sooner than he might otherwise have expected. Peter never did practice the exercise suggested in the dream, though his doctor said it might be helpful; therefore, it could not be credited with the positive outcome.

Psychosomatic medicine focuses on the role of psychosocial variables not in causing disease but in altering individual susceptibility to disease. It studies the reciprocal relationships of biological, psychological, and sociological factors in maintaining health and in influencing the onset and course of disease. Many medical researchers now believe that all illness is influenced by psychosocial factors.[6] These factors can be effectively uncovered and confronted in the dream state. People suffering from chronic pain can also use incubation to discover the psychosomatic dimensions of real pain. Perhaps one day specialists in the control of chronic and severe pain will have the skill to study their patients' dreams incubated on such questions as, "How can I reduce my susceptibility to sensations of pain?" "How and why do I amplify the pain I have?" "What secondary gains do I get from my pain?" and "Show me a good alternative to focusing on my pain."

Working on Bad Habits. Sometimes dreams will come to us quite spontaneously with warnings that we have been neglecting our bodies or are about to fall ill. In dreams where you appear extremely fatigued, you may be telling yourself to slow down and get more sleep. I have heard many dreams in which the dreamer sees or desires fresh vegetables or fruit but is disappointed or angered to be unable to find them or to be presented with potatoes and candy instead. These dreams usually occur after a period of unhealthy or excessive eating on the part of the dreamer. They usually have the short-term effect of tempting the junk-food eater to enjoy more nutritious, fresh food. In another version of this dream theme, the dreamer finds himself gorging on foods which are not good for him or of which he has been eating too much. These dreams act like aversive conditioning in that they literally leave a bad taste in the dreamer's mouth and discourage his eating of the food.

This same sort of aversive conditioning occurs in what I call pipe dreams. In these, the dreamer sees herself engaging in what she considers a bad habit, such as smoking, overeating, or drinking, but in the dream the experience, for one reason or another, is highly unpleasant. If you are trying to kick a habit, it may be useful to induce a dream in which you are either vividly impressed by an unpleasant experience with it or where you see yourself already liberated from it, free to enjoy the benefits of not indulging in the habit. Inducing a dream where you choose the specific action ahead of time is rather difficult to achieve, even with the aid of a skilled hypnotist.[7] My students and I have had much more success by incubating a dream with a phrase such as, "Why do I drink so much?" "Why am I fat?" or "Help me, inspire me to drop this habit."

Approaching the problem in this way allows your dream producer to explain the psychological dynamics which perpetuate your habit. We often use a compulsive habit as a substitution for more basic, often more healthy, but unrecognized psychological needs. This method also leaves the producer free to use the imagery that will best elicit in you understanding and a desire to kick your habit. You can also suggest to yourself, or make a long-term incubation request in your journal, that from time to time you will receive dreams to aid you in firming your resolve to drop your habit. In cases of drug and alcohol addiction, I have been told of dreams where the addicted person, or someone close to him, dreamt dreams warning of future temptations that would threaten the addict's progress in fighting the habit. These dreams served the function of forewarning and thus forearming the addict against the temptation which, in the three cases I know of, did occur a few days after the dream. Incubating dreams on the dynamics behind troublesome habits might also be very useful in dealing with such habits as compulsive lying, gossiping, bragging, talking, cheating, or stealing. Habitual responses which seem counterproductive in stressful situations that elicit them can also be explored in this manner with such incubation questions as: "Why do I always get so nervous when . . . ?" or "Why do I always get so jealous (angry, frightened) when . . . ?"

Coping with Anxieties. Two women in the Dream Meetings asked their dreams if they were safe taking the birth-control pill. They had not had any trouble on the pill, but they were concerned about the reports of possible dangerous side effects. Each received very clear warnings to get off the pill. One dreamer decided not to listen to her dream, and she is still fine two years later. The other took her dream warning to heart and quit the pill. To her surprise, just over a week after quitting the pill, she experienced a new sense of buoyancy and what seemed to be increased energy. Her doctor said the change possibly was the result of going off the pill. (There is evidence to suggest that the pill has a minor depressive effect on some women.) This dreamer was very glad she had listened to her dream, because she felt her increased energy and optimism had helped her to eat less and thereby lose ten pounds.

Four women I know have asked their dreams if they were pregnant when they had missed one menstrual cycle. In each case, the dream response proved to be correct. Many researchers have theorized that subconsciously we have access to very detailed knowledge about the functioning of our bodies. Dream incubation might be a simple and effective method of tapping that knowledge.

One man, who had never incubated a dream before, decided to use this technique in an interesting way. His dream, and the interview which followed it, will provide one more idea on using incubation creatively as well as practice and review in using the interview to interpret a difficult dream.

A psychologist named Skip had suffered from moderate insomnia for three nights, and each morning he awoke feeling anxious and fatigued. He discussed this with his training psychiatrist and could find no explanation for it. His wife was a member of one of our Dream Meetings and had been encouraging him to study his dreams for some understanding of the middle-of-the-night stress he often experienced. Skip decided to follow his wife's counsel and incubated a dream, asking, "Why this nighttime anxiety, especially lately?" That night he dreamed:

I'm at a ski resort. The weather is stormy and rainy. The snow is sticky, so skiing is out of the question. I am inside with Rick, who is wearing a black shirt and a blue tuxedo dinner jacket. I am wearing my black tuxedo but am worried about wearing my ordinary old brown shoes with it, rather than my blue snow boots. ("Blue Boots")

Skip brought his dream to a special dream session for the spouses of members of the Dream Meetings, and he asked me to interview him.

Gayle. Do you have any idea what the dream is about, Skip?

Skip. Before I awoke, just after the dream, I understood it perfectly. It was amazingly clear. But as I awoke, I forgot a lot of my insight. All I remember is that I use self-detachment as a defense against experiencing my feelings. I need to let myself experience the emotions of my body, instead of analyzing my emotions as if they were thoughts. But I fear that sensual feeling will take over and vitiate my objective intellectual powers and therefore my self-esteem and work achievement. In the dream, I had a very immediate understanding that there are two modes of perceiving life. One is experiencing the self, knowing first-hand its feelings, emotions, etc. The other is objectifying the self, or viewing my life experience as an observer with my intellect. I saw that I need to use the first mode more if I really want to live, though the second mode is important, too. Now it's hard to see how all this relates to the dream.

G. It sounds as if you had quite a vivid experience of insight in this dream. Does this happen to you often?

S. No. In fact, I rarely remember my dreams. That the incubation worked at all was a surprise.

G. Congratulations. Now I'll ask you a few questions about your dream. Just pretend that I come from another planet and know nothing about earth life, O.K.? [Skip nods in assent.] Would you describe to me what a ski resort is?

S. It's a place where one can get good exercise and relaxation sliding down beautiful snowy mountains with specially designed boards on your feet that distribute your weight for maximum speed and smooth going. I love to ski, though I don't do it often enough. Skiing reminds me of the pleasure of physical existence that is free and loose and uncomplicated. When I ski, I feel that I am flying and at one with my feelings. I'd like my life to be more like ski resort life.

G. Suppose you were the writer-producer of this dream movie. Why would you write in the bad weather at the ski resort?

S. To represent the emotional stress I've been feeling lately. The rain and storm are making it impossible to enjoy my emotional, feeling life lately. The weather (my emotional life) is too turbulent to get outside and enjoy my (feeling) environment.

G. Who is Rick and what is he like?

S. He's a friend who likes to martyr himself. He hangs on to his problems and seems fascinated by them. He rarely seems motivated to do anything about them.

G. Is there a part of you, like Rick, that likes to hang on to problems?

S. My wife thinks so. She thinks that I use my personal psychoanalysis to talk about problems without doing much about them. Yet I think talking brings understanding. You can't just pretend problems don't exist and sweep them under the rug with positive thinking.

G. What do you think about Rick's black shirt and blue dinner jacket? What sort of person wears a black shirt? What sort of person wears a blue tuxedo?

S. The black shirt reminds me of a priest's shirt. In my analytic session today, I touched on this dream and I thought it was about my psychiatrist, who is like a priest-confessor. That's about as far as we got with the dream, because my associations led me to other things for the rest of the hour. The blue dinner jacket? There's something false about people who wear them, sort of a fake sportiveness. Rick's wearing one is inappropriate because it is winter, when a black tux is called for not a springtime blue. Besides, the black shirt looks awful with it.

G. Inappropriate. Does that remind you of anything?

S. Well, President Carter has just made an announcement that he considers "inappropriate" our U.N. delegate's statement of confession for the United States role in the political affairs of Chile.

G. How do you feel in a tuxedo like the one you wear in the dream?

S. I love it. I always feel well dressed and very self-confident. You can go anywhere dressed in a tuxedo.

G. You are appropriately dressed then?

S. Except for my ordinary brown shoes. I'm concerned about that.

G. Describe your brown shoes.

S. They are old and scruffy. They are very comfortable, but they're no good for walking in the snow at the ski resort. Even in ideal weather, they slip in the snow and I get cold feet. I want to go out into the stormy weather and at least enjoy the outdoors if the weather is not right for skiing, but I can't with these shoes. I wish I had my blue boots on.

G. Describe your blue boots.

S. My wife convinced me to buy them on our last ski vacation. I had resisted doing so for a few days, but I finally got tired of slipping and sliding in the snow-mushy streets with cold wet feet. The skiing was not great, so my wife suggested we go for a hike to a small restaurant in the mountains. I knew I'd need a firmer footing if I wanted to go hiking instead of remaining in the hotel all day. So I gave in to her pressuring. She knows a lot more than I about ski resort survival since she has skiied more than I have, so she picked out the boots she thought would be best. They are very warm and have huge nonskid soles like tractor wheels. I was very glad she nagged me into buying them. I wondered why I had put up with wearing my old brown city shoes at ski resorts for so long. With the boots, I could really get out and enjoy the outdoor mountain life even in bad weather without fear of slipping and breaking my neck. The boots seemed symbolic of something very important in my life, but I wasn't sure what.

G. How old are your brown shoes?

S. Five years.

G. How long have you been in psychoanalysis?

S. Five years!

G. Does that tell you anything?

S. You mean that my nighttime anxiety is like the dream storm and that my psychoanalysis doesn't provide me with the footing to deal with it?

G. Maybe. What might the blue boots signify?

S. My wife's telling me that I should work on my dreams to explore the reasons behind my nighttime distress. She has mentioned that shoes can represent understanding in dreams. Perhaps dream work would give me a better understanding than my city, verbal analysis can of my bad-weather nights.

G. Maybe you have represented your feeling life as a ski resort. Your wife knows her way around in this environment better than you, perhaps because she is more comfortable with her feelings and emotions, which are the raw material of our dream lives.

S. Yes, and the storm is only temporary, I'll be able to ski and fly soon, but in the meanwhile my dreams may provide me with the understanding I need to feel comfortable in the outdoors. The ski resort represents the experiencing of the self through feelings, and my brown shoes, which are fine for the city, are representative of the second mode of perceiving life, that of objectifying the self, which I do a lot of in my analysis. Even though I do get into my body and emotions while we explore the transference, it's not as vivid or as immediate an experience as I've had in my dreams. I'll have to think about this.

G. I'd rather you not think about it so much, Skip! Why not just relive the dream a few times each day for two or three days and see what happens?

Dreams in Old Age. Many older people complain of insomnia because they can't sleep more than three or four hours at night, and they must take brief naps in the daytime. Actually, for someone over fifty-five or so, three or four hours of sleep with a nap may be quite sufficient. As we get older, we need less and less sleep. These "insomniacs" usually think that they "should" have eight hours of sleep, which sends them running to the medicine cabinet for sleeping pills. Many older people complain to me that they know they need more sleep than they are getting because they awake fatigued. These people frequently are not enjoying their lives, which tend to be somewhat inactive. They say that they don't want to remember their dreams because they are generally unpleasant.

One study on the dreams of older people found that many older people dream of losing their resources.[8] Dreams in which the dreamer is wandering in a strange place or is lost and looking for help, in which he cannot remember who he is or the names of old friends, in which he has lost something familiar and struggles to find it are all common among older people who have relatively passive attitudes toward their lives. These themes were not nearly as frequent in the dreams of older people who were deeply involved in making something of their lives in later years; their dreams were more oriented toward solving daily problems and achieving goals. Their dreams were also more varied, more detailed, and more richly elaborated than the dreams of the more passive group. It is reasonable to surmise that the older people who dream frequently of lost resources do so because in life they are throwing away their resources by not using them fully.

Though it is normal to worry about losing one's memory, sight, hearing, and mobility, concentrating excessively upon the unpleasant aspects of the aging process leads to a withdrawal from an active attitude toward life and a retreat from it. Dreams that taunt the retreating old are trying to show them what they are missing, not because they must but because they refuse to use the spirit of living within them. Dreams in which the dreamer cannot remember where he is going may be encouraging the dreamer to take some direction in his life rather than wandering about lost and lonely until death. A few dreams of losing physical faculties are probably anxiety dreams reflecting an aging person's fear of the future;

however, I think that the vast majority of these dreams are symbolic of the dreamer's mental attitudes toward living. Ask the dreamer who can't find a lost dream wallet or forgets where he is going if he has a sense of identity or purpose in his life right now. If you are growing old and feel that no one needs you anymore, that there is no more purpose to your life, ask your dreams why you have chosen to see the world this way when rationally you know there are thousands of young children and old people who need and could return your kindness and love. Ask your dreams what useful and satisfying thing you could do in your life now that the struggles of youth have passed. If you take a more active stance toward your day and dream life, both will reward you far more richly than you might imagine.

One woman who could neither hear nor see did not let those handicaps stop her. Helen Keller decided to make the best of her life. Her waking life and dream life responded to her attitude and became great sources of happiness and satisfaction to her. Because she took pleasure from her life and valued, instead of hiding from, her days and nights, she remembered many more pleasant dreams than many of us who deliberately close our eyes to them. She described her dream life as follows:

I believe I am more fortunate in my dreams than most people; for as I think back over my dreams, the pleasant ones seem to predominate, although we naturally recall most vividly and tell most eagerly the grotesque and fantastic adventures in Slumberland. . . . It is true that my dreams have uses as many and sweet as those of adversity. All my yearning for the strange, the weird, the ghostlike is gratified in dreams. They carry me out of the accustomed and commonplace. In a flash, in the winking of an eye, they snatch the burden from my shoulders, the trivial task from my hand, and the pain and disappointment from my heart, and I behold the lovely face of my dream. It dances round me with merry measure, and darts hither and thither in happy abandon. Sudden, sweet fancies spring forth from any nook and corner, and delightful surprises meet me at every turn. A happy dream is more precious than gold or rubies.

I like to think that in dreams we catch glimpses of a life larger than our own. We see it as a little child, or as a savage who visits a civilized nation. Thoughts are imparted to us far above our ordinary thinking. Feelings nobler and wiser than any we have known thrill us between heartbeats. For one fleeting night a princelier nature captures us and we become as great as our aspirations. [9]

Helen Keller discovered the beauty and freedom of her dream life, and it enriched the meaning of the daily life she lived. As you study your dreams, you too will discover the inspiration they can give to your life, no matter how old your physical body becomes.

Sexual Conflict in Dreams.

You may be saying at this point, "This is all very interesting, but what about the idea that all our dreams portray our sexual conflicts, desires, and wishes in disguised form? And what about those dreams where sex is not disguised at all?"

The classical Freudian theory, that dreams express repressed infantile wishes to make love with the parent of the opposite sex and kill the parent of the same sex, has been considerably modified since 1900. It has become clear to most dream researchers that dreams reflect not only more varied forms of sexual conflict but also the vast spectrum of the dreamer's conflicts, achievements, hopes, and efforts to solve daily problems in all areas of his or her life.

If you are having problems with your sex life, your dreams will naturally respond to your concerns and offer you helpful insights. You can incubate dreams about this area of your life just as you would any other. Several men and women in the Dream Meetings have used dream incubation to explore their inhibitions in enjoying sex. Three women asked, "Why does it take me so long to attain orgasm?" Interestingly enough, they all dreamt of making love to their husbands in the presence of one or both of their parents and being able to attain orgasm only by leaving the room where their parents were. These dreams pointed out the fact that the dreamers were still encumbered by early attitudes toward sex as a forbidden activity, attitudes which they also personified as parents. In two of the three dreams, the emphasis was on the discomfort at being seen by the parent rather than upon any explicit disapproval from the given parent. These women had not realized the extent to which they were still influenced by childhood attitudes toward sex as dirty, naughty, and sinful. Realizing this, they suggested to themselves using their journals to write up a long-term incubation of a series of "sex therapy" dreams, in which they would have experiences reinforcing their ideas of sex as a healthy, normal, enjoyable part of their lives. They did this by formally incubating the first dream of the series, using the incubation discussion and the incubation phrase the first night, adding only the request that similar dreams would follow every week or so. This is an effective form of self-therapy, which has been used successfully in a variety of situations where the dreamer desires to break the spell of old rigid ideas, fears, and beliefs and reinforce more realistic and appropriate attitudes.

In dreams where you engage in explicit sexual practices, you may be exploring sexual conflicts or you may be dreaming of "becoming one" with a part of yourself (represented by your dream partner) which you had previously not been very intimate with.

Now and then most heterosexual people dream of making love with someone of the same sex. These dreams have often been considered as manifestations of latent homosexuality. Though this may sometimes be the case, in my experience these dreams usually represent the dreamer's desire to attain or possess the characteristics projected on to the sex partner. For example, Jean dreamt:

I am in bed with Sara. We are making love, but I don't notice the details. Mostly, I am feeling warm and loving toward her. We are very happy. It all seems natural. Only upon awakening do I realize that the dream was one of a lesbian encounter. I awake feeling embarrassed about the dream content. ("Sara")

When asked who Sara was, Jean said: "She is an extremely talented and successful business executive. What is she like? She's a new friend whom I admire because she has not sold her kindness for her success. She's aggressive yet gentle. I wish I were more like her. Asked, "What is making love?" she responded, "It is a uniting, completing action motivated by deep physiological and emotional instincts. That reminds me— yesterday I practiced my own assertiveness by explaining to my boss that I deserve a promotion. I feel that my dream is reassuring me and encouraging me in my efforts to unite with or manifest the parts of myself that are like Sara."

This brings us to a controversial type of dream. Occasionally women dream of having penises. Do these dreams mean that the dreamers wish that they actually had penises? Rather than penis envy, these dreams can represent the female dreamers' desires for achievement of whatever traditionally male characteristics they see symbolized by penises. In interviewing such a dreamer, you could ask such questions as, "What is a penis?" "What are people who have penises like?" "How are people with penises psychologically, culturally, and socially different from those without them?"

Men having difficulty achieving and maintaining erections have incubated dreams on the issue, asking: "Why can't I get it up and keep it up?" or "What are the reasons behind my impotence?" These questions elicit dreams that help the dreamer get directly to the root of the problem and provide him with an opportunity to deal with the causes rather than the symptoms of the matter. Such dream responses have an enormous advantage over intellectual formulations that unconscious guilt, shame, anger, or performance anxiety inhibit one's sexual functioning. While dreaming, one is often led to an immediate experience of the guilt, anxiety, or whatever is getting in the way.

Joe used the incubation phrase, "Why can't I get it up and keep it up?" Here is his dream producer's response:

I am outdoors in front of the house of an extremely attractive lady. She is on the porch watching me as I show her how I can jump very high. Then I notice my old friend, Lila walk by. The next thing I know, I can't get off the ground when I try to jump. It feels awful. ("Jumping")

Here is a synopsis of Joe's journal interview:

How does the dream open? I am showing off my ability to jump high in the air. I feel proud of my prowess. It seems that, while I am light-hearted and oriented toward fun, I can show off and I can perform before this sexy lady. Then I see Lila.

Who is Lila? A high school classmate. She always seemed to look down at me. I always wanted to show her that I was a neat guy, but I was too shy to do anything about it.

I get it. When I am light-hearted about it, I can get it up easily. But as soon as I focus on the way I felt around Lila, the show's over. It's the old performance anxiety syndrome. So what else is new? I didn't realize that I was that uptight. There really is a Lila in me that says that I'm not cool and not good enough. As I relive my last few sexual mishaps, I can feel Lila operating. Now that I know she's there, will I be able to get rid of her?

Some dreams of sex are wish-fulfillment dreams, especially those portraying wonderful, satisfying sexual encounters on nights when the dreamer feels he or she has gone without sex for too long. Many sexual wish-fulfillment dreams can be explored further, however.

A rather timid wife told our Dream Meeting that her husband had had a dream that revolutionized their sex life. For a long while, she had been wanting to tell her husband that she desired and needed more sexual foreplay, especially clitoral stimulation, if she was to fully enjoy sex with him. She had broached the subject with him several times, but each time she received the impression that he was not open to discussing it. One night the husband dreamed that, in making love to his wife, he included a good amount of foreplay. To his delight, his wife was taking great pleasure from all this in the dream. When he awoke, the husband told the dream to his wife. She asked him to show her how he had been dreaming of making love to her. She was overjoyed when her husband turned into her Don Juan, and she told him so. Their love life was considerably improved.

A series of spontaneous dreams monitoring the quality of a couple's sex life was told by Laurel and Frank. Laurel had dreamt of a drooping, ailing palm tree three times in one month. Each dream consisted only of her seeing and feeling sad about the palm. She had no feeling for what the dream meant. She defined and described palm trees as very exotic, beautiful, and sensuous plants. The one in her dream had been given to her by her husband for her birthday and was growing quite well in their bedroom. She conjectured that the dream might have something to do with her health, but the corellations between the dream plant's illnesses and her own did not quite fit.

Then one night she and her husband both dreamed of seeing the gardenia plant that is in their bedroom. The dream plant had clearly been through some rough arid times, as the lower leaves had dried up and fallen off. However, the plant was now in exuberant good health and was very full. There were even two big gardenia blooms at the top of it.

In telling each other their shared dream, Laurel and Frank recognized what the drooping palm trees had been trying to say. The plants in the bedroom had perfectly mirrored their sex life. They had been going through a dry period, in which they were often irritably bickering and unusually occupied by their careers. The palm tree dreams could have served as reminders to tend to their drooping marital relationship if they had been understood. The blooming gardenia dream came as soon as they had realigned their priorities in such a way that they again had plenty of time for sex.

A happily married man named Louis dreamt that an intruder had entered his house while he was asleep upstairs with his wife. In the dream, Louis went downstairs to see what all the noise was about. The intruder was an unknown woman, who was taking his wife's favorite food from the pantry. Louis was enraged by the intrusion and insisted that the woman leave at once.

Louis knew right away that his dream producer was telling him that his casual affair with a woman he hardly knew was threatening his cherished marriage and had to be terminated. Specifically, the affair was using up his best romance and sexual energies—his wife's favorite food. Louis was surprised that his dream producer took his fling so seriously, but he could not deny his own fury at the dream woman's intrusion into his home. He got the message and acted on it.

Sex dreams come in many guises, often in productions with no explicit sex in them, as in Louis' dream. It is also true that many dreams using sexual imagery often concern other than sexual issues, as in certain female penis dreams.

One of the most exciting kinds of sex dreams and the most difficult to describe are "high" sex dreams. In these dreams, one can enter into a new level of intimacy with one's partner and into a heightened sense of unity with nature. High sex dreams sometimes have religious or mystical connotations to the dreamer. Many of us have heard of Tantric Buddhism and other sects in which sexual intercourse is a sacred religious ritual. Some dreamers have reported dream experiences of great light and love filling them and their partners during lovemaking. In some cases, the dreams acted as triggers to freer, less conflicted, and more joyous waking sexual experiences for the dreamers. These dreams are difficult, but not impossible to incubate. Phrases such as, "Show me the higher dimensions of sex." "What is sex like at its best?" and "I'd like an experience of true intimacy with my partner" have been put to good use. It is interesting to note that, even when these incubations fail to hit the requested target, they tend to portray the dreamer's blocks to attaining the desired experiences.

You will discover the meaning of sex dreams if you interview your dream writer-producer in a nonjudgmental manner without any preconceived notions about the meaning of such dreams. For example, one woman who dreamed of making wonderful and passionate love to Richard Burton was not disguising a wish to have sex with her father. When asked who Richard Burton was, she responded that he was a romantic, brilliantly creative actor and that, whatever his later years bring, she will always admire his art. She immediately realized that her dream writer was both reassuring her of her sexual attractiveness in a time when she had begun to doubt it and encouraging her to use her own Burton-like creativity. In interviewing the producers of such dreams, be sure to ask about the obstacles that appear in the dream to frustrate the dreamer's desire. These will reveal the nature of the obstacles that face the dreamer in this area of waking reality. In dreams where the sexual experience is frightening or unpleasant, the interviewer should ask questions about the fearful figures or circumstances, keeping lookout for such verbal and visual puns as are common and revealing in the telling of dreams with sexual motifs.

6

Dreaming in the Office

One of the most popular topics for dream incubation concerns the dreamer's relationship to work. Many a stormy relationship between boss and employee, or between fellow workers, has been clarified and improved with the help of dreams. Important decisions have been made and new ideas received using dream insights.

I have spoken with a number of successful executives who think dreams are nonsense, but who go on to tell me stories of great ideas and fruitful intuitions they come up with upon awakening in the morning or after a nap. It is interesting that in most business circles intuition is seen as an important attribute of a person who has risen to the top of a field, but dreams are usually dismissed as time lost sleeping. Nevertheless, dreams seem to be the most active laboratory in which intuitions are developed.

Bill, a successful reinsurance broker, on a flight between Chicago and Los Angeles puzzled over how he might rewrite a proposal which had just been turned down by a prospective client. He came up with nothing and so decided to sleep on it. As the plane was preparing to land, he awoke with an idea to change the proposal in a way that made good sense to him. He resubmitted the modified proposal, and it was accepted. Bill had not recalled a specific dream, but he did get what he asked for.

A nurse named Vera Leonard, who works in a hospital in Greensboro, North Carolina, reported that a dream had given her an important idea. From a dream inspiration she designed the "evacuation gown" to be worn by nurses working on infant hospital wards. The gown is made of heavy duck material and has four large pockets on it. In case of a fire or other emergency, a nurse wearing the gown can carry one infant in each pocket and one in each free arm, thus saving six infants each trip. Vera's patent is pending.[1]

Lawrence Lee and Barry Gifford recently wrote a book on Jack Kerouac. The title remained a frustrating and unsolved problem until Barry finally had a dream on the matter. He dreamt that he was an omniscient eye above the book department of a large store. A big crowd of people was buying his book. He leaned into the crowd to see the book and read its title. Upon awakening however, he forgot the title he had seen. The next night he succeeded in dreaming the same dream, and this time he remembered the title: *Jack's Book.* Everyone was pleased with the title, and the book has done well.

My dreams were indispensable to me as I wrote this book. They furnished me with ideas and additions and corrections to be made, but more importantly, they were crucial in motivating me to keep up the furious writing pace when my energies were flagging. My dreams made it possible for me to meet all my deadlines by clearing my head and refreshing my spirits when necessary and by charging me with energy and the desire to keep at it when I needed that.

In addition to incubating dreams for creative ideas to use in work, dreams aimed at resolving interpersonal conflict at work can be extremely useful. If you can't get along with someone you work with or if you can't elicit the kind of cooperation or work you would like, you might ask for dreams that will show you a new approach to the problem. Rapprochement dreams can work small miracles between warring parties in the same office.

New training and promotional programs can be designed in the dream state. You can try incubation phrases such as, "How best can I design this new program?" or "I need a new angle on this product." or "How can I best make this matter clear and convincing in next week's presentation?" If you need a good idea, don't forget to take advantage of the creative input available to you while you sleep.

Alcoholism contributes to many cases of office blues. Everyone who has contact with the problem drinker is adversely affected, yet rarely is anyone willing or able to do anything useful for the problem drinker until the problem gets out of hand. Business lunches, where one can easily feel obliged to drink excessively in order to keep a client, boss, or colleague company, provide the perfect excuse for afternoons lost to intoxication.

Not infrequently, the problem drinker feels that he or she would like to drink less at lunch but dares not for fear of offending a client or associate. Dreams incubated on a question like, "How can I drink less given the obligations of my job?" can help the overdrinker to face up to his or her conspiracy to excuse or ignore the excessive drinking.

Associates who work with the overdrinker can dream up ways to approach the problem without losing a friend. Once the problem is recognized by the overdrinker, the reasons behind it can be explored with dream work.

A few of my dream clients have challenged themselves to ask dream questions such as, "How honorably am I conducting my business?" and "What can I do to improve the environment my industry has helped to pollute?" A frequently employed incubation question is, "Success isn't as great as I thought it would be. Why not? What's missing?" The adjustment to retirement or the rejection of that concept also can be facilitated by looking inside and asking, "What shall I do at this time of life?"

Dreamers in our classes have asked their dreams for ideas and advice in finding a more satisfactory way of using their creative and productive energies. Maria's dream of the "Shiny White Car" in Chapter 2 is a good example of a dream response to such a query. The dream usually presents alternatives along with the reasons the dreamer fails to take advantage of them.

Another student asked her dreams if she should take a job offered her at a bank. She dreamt:

I was at a meeting of judges. We were all in judges' robes. I knew I could make business contacts here. Then a judge said to me, "If you go into banking, how will you have time to pursue your art work?" I answer that I'm about ready to sell out and take any job. But as I awake, I realize I must not sell out, that I should find a job that will afford me more free time for my art work. ("The Deciding Judge")

Another woman, named Lisa, disliked her present job and asked her dreams for an idea for a new career. Her dream producer responded with a vivid suggestion that she go back to school and study horticulture, a subject which she enjoyed as a young woman and found very satisfying in her dream. She looked at the suggestion as a metaphoric one, but she could not determine its meaning. So she incubated a dream for a specific, literal suggestion. Her incubation phrase was, "I need an idea." Her dream producer's response:

A young woman had her boyfriend at home. She fixed food and gave him light, but he would not leave. He acts like a demanding child. ("The Spoiled Brat")

Lisa wrote in a letter that this was a very unpleasant dream, and that she had felt fearful of the young man. No wonder! Lisa interpreted the young man to represent her creative energies, which had been given both food for thought and direction to light the way, but was still not ready to set out for the adventure. The dream suggested that, if she kept her creative forces pent up within her much longer, they would start to work against her. She wrote that the young man "is the part of me which is like a 'spoiled brat' who has been given the answers but is still asking for more." When you ask your dreams for an answer you have already received, they will often give you the answer in another form if you have worked with the first answer to the best of your abilities. But if you have not made a conscious effort to understand and act upon a dream answer the first time, the second incubation on the same subject either will result in a repeat of the first dream response, as in the case of Maria's "Shiny White Car" dream, or it may result in a dream like Lisa's, in which the dreamer is reminded that she already has the answer.

Besides asking for ideas on new careers, our class members have had good responses from their dream producers to such questions as "How can I be more effective in my job?" "How can I be more creative and satisfied within the context of my present job?" and "What hobbies or sports would give me a good outlet for the parts of myself I cannot express ⸱ in my work?"

7

Cinema Vérité

This chapter explores the use of dreams to discovering how we honestly see ourselves, how our dream producer sees us, and what we can do to improve our self-image using dreams.

How Do You See Yourself?   Virginia realized the importance of having a positive self-image. She understood that her own estimation of her strengths and weaknesses was a major determinant in the quality of her life experience. She knew that not only did what she thought of herself predispose her toward setting goals in accordance with her sense of self-worth, but her opinion of herself also communicated itself fairly clearly to the people she came in contact with, who then responded to her in comparable ways. Virginia had been having difficulties attracting the kind of man she wanted to marry, and she began to wonder if she was sending out nonverbal messages that had attracted dull men, vultures, or no men at all. She wanted to attract a man who was bright, assertive, and exciting. Somehow she wasn't sending out the right signals. After discussing this in her journal day notes, she decided to incubate a dream on the matter of her self-image. She asked, "How do I see myself?" She awoke with a dream fragment of "something about a TV and a small square table."

At first, Virginia thought she had not received or recalled a response to her incubation. Then it struck her. She wrote "Oops! Was that actually a big clue? Do I see myself (TV) as square and conservative, like the insignificant table? Is that the image I transmit?" Virginia began to ask her friends if her dream described an aspect of the image she projected. They said that, though she was lovely, kind, and charming, she did seem at first far more conservative than she turned out to be after they had known her for awhile. Virginia began to get in touch with a part of herself which felt small and "square." She had discovered an attitude she had long held about herself without realizing it. This attitude had not been unconscious, she had always felt it off in a corner of her mind, but she never turned around to look at it and consider its accuracy, value, or effect upon her life. She had preferred to push that self-image aside and replace it with another, which included seeing herself as a bright, liberated, adventuresome woman. Her dream producer was helping her to see a part of her self-image which she had tried to ignore but which was still alive and frustrating her efforts to attract a man who would be attractive to her.

Although many of your dreams will present you with images of how your wiser and more objective dream producer sees you, it will be harder to recognize the way you see yourself from a conscious point of view. You can ask your dreams to show you what beliefs about yourself determine your self-image; how others see you; and how daring you are in setting your personal, interpersonal, professional, and spiritual goals. If you don't think much of yourself, it would benefit you to realize it, because this attitude surely influences your behavior and all of your relationships in one way or another. You can use your dreams to discover aspects of your self-image which you have been spending psychic energy hiding from your full awareness.

Virginia had some resistance to admitting that she saw herself as "square" and insignificant, because she also saw herself as the interesting, likable, exciting woman she in fact was. Yet after another dream, in which she was told that she belonged with "the big people," not with the little or insignificant people she had thought she belonged with in the dream, she took a closer look at her insecurities. To what degree did she see herself as a little person, too humble or square to be an equal to the big, important people, who represented a higher appraisal of her self-worth. Virginia began a close examination of the attitudes and beliefs she held about herself and her potential. She wrote in her journal lists of the attitudes she held about herself—about her attractiveness, her desirability to men, her needs for independence and dependence, her professional achievement, security, and adventure. She also began a "first-draft" description of the kind of man she wanted to marry. Exercises like these have proved helpful in assisting Virginia and other members of the Dream Meetings to bring to consciousness attitudes and beliefs which often lurk just below the level of awareness. As Virginia was able to see the beliefs which she held and which led to her diminished self-esteem, she was able to examine and defuse some of their power and influence in her life.

She now took the opportunity to question the appropriateness of certain beliefs she had about herself which may have been formed in past circumstances far different from the psychological environment she presently lived in. The belief in herself as a little, insignificant person struck Virginia as being less than accurate in light of her personal development and professional achievements or recent years. She began to try on new self-images to see how they fit the Virginia of today. Then she began to try on desirable self-images of Virginia as she might like to be in the future. She wasn't trying to plaster a new, ideal self-image over her present one; she was trying some new and different ones on for size, some for laughs, and some for inspiration. Slowly, her image of herself was changing. Her dream producer responded to her waking efforts to see herself more clearly by placing her in the starring role of this dream:

I am in a bright red dress with a plunging neckline. I am thinking that it is pretty but probably not flattering in color or neckline. It seems appropriate for Christmas. Then I look at myself and see that it actually looks very becoming! ("Red Dress")

In her dream commentary, Virginia wrote that in the past she had thought that red was not a good color for her; that it was too bright, a color for floozies to wear. She had even disliked the color. About a year before this dream, her attitudes had changed and she bought several red blouses and accessories. By the time of this dream, she thought of the color as "bright and lively." She wrote that it "calls attention but, or rather *and,* that's O.K." Virginia was seeing herself in a new way. A part of her still believed that her red dream dress was too daring and too bright. Her dream producer was showing her that it wasn't at all, and that she was very attractive in the dress. If the dress fits, wear it. . . .

A New Passport. In *cinema vérité* dreams, you see what you really think of yourself, or what your more objective dream producer thinks of you. As we have seen, these two images are not always identical. Of course, any one dream will deal not with the only, or even necessarily the major, way you see yourself, but with important aspects of your self-image as seen by your conscious self or by your dream self. The insights gained from such dreams can have a profound influence on the life of the dreamer who takes them to heart. In 1972, I had a *cinema vérité* dream which unfortunately I did not take to heart until several years later. Here is the page from my journal which describes the dream. Notice also how the feeling that a mistake has been made parallels a similar feeling in Ardell's "In Bed with Bob" dream (Chapter 1). In both cases, a lack of self-confidence can be seen to explain the assumption that a mistake has been made.

8/21/72
Zurich

> *Day Notes.* A peaceful, quiet day. Wrote a letter to Lynn [my oldest and best friend]. I am sick of being a second-class friend to her. Whenever she has a boyfriend, she drops everything, and treats me as a second-class citizen. She seems to drop everything she's doing when she has the alternative of being with even a mediocre male. Walked in the park by Zurich lake. Read Rossi's book *Dreams and the Growth of Personality.* It is great. It started me thinking of the shy child who has been showing up in my dreams lately. I have lost some of my self-confidence lately. When in my life have I felt most confident? When I was skating every day, training for competitions. It's been five years since I've done any serious skating. Rossi writes that new growth in the personality seems to manifest itself first in dreams, in the form of new and unusual dream images.

ID *Discussion.* I need and want some new awareness, some new growth in my personality to break through old habits of perception and reaction to the world. I know there is within me more creative energy than I am using, but how to let it out?

☆ How can I release and express my deepest, most energetic creativity?

\# *MY NEW PASSPORT*

> *I had sent some photos to Philadelphia so that the passport people could choose the appropriate one when making up my new passport. I received my new passport in the mail and opened it to examine it. Instead of just one picture, the first four pages were filled with color pictures of myself ice skating. Fabulous pictures I seemed to be seeing for the first*

time. I thought: "I didn't know I was that good after so long away from serious skating. Could I be that good?" Many pictures were vivid action shots. In one particularly my body was just right, perfect balance and form. It was exciting to see. In another picture I was about forty-five. I reached into it and examined the muscle tone of my leg. I was amazed that it was good enough for exhibition skating at that age. But this is a passport, *and four pages of myself is really excessive and far too intimate and revealing. On the last page of pictures, I find my actual (present) passport picture. It is in the usual black-and-white, pleasant, calm,* standard. *While this should be the only picture in the passport, it was just one, an insignificantly placed one, among many. "But this can't be," thought I. "It looks as if I'm trying to show off. Why did the passport makers do it? What shall I do?" Then Lynn tells me she just received her passport with one page or so of extra pictures. Her father, a lawyer, had chemically steamed off the extra pictures. He did it very carefully so the police would not detect his tampering with the document. "My father will do it to your passport if you like," said Lynn. At first I was relieved. Then I hesitated, not wanting to tamper with my passport, for it is written on the passport itself that any alterations discovered will result in the revocation of the passport.*

Commentary. I awake, thinking, "Is this my true identity, expressed through skating? Did the passport people *not* make a mistake? Do they know better than I what is my true identity?" The warning printed on the passport application kept running through my head, "Passport photos must show a good likeness of the applicant, or they will not be accepted." Fully awake, I realize the impossibility of it all. I've not skated seriously for too long. I've lost too much time. I'm already twenty-three years old. Even if I were to give it another try, give up school for ice skating, where would I find a partner? There are so few men to choose from in ice dancing. As in the dream, I'd like to believe it possible that I could have a career in exhibition and movie ice skating, but I cannot. The dream was so vivid, and seemed so real in a literal sense, that it is hard to see behind the metaphor. The literal-objective interpretation can't be right, so I'll try a dream interview to get to the bottom of this.

Setting. It is time for a new passport (identity). I've given the passport people a variety of self-images from which to choose the one showing the truest likeness of my identity. The passport I receive is new. The dream is surely dealing with my incubation request for new awareness of myself, and perhaps with a way to express it.

What is a passport? My favorite document. It shows one's identity and permits free access to the world. Free movement. Horrible to lose it or have it revoked. You can't see the world without it.

The black-and-white photo? The same as the one I have in my present passport. It's a good one, but it is standard. It represents my conscious self-image as a bright graduate student in psychology. It's not very exciting. My dream producer seems to be of the opinion that this is indeed a part of my identity, but not the most important part by any means.

The color photos? These represent my dream producer's idea of my true identity. It seems that I see them for the first time in the dream, or that I have been unaware of this self-image until now. These pictures showed me skating with and without a partner, in professional rather than competitive (amateur) settings, such as ice shows and movies. The photos showed me at different ages ranging from twenty-five or so to forty-five. I was terribly pleased to see them, but did not dare let myself believe they represented my true identity. Yet the photos were undeniably of me; I could even touch my future self-images as if they were three-dimensional and real.

Why would I send these off to the Philadelphia passport office, rather than the one I usually use in New York? Because Philadelphia is a more sensitive place, more aware of beauty and graceful living, than New York, which is so work-oriented and pressured. I have been identifying myself with New York since I quit skating, haven't I?

Why can't I accept the passport people's choice? First, it seems impossible that I could become a really good skater again. Second, I'm afraid the photos are too ostentatious, revealing, and intimate.

How does that relate to my life? Perhaps in that I have become rather too sedate lately, in an effort to be acceptable to the intellectuals I have been surrounded by. I've somewhat repressed my flamboyance and the more free-spirited aspects of my personality because they don't seem socially acceptable in academic and professional environments. I regret this, but it seems appropriate. Perhaps I could find some outlets for my more outrageous, flamboyant characteristics. Perhaps a little skating on the side, a few times a week, would do it. Yet the dream is making a special point that my skating-self is the greater, more significant part of my personality.

Who is Lynn? A good friend who is too man-oriented. This has hurt me, as well as her own career. She puts herself down a lot and doesn't realize that she is dynamite as a woman, as a dancer-actor, and as a law student.

Is there a Lynn in me? I know the dream is telling me there is, but I can't believe it. Do I have more talent and "pizazz" than I realize or have the courage to express? A little maybe. Am I too man-oriented? Yes.

Who is Lynn's father, and what is he like? I like him a lot. He's sort of old world, a hard-working lawyer. He encourages Lynn to keep her nose to the academic grindstone. He likes to take car trips with Lynn. I'd rather fly. In fact, when I have traveled with my father it has always been by plane. Lynn's father, and her following in his footsteps, must represent my more conservative, cautious, security-conscious attitudes, which are capable of defacing my passport or true identity if I let them. I think Lynn has allowed these attitudes and a lack of belief in her talents to restrict the most exciting aspects of her identity.

Summary. O.K. The dream is saying that my most colorful, lively, and true identity is represented by the skating pictures, and that the sedate, hard-working, nonadventurous aspects of myself, with which I now almost totally identify, belong, as does the black-and-white photo, in a subordinate position to my skating-self. Just like Lynn, I tend to reject my skating-self because of self-doubt, and because of an exaggerated concern for appearing respectable to people in my profession as well as to the part of myself which is like Lynn's father. As Rossi would say, Lynn's father represents my work and security-oriented attitudes, which block my realization of my true identity. These attitudes limit my personality and tend to standardize it. It is no wonder that, when I looked at myself through Lynn and her father's eyes, I felt inadequate and incapable of becoming that skater. I couldn't see the part of myself that is already like her. What does that skater represent? It seems reasonable to think that she stands for the flamboyant, risk-taking, courageous, and adventuresome part of me. Yet the sensation of skating is so real, even now, that it is hard not to take her as a literal, objective representation of my future. The fact that every one of the pictures, except for the black-and-white one, show me ice skating and not doing something else, is very interesting. It would seem to suggest that the dream is dealing with my objective professional identity rather than with a subjective metaphor for my whole identity, as that would have had to include several different representations of the other aspects of my personal identity. Perhaps I am being like Lynn now, but becoming a professional ice skater does seem to be out of the question. Therefore, I shall interpret the dream to mean that I need to recognize, accept, and actualize the symbolic ice skater within me—if I dare.

This dream was a harbinger of such good news on the objective level that I was tempted to place it in the category of a wish-fulfillment dream. Yet as usually happens in the course of a dream interview, it soon became clear that on the subjective level the meaning of the dream was more profound than that. Unhappily, I found both the objective interpretation (that I would skate professionally) and the subjective interpretation (that I was rejecting my flamboyant self) threatening to my current self-image and to my current professional and romantic involvements. Even after my dream interview, I decided to ignore the dream.

Finally, of course, day and dream events conspired to convince me to take the message of this dream seriously. About a year after the dream, I began to express more and more of the symbolic skater within. Two years after the dream I put my skates on again and went to a local skating club session. There, miracle of miracles, I met Bob Castle, a spectacular gold-medalist ice dancer who just happened to be looking for a partner! Male ice dancers are rare, but ones with gold medals and no partner are harder to find than water in the desert. Since Bob and I have been skating together, we have been to ice rinks in Sun Valley and Europe, and my skating is better and more fun than ever before. I never would have believed this possible in 1972. I have not turned professional, but who knows—even that might be in the cards for me, though I still doubt it. Be that as it may, the quality of my life has improved markedly. Much more of the skater within has moved into every area of my life, and I have recaptured that sense of adventure the longing for which had prompted me to incubate the passport dream.

Our personalities will mature and grow in spite of ourselves with time and a little luck. But if we participate actively and enthusiastically in the growth process, we can save ourselves a lot of time and suffering.

Finding the "Real" You. Following is a list of questions you might like to use to incubate a few *cinema vérité* dreams of your own:

How do I see myself, really?

What beliefs do I have about myself which I need to be more aware of?

How does my wiser, more objective dream producer see me?

What attitudes do I hold about myself that limit my enjoyment of life?

What are my most restricting fears or inhibitions?

What beliefs do I have about "the way I am" that lead me to attract people who do not treat me as I would like?

What are my greatest personality assets, and how can I manifest them more fully?

You may want to put these questions into your own words, and perhaps make up your own *cinema vérité* incubation phrases. In either case, you will probably receive dreams that surprise you, because you will be asking your dream producer to tell you something you don't already know. Using the dream interview technique to explore both the possible subjective and objective interpretations of these dreams is a good idea. If you ask a friend to play the role of interviewer, you will be less likely to decide to ignore a very important dream, as I did.

As we turn to Part III, we will explore some of the more exotic ways of dreaming which can lead into a new awareness of many dimensions of experience. The kinds of dreams we are about to consider are neither more nor less important than the dreams we have already discussed. These exotic dreams can change your life overnight; but, like most dreams, they will usually help you to improve your experience of life bit by bit. They will enlarge your horizons by introducing you to sources of perception and inspiration you may not have known were available. They can show you that life without a body, both while you live and after death, is more than a saint's or mystic's hallucination. All these dreams are exciting and at times very important. People who believe that only certain kinds of dreams, which seem particularly intense or special, are worth remembering,[1] apparently have never known or have chosen to forget the vital importance of the insights our more normal dreams provide. Anyone who knows how to interpret dreams will know better than to disparage any dream and will more fully appreciate the significance of all dreams.

PART THREE

Day Dreamers
and
Night Trippers

8

Mission Possible

Asking Your Dreams for Inspiration and Creative Ideas

It is well known that throughout history saints, mystics, and artists have used their dreams for spiritual and creative inspiration. It is less well known that scholars and scientists have been led to important discoveries through the dream resolution of their research problems.[1] Examples of spectacular dream inspirations and discoveries abound in the literature on the history of dreams.

At the age of twenty three, René Descartes, the greatest of French philosophers, spent a night dreaming dreams that would determine his life's work. Descartes' dreams of November 10, 1619, revealed to him the fundamental ideas upon which he based his work in methodology, algebra, and physics, and metaphysics.[2]

Voltaire wrote: "I have known advocates who have pleaded in dreams, mathematicians who have sought to solve problems; and poets who have composed verses. I have made some myself which are very passable. It is therefore incontestable that constructive ideas occur in sleep as well as when we are awake . . ."[3]

Mahatma Gandhi used his dreams to find a nonviolent mass response to England's Rowlett Act, which harshly supressed any agitation aiming at the liberation of India. One of the most important manifestations of Gandhi's doctrines of nonviolence and civil disobedience was the general *hartal,* or mass strike. Gandhi, having meditated for weeks, to devise a non-violent, yet effective expression of the populace's refusal to submit to the Rowlett Act, found the solution in a dream, which suggested that for twenty-four hours the people of India suspend their businesses and spend the day in fasting and prayer. The resulting *hartals* of 1919 were major turning points in India's fight for the right of self-determination.[4]

In the spring of 1940, D. B. Parkinson, a young engineer at Bell Laboratories, was working with a group to develop an improved automatic level recorder. This recorder, to be used to improve the accuracy of measurements in telephone transmission, was "a sort of recording voltmeter. Applied voltage caused an inking pen to move across the width of a strip of paper, the paper being driven at uniform velocity along its length . . . [T]he pen motion was not linear with applied voltage, but rather with the log of the voltage. . . . The system was, for its day, very fast. To all intents and purposes this small potentiometer could be said to control the motion of the pen."[5]

While Parkinson was working on telephone technology, the Nazis were marching through Holland, Belgium and France. Like most Americans, Parkinson was troubled by these reports and one night he had the following dream:

I found myself in a gun pit or revetment with an anti-aircraft gun crew. I don't know how I got there—I was just there. The men were Dutch or Belgian by their uniforms—the helmets were neither German, French nor English. There was a gun there which looked to me—I had never had any close association with anti-aircraft guns, but possed some general information on artillery—like a 3". It was firing occasionally, and the impressive thing was that *every shot brought down an airplane!* After three or four shots one of the men in the crew smiled at me and beconed me to come closer to the gun. When I drew near he pointed to the exposed end of the left trunnion. Mounted there was the control potentiometer of my level recorder! There was no mistaking it—it was the identical item."[6]

Upon awaking, Parkinson soon realized that "if the potentiometer could control the high-speed motion of a recording pen with great accuracy, why couldn't a suitably engineered device do the same thing for an anti-aircraft gun!"[7]

In his dream, Parkinson, who had no knowledge of the technology of fire control, had dreamt the key to the development of extremely effective gun directors which "used computers to translate radar data on the existence and location of a target into gun orders designed to direct artillery shells to, and cause them to burst at, a point where the target and its hostile mission are most apt to be adversely affected."[8] The first all-electric gun director which evolved from research based on Parkinson's dream inspiration became known as the M-9 electrical analog computer. The M-9 was not only easily and relatively cheaply mass-produced, it was also very accurate. In the Second Battle of Britain, "[i]n the one month of August 1944 nine out of ten German V-1 buzz bombs originally destined for London were shot down over the cliffs of Dover. . . . In a single week in August, the Germans launched 91 V-1's from the Antwerp area, and heavy guns controlled by M-9's destroyed 89 of them."[9] The M-9 was the precursor of guidance systems for antiaircraft and antiballistic missiles developed after the war.[10]

Robert Louis Stevenson had stated that half of his creative work was done for him in his dreams.[11] His *Strange Case of Dr. Jekyll and Mr. Hyde* was inspired by a dream in which Mr. Hyde transformed into Dr. Jekyll in an effort to escape pursuers. Friedrich Kekulé realized the molecular structure of the benzene molecule to be a ring when, in a reverie, he envisioned a snake swallowing its tail. Kekulé was so impressed by the relationship of dreams to scientific inspiration and problem solving that he addressed his colleagues at a scientific convention in 1890, saying, "Let us learn to dream gentlemen, and then we may perhaps find the truth."[12] Ten years later, with the publication of *The Interpretation of Dreams,* Freud commenced our modern preoccupation with the psychodynamic nature of dreams. Carl Jung, particularly in the 1940s and 1950s, emphasized the important creative and inspirational functions of many dreams in his own life and in the lives of his patients.

Although all dreams can be seen as inspiring us to grow, mature, and change our lives, in this chapter we shall focus on examples of dreams which treat our more spiritual and creative needs centering around our philosophical, religious, artistic, and work life.

Soul Food. Many people who will never be saints not well known for their insight into the nature of the universe have had dreams which have brought them an unshakable sense of the meaning and purpose of their own lives and of the world they live in. Others have found new hope, energy, and insights in dreams which have soothed and encouraged their troubled or questioning souls. Dreams can provide some of the most beautiful and inspirational experiences of your life. These dreams may give you significant mystical or religious experiences of the harmony of the universe which you will never forget. Some inspirational dreams may show you a purpose in your life when you thought there was none, or they may show you the love of your fellows when you could feel none. These dreams will come whether you ask for them or not. They will probably affect your spirits whether you remember them or not. However, if you cherish them, allow yourself to recall them, and even seek them out when you need them, they will become a far more frequent, potent influence upon your life. Simply expecting inspiration from your dreams will open you up to receiving it.

Where does this inspiration come from? Our higher self? Our innermost being, which has access to universal wisdom and maybe even a God? Or perhaps inspiration comes from a subconscious state of awareness in which we have access to all the impressions and experience of our personal lives, which, when creatively rearranged, furnish us with inspirations that only seem to be beyond our normal powers of perception. In laboratory studies, sleeping subjects have been awakened at various points in the stage of sleep preceding the onset of dreaming (pre-REM sleep). The awakened subjects have reported that their minds seemed filled with more or less ordinary thoughts and memories which apparently became more bizarre and dreamlike as they approached the dream state.[13] These findings have been interpreted to mean that, in sleep, we neither struggle with a seething cauldron of instinctual drives nor communicate with some wise or universal force within us or "above" us. However, laboratory studies do not usually provide settings conducive to inspirational dreams. Furthermore, they do not generally study a subject population with a high degree of awareness of the various states of consciousness which can be encountered while sleeping. These subjects' reports may not tell the whole story.

Those who have studied the mental contents and experiences of altered states of consciousness through meditation and various disciplines, including maintaining consciousness in the sleep state, know that the mind is capable of operating at several different levels at once. For example, if you close your eyes, relax, and count your breaths carefully up to, say, five hundred, you will probably become aware of at least one if not two or more levels of thought and awareness which occur simultaneously with your counting.

Carl Jung proposed the theory that at times in sleep we have access not only to our personal unconscious or subconscious but also to the more universal state of awareness he called the collective unconscious.[14] Jung hypothesized that the contents of the collective unconscious form:

as it were, an omnipresent, unchanging, and everywhere identical quality or substrate of the psyche *per se.* This is, of course, no more than an hypothesis. But we are driven to it by the peculiar nature of the empirical material, not to mention the high probability that the general similarity of psychic processes in all individuals must be based on an equally general and impersonal principle that conforms to law, just as the instinct manifesting itself in the individual is only the partial manifestation of an instinctual substrate common to all men.[15]

The empirical material referred to is the sum of fifty years of Jung's study of his own, his patients', and history's accounts of dreams, fantasies, and myths. Jung called the part of ourselves which has direct access to both our universal consciousness and our personal experience "the self." Others have described the profound and comprehensive center of our psyches as our inner or higher self, our soul, or the god within. This higher self operates at a level of superconsciousness and is intimately related to, and a part of, universal, creative forces, being itself, or God.

Whatever the explanation of where dreams come from, the fact remains that people do have dreams in which they feel they experience or glimpse some ultimate reality, and these experiences have led to the enhancement or even renaissance of their lives. The experiences of unity and totality in some of these dreams are valued among the most beautiful and important of any life experience by those who have them. Perhaps a discussion of a few of these dreams will inspire you to remember and incubate your own. In that way you will be in a better position to judge their validity.

The Many Faces of Inspiration.   Inspirational dreams come in many guises. Some seem exquisitely profound and others seem to be just slightly more real or insightful than our normal perceptions. They deal with our deepest philosophical concerns and with the use to which we put so much of our life energy in the context of our vocations and avocations. In the more intense and obviously inspirational dreams, perception and expression seem direct, without relation to sensory data, and seem to occur simultaneously. The dreamer may describe the dream as a timeless experience of "pure knowing," or "basic being."

These "dreams" may be very difficult to recall, probably because they offer few tangible handles by which to pull them back with us into waking consciousness. Several people have told me, and I too have noticed, that it is difficult to retain the awareness of imageless, timeless perception in waking consciousness unless it is followed by a dream with recognizable images. Some dreamers feel that after they have had an experience of direct knowing they proceed to create a dream which serves as a symbolic interpretation of the experience. The symbols form a sort of parable, which captures as much of the essence of the experience as the dreamer's consciousness can handle. The dream is a translation of the primary experience into terms which the dreamer can relate to and recall; however, the dreamer usually recognizes that translating these experiences unfortunately limits their richness and scope. In such situations, dreamers seem to experience an unusual degree of awareness. They may even be aware of choosing the images and producing the dream translation. Very often, only the dream translation is recalled, perhaps with an inkling that "there was much more to the dream, but I can't remember it."

I had an experience like this, in which I understood that the universe worked perfectly. Its purpose was just to exist, and its existence was completely joyous. I knew that I was an individual particle in this universal aliveness and yet one with it. I felt a profound sense of individual integrity and, at the same time, of unity and harmony. It was very clear to me that beneath appearances all things worked in total creative and blissful harmony, and I was a part of it all. Thus far, I was aware of no images, only of this direct and immediate perception. Then, realizing that I might need something specific to remember, I decided to imagine this experience in images. I somehow "chose" to represent the universe by a glowing, glistening, flowing circle of countless stars which were all the individual consciousnesses of the total oneness. I was one of those stars. The feelings of completeness, harmony, and joy permeated the dream. Upon awakening, I seemed to remember both the dream and the much fuller experience that preceded it. My life had been irrevocably changed. Ten years after that experience, I have never lost the faith that at bottom the true nature of existence is one of joyous harmony, and that my life's work is to discover, or rediscover, that fact. In times of distress, the living memory of my momentary glimpse of that harmony has not only comforted me but has encouraged me to understand the meaning behind my difficulties.

Barbara, one of the women in our Dream Meetings, has dreams in which she can communicate with trees, mountains, oceans, and clouds; even with the wind and stars. They tell her without words about the world and her life and about the nature of reality. She says that the difference between our consciousness and that of a mountain or an ocean is that their consciousness is a "larger, more collective one, with an emotional disposition that expresses its feelings in nonhuman form. This expression is of a wise, pure knowing." Barbara says that, in these dreams, she feels at one with the forces of nature and of the universe. They accept her, guide her, and play with her. One night she had what she described as "an hilarious conversation with the raindrops." Another night the ocean revealed the splendor of its being to her.

Although most dreams of nonverbal experience lose much in the telling, some inspirational dreams are easier to convey because they seem more like normal dreams with people and events which can be described, at least in part, by words. Sometimes dreams of what seems to be a superconscious origin involve religious figures of importance to the dreamer who advise or enlighten the dreamer. Barbara had a dream once where Moses smiled, shook his head, and said, "Barbara, I don't know what we're going to do with you." He was trying to show her that she was "really botching up" a part of her life, but at the same time he was reassuring her that she was loved and accepted and basically on the right track. Others have dreamed of Christ communicating love and profound understanding to them, or of Buddha inspiring the dreamer with compassion or tranquility. At times, the dreamers feel that their dream Christ or Buddha is an actual communication with the spirit of the historical figure; at other times the holy person represents that part of the dreamer's self which is divine or wise. In both cases, the experience is usually a positive one from which the dreamer takes comfort or learns some basic truth about existence.

These dreams often have a marked transformative effect upon the dreamer. This may be impossible to detect if one looks only at the manifest content or story of the dream. For instance, a dream about two triangles forming the Star of David may not mean much to an outside observer. Yet this could constitute the most intense experience of the dreamer's life if in the dream is seen the unity of heaven and earth. Though it seems we cannot command the gods to send a specific dream of integration, it is possible to successfully incubate inspirational dreams. If you have tried your best to understand a philosophic or religious problem and then ask with all your heart for enlightenment in a dream, you are very likely to get an answer.

A middle-aged man who had begun to feel that his spiritual and emotional life was stagnating incubated a dream, asking that it remind him of the vivid beauty of the inner world. He said that he had forgotten "the first and most important part of the dream" but that he remembered this much:

I am on a hike in a new and beautiful land. I pass a tree with incredibly gorgeous birds in it. The birds are of different vivid living colors: reds, roses, oranges, and purples. I am enchanted by their beauty and the peace and happiness which surrounds them. I lie down under the tree to rejoice in their lovely song. Then I wonder if, by wishing it, I could turn their song into classical music with familiar instruments interpreting their song. Yes! What a joy! I have never heard music so heavenly. I feel a contentment and participation in the beauty of the universe that fills my soul with great happiness. ("Classical Birds")

The fact that the dreamer experienced this happiness while asleep made it no less real to him. He felt that his prayer for a renewal of his inner life had been answered.

One of my students named Kirsten incubated a dream asking to meet her spiritual guide so that she could begin to study under him or her in the dream state. She had read of dream guides and was eager to see if she, too, could contact one who would guide her in her life. Kirsten dreamed that she met her guide, and he told her that he had been at her side for a long time before the dream meeting. He assured her that, now that she seemed ready to study with him, he would appear often in her dreams to guide her. In the following two months, she dreamed of this same figure eight times. Each time he seemed to fill her with peace and confidence. He counseled her on a few life problems, and for the rest he instructed her in experience and perception of a spiritual nature. Then for the next two months or so Kirsten remembered no more dreams about her guide, and was rather disappointed. She incubated a dream with the request, "Good guide where are you? Please come back, I'm ready to work!" Her dream response:

I had accepted a new temporary job at a desk from a man for money. One day I suddenly realize that I've forgotten all about the job and did not go to work last Monday. Oh dear! He was so good to give me the job. I must go back, face him, and apologize, in spite of the embarrassment I feel. ("Forgotten Job")

Upon awakening, Kirsten knew precisely what the dream was about. She had promised her brother that she would type his master's thesis for him, but she had been procrastinating as the deadline moved closer and closer. She had accepted the job as a service of love, and she realized that this was the job she had been neglecting. She knew that acts of love reward the giver with good feelings, and that her dream was telling her that, if she was indeed ready for spiritual work, she had better remember that she already had more than she could handle. After Kirsten finished her brother's thesis, the guide reappeared in a dream and congratulated her on having understood and acted upon his dream message to her.

Inspirational dreams are often striking in their use of imagery. Some seem almost entirely composed of sound as music or voices, or of color where form is quite secondary. Others may consist of very strange images or geometrical forms which seem to glow or vibrate in beautiful ways. Still others involve images of familiar holy figures or of unknown but unquestionably wise old men and women, as well as wise stars, mountains, and trees.

If you wish inspiration, encouragement, or comfort from your dreams, ask for it. If you are discouraged or sad and depressed, ask for a pleasant or joyful dream that will lift your spirits. Remember past dreams from which you awoke refreshed and cheerful and incubate a dream in which the same images will reappear. Even if you don't remember these dreams, they can break the cycle of unhappy and depressing thoughts which held you prisoner. But don't expect your dreams to continue giving you beautiful inspirations if you don't use them in living. Your dreams seem intent on giving you what you need and what you can use. They will cooperate with you if you cooperate with them. If you seek to live a life of beautiful dreams and stagnant days, your dreams will not let you. They will remind you of all the things you may be trying to escape and forget in your life.

Everyday Inspirations. Many people who need a new idea or a new way of looking at a problem have discovered that in the dream state they can tap levels of creativity which seem to surpass those they know while awake. Members of our Dream Meetings have successfully incubated tutorial dreams[16] on the spiritual significance of the crucifixion, Easter, or Christmas. One member asked, "What do I most need to understand in my search for wisdom?" She dreamed, all through the night it seemed, that she kept moving to the center of the earth and back to the surface over and over again. The experience was a very pleasant one of finding vast resources of wisdom every time she came to the center of the earth. A voice explained that she would find wisdom by going within herself and into her life on earth. The voice commented that, though she thought she was looking within herself, she was actually hoping to find wisdom in some altered state of consciousness or astral plane. Her tutor explained that what she needed most now was an appreciation of the learning and wisdom her life with its everyday beauties and challenges could offer her.

The voice finished by saying, "You didn't come to earth just to get away from it. You are here to taste and experience earth life as fully and as vividly as your understanding allows." As you might expect, this dream had a beneficial effect upon the dreamer's zest for everyday life. A friend who was a member of a tap-dance company, used to use incubation to call upon Fred Astaire and Gene Kelly to help her with her dancing. The two were such gentlemen they never refused. When I began writing this book, I recorded a long-term incubation request in my journal for specific dreams which would help me with my project. Almost every day, while I continued to remember dreams on other issues, I awakened with a helpful dream or several good ideas or corrections on my mind. At one point, I got so sick of dreaming about how to clearly explain the uses of dreams in my book that I asked for a few nights off. My dream producer obliged with some very recreational productions.

On the night before my wedding I was faced with a terrible problem. At every wedding I had attended, I had cried. At my sister's wedding, I cried all through the ceremony and the receiving line. I did not want to spend my wedding day in a flood of tears, however sweet and intense the emotions. I asked for a dream that would help me enjoy my wedding without all the tears. In the dream, it was my wedding day. All my long-lost relatives and old friends had gathered, and I was full of happiness at seeing them again. I told them that, "Since there isn't enough time to visit with each one as I long to, I wish that I could make you all into a soup, then I would be a piece of bread and soak you all up at once!" I awoke feeling flying high on the joy of the reunions my wedding would occasion. Throughout that wonderful day, I shed not a tear and I was exquisitely aware of the happiness all around me and in me.

Another interesting use of dreams is in the area of artistic inspiration. Spontaneous dreams frequently provide writers with ideas for stories and novels, and painters often receive dream inspirations for their paintings. You can take advantage of your dream producer's creativity by incubating dreams for ideas on specific projects or by simply making a special effort to recall your spontaneous dreams when you are involved with an artistic problem. You needn't be a great artist to receive dreams which surprise you with their inventiveness, though realization of your dream inspirations will be limited by your skills. Your dreams will tend to help you solve the problems you are actually working with, or are capable of handling. For example, in dreams where I see a good suggestion for a painting, it is clear that my dream producer knows better than to propose a composition that requires much in the way of drawing skills. My dream paintings are within the range of my very modest capabilities, and yet they always seem to lead me into an exciting experience in the medium. It is said that people do not dream of creative ideas and inventions in fields with which they have no experience, and this seems generally to be the case. However, I have had several dreams which have clearly urged me to experiment with sculpture, something I have never done. The sculpture of my dreams has been very vivid and not entirely beyond the capabilities of a beginner.

If you are working on a book, a story, a painting, or a sculpture; or if you are designing or decorating a room; or developing a new training program at work, why not ask your dreams for some inspiration? You may be surprised at the creativity of your dreaming self. If you don't remember a dream answer on the first try, make the same request for the following two nights, and try to remain open to new ideas or hunches which may come to you during the day. If you are unsuccessful after three trials, you are probably trying too hard. Let yourself forget the problem for a few days before trying again. Dreams seem to be very supportive of even our slightest interest in expressing our creative impulses, no matter how unsophisticated they might be.

It is also fun to use your art work to influence your dreams. If you want to dream of flying and soaring like a bird, study the flight of birds in the sky and paint or sketch them before you go to bed. Then incubate a dream in which you will fly and see what happens. If you are interested in a subject which you would like to dream about, use your daily activities to increase your focusing and understanding of the matter. While I was studying Buddhism, I bought a very difficult jigsaw puzzle of a marvelous statue of the Buddha. I worked intently with the puzzle for three days and used the piecing-together process as a meditation. Each night after working on the puzzle, I would have the most peaceful and enlightening dreams, in which I was piecing together my understanding of the Buddha's teachings. The more you immerse yourself in a subject or activity, the more likely you are to dream about it whether or not you formally incubate a dream. What you do in the day will influence your dreams, just as your dreams will influence your days.

Life Is But a Dream.   How many writers have told us that life is but a dream? What is the true reality of our existence? Is life but a momentary experience in three-dimensional reality? Do we exist on other levels of reality from which waking life may appear as a dream and a forgetting?

In any case, it can be very instructive to look at certain life events as if they were a dream and, supposing that there are no accidents, only meaningful coincidences, interpret them accordingly. Jung noticed that, in the course of an analysis, the synchronistic events (or meaningful coincidences) in a patient's life could reveal insights very important to the progress of the analysis. He had one patient who refused to talk about her sex life, in fact, she told him that she had come to him because she knew that he would not get carried away with all that Freudian nonsense about sex. Jung felt that this patient did have serious sexual conflicts, but he got nowhere with her until he discussed the subject with her in a session he conducted in his garden. Just as he insisted that her analysis could progress no further until she dealt with her conflicts about sex, two birds landed on the ground between Jung and his patient, copulated, and flew away. Both the analyst and the analysand laughed, the barrier was let down, and the patient began to discuss her sexual conflicts.

A Dream Meeting member told us one evening that he had had a particularly harrowing day at work and that in the midst of it his wristwatch, which had belonged to his father, had broken. When one of the other class members asked Stew how he would interpret his day if it were a dream, he replied that he would interpret the watch stopping as a signal to stop and look at how he was spending his time. Then when he thought of the fatigue of the day, he saw the meaning of the day as he might the meaning of a dream. He seemed to say "aha!" He told us that he had been thinking of taking a less demanding job in the country where he would earn less money and less acclaim but where he would be freer to live life more fully than he presently could because his work used so much of his energy. Stew's father had always encouraged him to work very hard because "life is hard and disaster is just around the corner." Stew interpreted his day as suggesting that perhaps he should stop living by his father's values regarding the use of time and pace himself according to his own values and needs.

Sometimes day events take on an aura of meaningfulness which is impossible to ignore. One evening I happened to glance at my huge philodendron plant. I looked at the root stubs behind each leaf where I had cut off the long roots I knew were not necessary for the plant and which I found unattractive. I was overcome with remorseful tears. Who was I to deform this noble plant? Who was I to cut back its natural growth and reaching for new life? I was profoundly appalled at how I could have been so insensitive. I wondered what in the world could have rendered me so sensitive now to something that had never bothered me before. I was not intoxicated or ill or particularly fatigued, and yet I was responding out of all proportion to the fact that I had trimmed the roots from this plant. I stopped trying to analyze my response and just let myself cry and experience the terrible sadness of my soul. Then it dawned on me: I had just seen three beautiful ballets by Balanchine on television. I had resisted acknowledging my sadness in watching the dancers that I was not one of them or at least a serious ice dancer. When I let my heightened perception of the plant fill my heart, I recognized that, by giving up my ballet and ice dancing, I had needlessly deformed myself. And even now I was continuing to deny my impulses to ice skate. That night I dreamt:

I am visiting Harry and Ella Stafford [my skating teacher and his wife, whom I love a great deal] at their summer skating school where I trained as a teenager. Harry drives me to see a woman my age who is mistreating a sick and cancerous dog. I am appalled and cry, "How could you?" I begin to show her how the dog's skin cancer can be cured by gentle care and healthy exercise. But she grabs the dog and throws her into her purse, saying that she is going to start from scratch with a new dog. I am horrified by her treatment of the poor sick dog, and awake feeling raw. ("Dancer Brutalized")

I was one of the first students to come to the Staffords' summer school, and the first dog they had there was named Dancer. So much for the setting and the identity of the dog! I continued the interview as follows:

What is cancer? Cancer cells consume vital organs. I have been eating my heart out not dancing for the past eight years, although in the last year I've begin to dance on ice again.

What is skin cancer? It is one of the few curable forms of cancer. Skin is a vital organ, and our largest. Skin is what allows us to touch and feel the world around us.

What it the dog's cancer like in the dream? The dog's skin is raw. I feel the terrible pain and rawness of the dog as I awake. The dog is the dancer within me whom I have mistreated by not exercising her and by criticizing her brutally for not being in perfect condition. Instead of trying to heal her, I've thrown her, like a used kleenex, into my purse. My pride has kept me from skating much even this past year. Like the other woman in my dream, I tell myself that I've lost my best skating abilities and might as well start from scratch with other pursuits I am good at. Yet I could heal the dancer in me by letting her dance and I would grow strong doing it.

What is Harry like? He has been my loving mentor in ice dancing and has taught me much about life. I trust him completely. His advice has always been very good. He must represent a wiser part of myself who is trying to make me see what I have been doing. I guess that my need to express myself through dancing on ice has not been appeased by my half-hearted attitude toward skating. When will I let myself skate as much as I can and need to? There is really nothing to stop me from skating twice as much and far more fervently than I do now. Especially now that I have such a great dance partner.

My dreams and my day life were not going to let me forget that I was still brutalizing the Dancer within. The impact of this dream and another one like it the following night was considerably intensified by my waking experience with the philodendron plant. In the year that has followed these experiences, I have done more skating and enjoyed it very much more. Yet as I rewrite this account now, I recognize that I am still holding back. This is an example of how the meanings of some dreams take years to realize, and periodic reviews of our dream journals can show us much fruit we have neglected to gather from past dreams and daytime experiences.

Many religions and some philosophers have held that the events of our days are not coincidences but meaningful events that mirror the inner state of our minds and hearts. Some have seen the coincidences, the good and bad luck of our lives, as omens from God. Others have seen them as the natural physical manifestations of thoughts, attitudes, and beliefs which sooner or later will attract what we expect into our lives. Some psychologists are beginning to think that our thoughts create our reality in a predictable and tangible way. The belief that we are not the victims of our circumstances but are, to some extent, the creators of them, is held in a less extreme manner by a large number of psychologists, psychiatrists, and mental-health therapists. They believe, and feel they see daily evidence, that we create our experiences of our daily lives and of the events which take place in them. Surely our image of ourselves, and our beliefs about the world and our expectations of it, have an enormous influence upon how the people we meet react to us and how we react to the people and events we encounter. If we can see ourselves, to some extent at least, the creators rather than the passive recipients or victims of the events of our lives, we will be in a better position to use those events as significant learning experiences.

For a few hours each week pretend that your life has as much purposeful composition and meaning as your dreams. Imagine that, just as you, the dream producer, create your dream experiences, you, the director of your thoughts, create your daily experience. You might also ask your dreams for some feedback on your experiment and see what happens. Our dream and waking lives can work together in surprising ways to enhance the creativity of our lives.

The words of the German poet Rainer Maria Rilke tell us where to find inspiration:

Seek those [themes] which your own everyday life offers you; describe your sorrows and desires, passing thoughts and the belief in some sort of beauty—describe all these with loving, quiet, humble sincerity, and use, to express yourself, the things in your environment, the images from your dreams, and the objects of your memory.[17]

9

The Twilight Zone

Psychic Dreaming; Esp;
Past-Life, Other-Life,
and Afterlife Dreams

Psychic Dreaming. Strange things happen in dreams. Many of us have had at least one experience of dreaming about an event before it actually happened. Some of us have dreamt of meeting dead relatives or of being in another body in another time and place. A few of us have shared the same or similar dreams. What could explain all this? Laboratory studies have not found the answer, although there have been a few provocative studies of psychic dreaming. It is true that many so-called psychic dreams[1] are no more than lucky guesses or logical projections into the future. The dreamer's subconscious, having had access to consciously forgotten memories and subtle, unrecognized perceptions, is capable of producing dreams that can seem psychic but which, in fact, are not. Certainly some accounts of "psychic" dreams represent little more than exaggeration and distortion of the dream and of the facts involved in the event described. However, anyone who has taken the trouble to investigate the subject would be likely to agree that perception by means other than our senses as we presently understand them is possible and does exist in at least some cases. Dr. H. J. Erpenck, Professor of Psychology at the University of London, has commented that, in view of the research thus far available to us:

Unless there is a gigantic conspiracy involving some thirty university departments all over the world and several hundred highly respected scientists in various fields, many of them originally hostile to the claims of the psychical researchers, the only conclusion the unbiased observer can come to must be that there does exist a small number of people who obtain knowledge existing in other people's minds or in the outer world by means as yet unknown to science.[2]

As to how psychic perception operates in both waking and sleeping states, there are many theories but no concrete answers. Theories of thought and information transmission via body waves, bioplasma, or as yet undetected brainwaves have not yet led to an understanding of the laws which psychic perception follows. Though we don't know how ESP[3] works, we have found some productive uses for it. In studying your dreams, you may find that you have had similar experiences. Perhaps you will want to experiment with incubating dreams which could demonstrate the validity of ESP to you in an immediate way or which might draw upon your psychic perceptions to solve a given problem. The dream examples below will give you something to think about as well as a few ideas which might inspire you to explore your own psychic abilities.

Certain Freudian psychoanalysts tend to see their patients' psychic dream perceptions about the personal lives of their analysts as neurotic acts aimed at gaining greater intimacy with the analyst or at "castrating" him by discovering one of his "secrets."[4] I have not noticed that my dream students have been psychically spying on me, but they are not so intensely involved with their weekly class instructor as a patient in analysis four or five times a week is with the analyst. Further, my students are a generally healthy group, and their dreams are not those of the deeply troubled patients seen by many analysts. I have however, found many instances in which the dreamer seemed to use psychic perceptions in an apparent effort to warn him or herself of an imminent difficulty or threatening situation. Ann Faraday calls this "underdog's psychic radar."[5] While my experience has led me to see this as a beneficial psychic function, not as a neurotic function of psychic dreaming, as does Faraday, I think the image of a psychic dream defense system which forewarns and forearms us against future difficulties is a useful one.[6]

One of the members of our dream group had planned a trip to Italy to visit some old friends. Before she left, she dreamt that her planned visit would be quite unpleasant because of marital discord in her friend's home. She had no conscious knowledge of any problems in her Italian friends' marriage at the time of the dream. But soon after she arrived at their house, she began to feel the stress and discord that filled the air. She was sad to see her friends so unhappy, and she was disappointed that her stay with them became an exercise in psychological survival rather than a peaceful vacation with friends. She felt that her dream had prepared her for her disappointment and that it had made her more sensitive to the delicacy of the situation she found her friends in.

In other members' dreams, their psychic radar tuned into somewhat more threatening future situations. One dreamer was warned that the next day at work she would feel very criticized but that she should try to be patient, let the whole thing blow over, and not act impulsively. The next day, her boss threatened to fire her for a small mistake she had made in typing an important letter. She was tempted to quit and save him the trouble of firing her, but she restrained herself, remembering her dream. The following day, her boss apologized for having been so unreasonable, explaining that he had recently been under a lot of pressure from his own boss and had taken his anger out on her.

Another class member, Al, dreamt that one of his best friends had died. In the dream, while grieving, he realized that his tears were for himself and that his friend was fine and had chosen to die and live another form of life after death. About a month later, Al received a telephone call from this friend, who had been in South America for the past two years. This was the first time the two had communicated in over a year—or so it seemed. Al's friend had become a follower of a fanatic religious cult and spent the whole call trying to convert his unenlightened friend to the Truth. After the phone call, Al said to himself, "I feel as though my best friend has died." Then he remembered his dream, and it consoled him. Even if he was now quite unable to share friendship with someone who considered him a sinner possessed by the devil, Al realized that what seemed to him a sad delusion of a formerly bright and accepting friend was, after all, something which his friend had chosen to believe and that might in the long run bring him peace. "To each his own" seemed to be the message Al took from his dream.

An argument could be made that, in each of the three cases described above, the dreamer did not need to use extrasensory perceptions to become aware of the threatening situation, especially in the dream state, where we have access to forgotten memories and subliminal clues. For instance, the secretary unconsciously remembering her mistake could have made a good dream guess that her boss would blow up, particularly if she had picked up subtle clues regarding the tension he was under at work. The dreamer who visited her Italian friends might possibly have sensed the marital discord from letters they had exchanged. In her waking state, she might have had a natural desire not to recognize subtle signs of trouble, but in her dream perhaps all she did was put two and two together. Al's dream is harder to see as an extension of good dream reasoning. All three dreamers felt their dreams provided them with information to which they did not have normal access. Whether or not these dreams are genuinely psychic dreams, the fact remains that in each case the dreamer's awareness of them was helpful in dealing with the pictured situation.

In the Dream Meetings, we have come across a few examples of apparently psychic dreams which seemed to have no particular purpose or use. It may be that sometimes we accidentally or randomly tune into events which do not concern us or which are quite unimportant in our lives. When we dream a prediction of an unimportant event which later transpires, we may have just happened to tune in to it, or, as sometimes seems the case, we may just be trying to prove to ourselves that psychic experience is possible for us. There are people who complain that their psychic dreams are very unpleasant and that they almost always about disaster which may not even involve the dreamer. Why would one dream of unpleasant events over which the dreamer has no influence? Are the dreams out to torment their dreamers? It has been suggested that this sort of psychic dream is a symptom of a person's concentration upon the negative aspects of life and of his or her fascination with the horror and disaster in the newspaper and the mass media.[7] Only one of my students has reported such a dream, and it could fairly be said that she was unusually focused upon the disasters of the world.

The idea that we attract to ourselves the kinds of experiences we expect, fear, or generally concentrate on is provocative and might explain why people who expect the best of life and dreams seem to have pleasant daily and dream lives. Those who expect the worst often find it. Which comes first, the chicken or the egg? Unfortunately, to date there is little information available regarding what healthy, normal people dream about in the course of their normal lives. There is still less data on the psychic dreams of people who are neither patients nor laboratory subjects and who use psychic perceptions in the natural course of their lives. Perhaps when such information becomes available, we will discover what types of personalities have what kinds of psychic dreams. All I can say at this point is that, if you suggest to yourself that you will not have unpleasant psychic dreams at all or not unless they deal with situations you can do something about, you will very likely not be bothered by such dreams.[8]

By far the majority of the psychic dream perceptions we have encountered in our Dream Meetings have occurred in both spontaneous and incubated dreams which dealt with solving problems. My first psychic dream came in 1970, when I was doing research for my college senior thesis on Carl Jung's and Edgar Cayce's views of the religious process manifest in dreams. One evening, after seven hours of struggling through reams of the sometimes cryptic Cayce readings, I had just about given up trying to figure out how Cayce conceived of and described the "higher self" so that I could compare it to Jung's concept of the self. I decided to ask my dreams for help, because I hadn't any better idea and needed the information badly.

I asked for a dream which would help me integrate what then seemed to be a hopelessly incoherent, apparently conflicting mass of cross references. That night I dreamt that the representative of the Department of Religion was telling me that my program of study was in good order except that I really should feminize it a bit and take one more course in a specific religion. I protested that I just didn't have the time. Upon awakening, I thought that to "feminize" my program would be to add more *eros* or sense of relatedness to it. Not having time to study a specific religion made me think of a Cayce study book on Revelations, which I had just bought but had no time to read or even look through because I had to finish my thesis. I had bought the book on the recommendation of a friend and planned to read it after graduation. The representative of the Religion Department, of course, set me thinking of a direction from my higher self (whatever that was) and of words from my wise man. So I picked up the study book on Revelations and started reading. Right there, on the page I just happened to open to, was an explanation of the overself, which showed me how Cayce related all those confusing terms. The dream may well have had more to say regarding a general need to better integrate my study of myself. In any case, it certainly answered my prayer.

Another situation where the dreamer seemed to use her psychic skills to solve a problem is provided by a dreamer named Sarah. She had recently heard about a new journal devoted entirely to the study of dreaming, *The Sundance Community Dream Journal.*[9] She followed the editor's suggestion that she consult her dreams as to whether or not it would be a good idea to subscribe to it. She wrote me, describing her very vivid dream as follows:

I was playing ping pong and always missed the ball. When I bent to pick up the ball, I picked up a letter written in characters I couldn't read. The paper was light yellow or cream with blue lettering, and the right margin was red, the red fading into the indentations formed by the ends of paragraphs.

I put the letter in my mouth and ate it. It tasted more delicious than anything I had ever eaten. ("Mmm, Good")

Sarah had not seen a direct correlation between her query and her dream, but she subscribed to the journal anyway. In the first issue, she had read the article I'd written inviting subscribers to participate in an experiment on phrase-focusing dream incubation. She later reviewed her dream journal, and it was then that she wrote me of this dream, adding the following commentary:

It was only after receiving my first issue of *Sundance,* that I reviewed my dream journal and I noticed the same combination of colors in the dream letter were on the *Sundance* cover. This, plus the dream content of delicious "bread," jogged me into writing this letter to see if it is too late to join your experiment in phrase-focusing incubation.

Even though Sarah originally did not notice the psychic elements in her dream, her later recognition of them encouraged her to become more involved with her dream study. One wonders how much influence the dream originally had on her decision to subscribe to the journal.

Instances of psychic dreams which have helped my students and myself to be more effective in dealing with everyday concerns occur with such frequency that most of us have come to consider them as a regular part of our dream life. One dreamer asked for help in finding an apartment in the city and received very detailed and useful information on where to look. My fiancé Steve was too anxious to wait six weeks to hear the outcome of his exams for board certification in his medical specialty. He asked his dreams for the results and received what turned out to be the right answer, that he had passed them. While Steve knew that his dream's answer was no great statistical feat, the conviction of having passed certainly reduced his anxiety during the waiting period before the results were mailed to him.

Afterlife and Other-Life Dreams. Most of us have dreamt of a close friend or relative who has died. Reports of such dreams often describe the dead person as reassuring the dreamer that the dead person is "alive" and well and that there is no need to grieve. Sometimes the deceased instructs the dreamer in some matter-of-fact concern in daily life. A few of the dreamers I know have successfully incubated dreams asking dead parents for advice, comfort, or simply the pleasure of their company. These dreamers could be dreaming of their images of the deceased person, or they might actually be in direct psychic contact with them. Who can say? The experience is usually a very intense one that seems real and helpful to the dreamer. You might want to experiment with this sort of dream direction and decide for yourself the nature of such dreams. I have read of instances in the Cayce readings where dreamers report that the deceased have asked the living to pray for them. This is reminiscent of some religious beliefs that dead souls need our prayers.

One of the most interesting dreams of my life came in response to an incubation in which I asked what it is like to be dead. I had the dream seven years ago, and it continues to be a source of extremely convincing reassurance that there is life after death and that the transition from one state (living) to another (life after death) is or can be a gentle withdrawal from attachment to earthly concerns. This dream considerably reduced my fear of death and gave me an increased sense of security in the world. I heartily suggest this experiment in dream incubation. It has been very interesting to three people who I know have tried it. Such a dream may represent a version of the truth about life after death, or it may represent our feelings about death. It will help to specify in your incubation whether you seek to know what it might be like for you after death or whether you would like to explore your present feelings about death.

There are those who believe that we or some part of ourselves can travel forward or backward in time and can apparently experience what it is, was, or will be like to see the world from another person's viewpoint. One student has described such an experience of a dream in which she "became" the child her mother had been. In the dream, she experienced the pain of loneliness and poverty her mother had known. The part of herself which was aware of being the dreamer was filled with compassion and understanding for her mother. She awoke with tears that were both her mother's and her own. She had asked for a dream which would help her understand her mother better so that she could relate to her with more gentleness and less resentment. Whatever the true nature of the dream, it gave the dreamer what she had asked for. Even if it is only in our dream imaginings that we can put ourselves in another's place, if this experience proves to give us a better feeling for another person's way of perceiving and reacting to the world, it is valuable.

Past-Life and Future-Life Dreams. If you have ever wondered if you live more than one life, you might enjoy exploring that possibility in your dreams. Many people dream of seeing themselves in other times and places and often in other physical bodies. While this dream motif does not constitute proof that we have or will experience other lifetimes on earth, it has often been interpreted this way. Edgar Cayce and Jane Roberts, speaking for psychic "sources," have said that dreams about reincarnational motifs come to assist dreamers in dealing with present life conflicts. They add that, in dreams where we are free of our linear concepts of time, we can draw upon the insights and strengths of other life experiences from both the past and the future as we conceive it. In the twelve "reincarnational" dreams I have studied, ten seem clearly to have been helpful in giving the dreamer insights into present life difficulties. And so again, if such unusual experiences are but flights of dream fancy used to represent psychodynamics of the dreamer's present life, they serve their purpose well. Whether or not they have a reality beyond this is impossible to say.

The first time I had a dream with this motif, it came unbidden:

This was a long dream about a voyage on a boat. Toward the end of the dream, it was time to disembark. I had found what seemed to be some lost clothes. From the deck I said to the captain above in his cabin that I had found these clothes which someone had left behind. To my surprise, he told me, "Oh no, they are yours." I tried on the skirt, which fit perfectly. Then I put on the full-length white wool coat, which I also had found. As I began to button the buttons that went from the mandarin collar to the floor, I had a very powerful memory flash. I realized [in the dream] that this coat had·been made for me by my servants in another life. I saw an image of myself in orange brocade robes beside an Eastern or Near-Eastern temple. I had once been a princess of a small principality who wanted very much to perform the·most sacred rites at the temple but could not, for tradition had ruled that only men could do this. I therefore had ordered this long and very heavy coat, a copy of the "altar boy" garb, to camouflage my femininity so that I might at last enter the temple unnoticed and come as close to God as the men. As I stood on the boat remembering all this, I couldn't believe that such a fantasy was a past-life memory, since I didn't believe in reincarnation. But the magnificent coat did fit. ("The Temple Coat")

This might not be a reincarnational dream at all, but it does hint at what I finally realized to be at the heart of my resentment at being a woman in our society: It has always been reserved to men to perform the most sacred rites. This dream clarified a lot of the feelings about male chauvinism which I had been experiencing at the time. It helped me to let go of some of my resentments as I realized that the society has only as much power over my spiritual life, or my self-esteem, as I grant to it. My resentments were in part an acceptance of defeat. In my present life, I know what I want, and there really is no insurmountable power that will stop me from living the life I choose. This dream helped me recognize my freedom.

Eileen, a healthy, vibrant young mother wrote me of an experience she had three years ago. At the time she wrote the letter, her five-month old son Adam had just undergone dangerous but necessary open-heart surgery to correct a life-threatening birth defect. Eileen and her family had been under tremendous strain during the past five months, especially around the time of the risky surgery. Here is an excerpt from her letter:

Adam is doing well now. He has a lot of catching up to do but is really progressing since his operation three weeks ago. He was almost too weak to roll over most of the time prior to that. One of the things that kept me going was something that happened about two years before he was born. We hadn't decided at that time if we would have another child or not. I was sleeping and either dreamed this or else it really happened at a stage in between sleeping and waking. I woke up and saw a young boy standing by my bed. In nonverbal communication, I asked him who he was. He said that he was the son I was going to have. He had been watching me sleep. He looked like Adam will look (slight build, 5'6", with brown hair, intelligent eyes, even features). I felt very comfortable and felt as if I knew him. I closed my eyes and went right back into a deeper sleep. I almost feel now that Adam was letting me know he would live past the surgery.

Eileen has also recorded several dreams in which she met and talked with her deceased grandmother, whom she has always loved and respected very much. In one dream, Eileen asked her grandmother "all about what happened after death" and received a response, part of which she could not remember. The part she did recall was vivid and meaningful to her. The answer dealt with her grandmother's afterlife reunion and relationship with her grandfather.

In another sleep meeting with her grandmother, Eileen dreamed:

There was a gathering of the family somewhere. Grandma entered the room. We were all overwhelmed and said that she was dead. She just laughed. The next part is hazy. Then the next part is vivid. Bill, Grandma, and I went for a car ride. Grandma didn't know how to drive in life. She started to drive Bill and me somewhere. Her driving was very fast. I felt the air hitting me in the face and could hardly catch my breath—like in the back of a convertible. Bill and I were both concerned and protested because Grandma didn't know how to drive. She laughed and said, "There's more to me than that old woman you thought I was!" ("Grandma")

Eileen said that, when she told her brother this dream, he filled in a few details for her, explaining that he had dreamt the very same dream! Neither Eileen nor her brother could remember where their grandmother was taking them, but they speculated that she might have been giving them a lesson in astral travel.[10]

This dream brings up the question of shared dreaming. Since the psychologist Hornell Hart first described mutual dreams as making up a special category of dreaming which he called "reciprocal dreams,"[11] very little attention has been paid to this rare phenomenon. Recently, however, interest in mutual dreaming has begun to grow.[12] The possibility of sharing dreams with other people is a fascinating one that poses many questions about the nature of dream reality. If dreams can be shared, then whose creation are they? How real are our dream landscapes? Who tunes into whose dream? The questions are almost endless. I have just begun to experiment with inducing shared dreaming by using the phrase-focusing technique of incubation described in Chapter 2.

If you would like to experiment with your own Twilight Zone dreams, and perhaps resolve a few problems in the process, ask your dreams incubation questions like these:

If I am experiencing existences in another time and place, or have done so in the past, show me!

What happens after death?

I would like to meet and speak with my dead father (mother, sister, friend, etc.).

What will be the sex of our new child?

Have I known my husband (mother, sister, etc.) in another life?

I would like to know what it was like to live in seventeenth-century Paris.

What would my life have been like if I had done (or if I had not done) such-and-such a thing?

What would result if I did such-and-such? (Here you can try out alternative solutions to problems, etc.)

What is it like to see the world from X's eyes?

Many other questions will probably suggest themselves to you. I would be very interested to hear what kinds of responses you receive to such incubations and would appreciate your letters. Perhaps in a few years enough people will be studying their dreams to make a broad survey of Twilight Zone dreams possible. In the meantime, we are all pioneers in this kind of dreaming as are those who are experimenting with lucid dreams and astral projection, which will be discussed in the next chapter.

10

Startrekking

*Conscious Dreaming, Astral Travel, and
Exploring Other Dimensions of Reality*

Have you ever had the feeling that a dream is like a movie you filmed
while away on a trip? When you see the movie upon your return, you
realize how much of the trip you have forgotten and how little of it could
be captured on film?

Many dreamers, having sensed that their dreams are but recalled highlights of richer, more complex experiences in the sleep state, have experimented with various ways of increasing their conscious awareness of those
experiences. Some have discovered that it is possible to become conscious
while sleeping or dreaming as well as to actually fall asleep without losing
consciousness. By increasing their conscious awareness of different sleep
and dream states, they have been able to consciously participate in both
the production and action of their dreams. Some have had experiences
of participating in the events "behind" or "before" the dream-making
process. Some feel they have been able to travel out of their bodies and
"visit," or at least perceive, different realms of reality. Almost everyone
who has achieved a moderate degree of consciousness within sleep and
dream states has been able to recall dreams far more vividly than before
and direct them in ways which are both beneficial and exciting.

By using the suggestions in this chapter, you will be able to increase
your awareness of your nightly activities both as an explorer of different
modes of perception and as a master producer of dreams.

Developing Conscious Awareness within the Dream State. The degree to which you can be conscious of your sleeping activities can range from recalling nothing at all about them to recalling vividly many dreams each night, to becoming aware of the fact that you are dreaming during the dream itself and participating in its creation. You can go further; you can become aware of your experiences in levels of consciousness which may form the raw material from which dreams are made.

Watching the workings of your mind while your body sleeps is a fascinating endeavor which will lead you to a much fuller understanding of your dreams. It will also increase your appreciation for the depth and variety of experiences available to you when your consciousness is free to focus its attention on your inner world.

In *lucid* dreaming, the dreamer is aware of the fact that he or she is dreaming while the dream is happening. You have probably experienced some degree of lucidity if you have been recalling your dreams at all. How many times have you said to yourself, "This is only a dream," while some dream enemy was chasing you? This is a form of *prelucid* dreaming in which the dreamer, while sleeping half realizes that some segment of the dream is only a dream. A fully lucid dream is one in which you definitely recognize that you are dreaming. In a lucid dream you can use your awareness to change the dream you are having in almost any way you choose. What would you like most to do in a dream? Fly and soar like an eagle? Meet with a wise old friend or relative? Ask each figure in a dream what it represents? Or perhaps you would like simply to watch the progress of a dream, knowing all the while that you cannot be hurt by the most fearsome of its images.

There is a joyous quality to many lucid dreams that is almost irresistible. Colors are filled with sunlight and moonlight, and one often has the impression that everything in the dream is more "real" and vivid than in waking reality. If you hear music in a lucid dream, it will probably be sweeter than any earthly sound you know. Tastes and smells will delight you by their intensity, and the degree to which you can direct the progress of events will amaze you.

In her book *Lucid Dreams*,[1] Celia Green, Director of the Institute of Psychophysical Research in Oxford, England, reviews the phenomenon of conscious dreaming. Patricia Garfield, in *Creative Dreaming*,[2] has made an important contribution to the literature on lucid dreaming by analyzing her own lucid experiences in relation to those of the lucid dreamers reviewed by Green, and by suggesting certain techniques for inducing such dreams. In this chapter I have drawn largely from these accounts and from the experiences my students and I have had with prelucid and lucid dreams.

You may have already noticed that dream incubation often has the wonderful side-effect of producing dream experiences in which you are more conscious of the dream process than usual. It seems that the conscious attention lavished upon the dream process while the dreamer is in the waking state is rewarded by an increased awareness in the dream state. The psychologist Kilton Stewart took advantage of this phenomenon in developing a theory of dream education which he called "creative psychology."[3] (His theory is popularly know as the Senoi technique of dream control. However, this may be a misnomer, and therefore I shall refer to his theory as the Stewart technique.[4]) Stewart evolved a set of directives which instruct dreamers to *"confront* and *conquer"* all harmful, useless, wasteful, rigid, obsolete, infantile, uncooperative, sick, or troublesome images in a dream. The dreamer is to kill, burn, melt, or somehow eliminate or change these images while he is dreaming them. At the same time, the dreamer is encouraged to help and to cooperate with all helpful dream images as well as to ask them for assistance and information. Stewart stated that, by studying and reviewing such directives in the waking state, one would eventually remember them in the dream state. The purpose of such directives and the dream action they encourage is to educate the dreamer to attain a greater awareness in the dream state so that he can outface and conquer dream representations of conflicting, fearful, and negative aspects of himself and thus unify his personality.[5]

The Stewart technique is different from dream incubation in several significant respects. When you incubate a dream, you consciously choose the issue the dream is to treat, but your autonomous, usually unconscious, dream process is free to deal with the matter in its own fashion. Stewart's directives constitute a form of dream guidance in which one is to guide or influence the action of the dream once it is in process. The directives are suggested to the waking mind, but they are meant for use by the dreaming mind, which is to guide rather than control the spontaneous dream action. Although dream incubation may precipitate lucid dreams, it does not require lucidity in the dream state. Dream guidance, on the other hand, does require at least a minimal degree of awareness while the dream is happening.

Because the degree of consciousness dream guidance requires is not very difficult to attain, it is often a stepping stone to lucid dreaming.

Dream guidance can greatly benefit the dreamer if it is used wisely. My students and I have used a modified form of the Stewart technique to increase our conscious awareness of dreaming and to simplify and accelerate the problem-solving process in both our spontaneous and our incubated dreams.

Confronting the Monsters. I agree with Ernest Rossi[6] and many psychotherapists that, until we can feel loving acceptance of negative (frightening, threatening, or frustrating) dream figures, we will not be free of their negative psychological influence. In the Stewart technique, the dreamer is told to take forceful aggressive action against any negative dream figure. She is to turn and confront pursuers rather than run from them. The dreamer is to create weapons or call forth friendly dream figures to help conquer aggressors, and, if all else fails, the dreamer must stand her ground and fight to the death in the consciousness that she is dreaming and cannot be physically harmed.[7] Although it is certainly better to turn and fight one's negative dream images than to run from them, I believe that the directive to "always advance and attack in the teeth of danger"[8] is unwise. The theory behind it is that "the spirit or essence of this dream character will always emerge as a servant or ally."[9] However, it is not at all clear that the essence of a slain dream enemy is or will be helpful to the dreamer's psyche. In fact, it seems that slain dream enemies keep popping up in future dreams in various guises until the dreamer finally understands and accepts them as a part of herself. In reviewing dream accounts in the literature and in my research files, I find that very much more is to be gained by confronting threatening dream images with a desire to understand rather than to demolish them. I have found that asking a negative dream figure "What do you want?" or "What do you represent?" results not only in the transformation of the figure into a friendly one, but also in valuable insights into the parts of the personality represented by the originally threatening figure. For example, Mary Ellen dreamed:

I am in my apartment when a gang of young thugs walk in and say they are going to do something terrible to me. I manage somehow to trick them out of the apartment and lock all the windows and doors. I hope I am safe. I am still frightened. They get back in, and now they are in a new and terrifying form. They look like huge monsters with tentacles, bulging eyes, and sea-monster skin. I remember that I was not going to let fear get the better of me in my dreams from now on. So I swallow my fear and concentrate on saying, "Well you got back in. Now what do you want?"

Immediately the monsters transform into friendly people who explain that they want to be my allies and help me understand myself. They proceed to demonstrate (in ways I've forgotten) why I've been so jealous of my best friend. Their explanations are "right on" and I awake feeling more self-confident and far less jealous of her. ("Eyeball Monsters")

If you persist in suggesting to yourself while awake that you will turn and confront your negative dream images, and that you will then ask them why they threaten you, you will succeed. This may happen for you right away or it might take a couple of months, but you will be able to do it and, when you do, you will feel a great sense of accomplishment. This feeling will carry over into your day and give you a new sense of courage and prowess. If you succeed in asking your negative dream image what it wants, you will also bring into your waking consciousness surprisingly helpful insights.

Joe, whose "Pet Lion" dream was discussed in Chapter 3, did not always have such a good relationship with his assertive, playful self. Before Joe came to his first dream meeting, he had the following dream:

I'm keeping order in some kind of institution. A BIG fellow, huge, keeps slithering backward across the hall floor. This is against institution policy. The first couple of times, I don't stop him. I'm afraid of him because he is so big, and he knows it. Finally, I go over to him and poke stiff fingers at his eyes. "What's that for?" he asks. I answer, "I'm gonna make you (obey? the rules?) *one way or the other, even if I die in the attempt." ("Law and Order")*

Joe sees himself as a nice, kind guy—which he is. He is also an assertive, aggressive human being. This was the part of himself he thought crazy and locked up. He saw this aspect of himself as very threatening, and had considered himself to be sliding backward on the path to maturity and spiritual enlightenment whenever he expressed even quite natural and appropriate assertiveness. Had Joe asked the threatening figure what he wanted, or what he was up to (instead of vice-versa), Joe would probably have gotten a clearer insight into his "nice-guy" complex. As it was, Joe had confronted and outfaced his dream enemy. Though he felt glad to have stood up to him, he did not get very much out of the encounter except a hint (which he missed) that he was risking the well-being of his psychological life by keeping this big fellow in line with the rules of his nice-guy role. We encouraged Joe to suggest to himself that his frightening dream figures were really friendly ones distorted by his fear, and that he should try loving them. Then he had a dream about a tiger. In this dream he was seeking his lost pet tiger, who was hiding from him. When he found it, the tiger was dressed in women's clothing. Joe was gentler with the rule breaker this time, and the tiger's response gave him an important clue to the dynamics of the conflicts which led him to dress his aggressive and assertive tendencies in nice-guy behaviors (women's clothes). When Joe had experimented with a more accepting attitude toward his assertiveness and with the enhanced sense of self-esteem that required, Joe had the dream about his playful, energetic, pet lion. He was learning to love the lion inside him, and in so doing discovered its natural nature was not hostile but helpful to him. I believe he came to this realization sooner by practicing a more loving, non-attack-oriented form of dream guidance.

Virginia dreamt of a "big, black screeching blob." In the dream, she recognized it to be an acquaintance of hers. She then authoritatively told it to stop playing the victim role. Virginia added that it was responsible for its own actions and could not blame its misfortune on outside forces. Virginia's dream action was undoubtedly a healthier response than fright or agreement. However, one wonders what would have happened if Virginia had tried to understand the "blob lady" as Ginger (Part V) tried to understand her attacking dream lady. Might the dream have continued and portrayed more complete representation and possible resolution of the conflict?

Another dreamer, Rick, had a dream almost every three weeks or so of being attacked by hateful, spiteful men. The men would appear as soldiers, tyrants, bullies, and landlords. Each time Rick had these dreams, he would manage to defend himself, and sometimes kill his attackers. Yet the dreams kept recurring in various forms until Rick was encouraged to reconsider what he felt was his justified hatred of his father. We thought that, if Rick could forgive his father and love him as a struggling human being, he (Rick) would be freed of the hatred and resentment that pursued him in his adult life. Although Rick's father had been dead for several years, he had strongly influenced Rick, who was still carrying his image of his father and a hatred toward him inside himself. Rick experimented with the idea of "hating the sin but loving the sinner" and began to see how he could forgive his father for his real or imagined wrongs. Rick even began to forgive the part of himself that was like his father. Although his hatred was still alive and strong, at least he could now consider that his attitude was not the only one available to him. During one of our meetings, Rick resolved to confront and try to understand his dream pursuers.

Before the next Dream Meeting, Rick dreamt that an armed soldier barged into his house. As Rick grabbed a gun to shoot him, he remembered his resolve and vaguely realized that he was dreaming. He put down his gun and mentally communicated to the soldier that he wanted to understand him. Rick said, "What do you want?" The soldier turned into a friendly contemporary of Rick's and said, "I want you to stop hating." Then the former soldier explained to Rick things he could not remember but which he felt brought him a profound understanding of something. Rick was feeling loving and grateful toward his unknown friend when the scene changed. Next, Rick was with his father, whom he saw as a man suffering with his own conflicts and who was far from malicious. For the first time, Rick felt a deep compassion and forgiveness for his father. Here the dream ended.

Rick told us that the dream had given him a taste of how it would be if he could give up his hatred for his father. He was encouraged to do so by the memory of the dream. Old hates rarely die overnight. Yet it is interesting to note that, since this experience, Rick has had only four dreams of attacking hateful, spiteful males in the last eighteen months. In each, he has been able to come to a compassionate understanding with his pursuer. Dream experiences like these have a wonderfully integrative effect upon the dreamer's personality.

To confront and understand threatening or perplexing dream images is, in my opinion, the best way to approach dream guidance, because the rewards of loving and understanding your enemies seem far greater than those of demolishing them. Most often, the conquering of a negative image ends the dream: The dreamer is left with a sense of achievement and courage. This is certainly preferable to having fled and not confronted the image at all. However, by not making the effort to understand the attacker, the dreamer has missed an opportunity to increase his understanding of that part of himself which the negative image represents.

In dreams where you are frightened by certain images, first try to tell yourself that you are dreaming and need not fear being harmed. Tell yourself that you are in another kind of reality in which time and space, cause and effect, operate according to dream, not waking, reality. Tell yourself that you are safe. Try to understand what is happening to you and ask your dream figures what they represent or what they want. If you can do this, you will surely learn much from the dream. You may also come to a clear realization that you are dreaming and become fully lucid. At this point, you will be free to experiment with your new state of awareness. It may take time and practice, not only to become fully lucid but to become conscious enough of the possibilities to take advantage of them.

Waking up in Your Dreams. Your first efforts to become conscious in the dream state may result in passing dream thoughts in which you reflect upon the dream process. They may not precipitate a full awareness that you are dreaming, but they are a beginning. One woman who dreamt she was on her way to a great council of all sorts of "people," understood that an elf would be present and wondered if her dream producer's representation of an elf would meet her high expectations of what elves should be like. After this thought, the dreamer lapsed back into a normal dreaming state. This is an example of a prelucid dream in which the dreamer had a glimmer of awareness of dreaming but did not quite grasp its implications. She did not become lucid, with a clear realization that she was dreaming.

Sometimes reflective thoughts about the dream process will lead the dreamer into a lucid awareness that he or she is dreaming. The next problem is for the dreamer to continue using critical faculties and not fall back into normal, nonreflective dreaming. The only remedy found for this is practice. Ten of us in the Dream Meetings have tried to focus on a given image in lucid and prelucid dreams, to examine it carefully, reminding ourselves to keep the image stable[10] or to transform it through an act of will. The idea is not to forget that we are in a position to direct our dream imagery. So far, only three of us have had any success in doing this. Our success in calling forth the dream environment and experience of our desires has been limited to brief moments typical of novices.

Lucid dream direction, even when practiced by very skilled dreamers, has not been experienced as an ability to entirely control dream reality.[11] Hervey de Saint-Denys,[12] after extensive experiments with his lucid dream states, wrote, "I have never managed to follow and master all the phases of a dream, I have never even attempted it."[13] The freedom to control even lucid dream environments is not limited but enhanced by the apparently autonomous or spontaneous characteristics of dream reality. It would seem that our deepest pleasures, joys, and comprehensions flow from the autonomous, often surprising and exquisitely creative elements of our dream experiences. The purpose in directing or guiding dreams is not to control dream reality completely or try to force it into the forms of waking experience but to taste dream reality as vividly and as fully as possible.

Lucid and prelucid dreamers sometimes find themselves deciding to practice manipulating their dream environment. Barbara, in her dreams of communing with trees and oceans and raindrops, often practices moving the clouds by her thoughts. I have had several dreams in which I have experimented with changing the size and quantity of objects around me. Once I dreamed I was in a nineteenth-century Bavarian bar. I looked at two beer steins on the table and decided to "think" them into three. It worked. Then I made one larger and one smaller, increased their number, and finally decided that there should be only one stein on the bar. This was great fun, and I had the distinct impression that I was perceiving and learning through play how to work with the true nature of reality. Since that dream, I have had others like it and have heard and read of similar stories from other lucid dreamers.

Perhaps lucid dreamers' fascination with altering dream images just to see if it is possible and what will be the results is a natural learning process. Some philosophical and spiritual texts[14] propose the idea that our thoughts (beliefs, attitudes, hopes, desires, and fears) create reality— not only our response to reality but the events and objects of reality as we know it. Such texts explain that, if it were not for the time it takes for thoughts to manifest in physically perceivable form, we would not consider such an idea so unlikely. In dream states, where we are free of the constrictions of linear time, perhaps we recognize at some deep level that thoughts create reality not only in dreams but in three-dimensional, physical states as well. Even this form of manipulating lucid dream images is usually aimed not so much at controlling dream reality as at exploring the different ways it works.

The practice of dream guidance will lead you to thoughts in which you reflect upon the process and nature of dreaming. These thoughts can trigger lucid dreams if you fully realize that you are in fact dreaming. You might also choose a "trigger object." While awake, select an object you are likely to encounter in a dream, such as a tree, a familiar street or house, a part of your body, a friend, or any of your frequent dream images. Suggest to yourself during the day that seeing the trigger object will make you realize that you are dreaming. Another way to trigger lucidity is to suggest to yourself that in dreams you will become aware of incongruous and bizarre elements and that they will signal your dreaming state to you. This happened to me in the following dream about "The Quickstep," which is a dance in a series of national test dances which an ice skater must pass in order to get a gold medal (like Karate's black belt) in ice dancing. In day life, this was the last dance I had to pass before receiving my medal in 1967.

I've just taken (danced) my test on the quickstep. It was pretty good and I think I've passed. But Lo! the judges fail me! All three of them! I think, "Oh well, I'll take it again as soon as the enforced two-month waiting period expires. I do want it to be a great test if it is my last before the medal. But I am disappointed, because I thought I had done well. I read the judges' comments on my score papers. "Lean back more here. Extend this edge there," etc. These comments are absurdly picayune and petty. They in no way justify my failing marks. I am angry but again think that it's O.K., because when I pass this test it should be so good that no one could give me anything but very high marks. . . . Then, Wow! Wait! This is 1976 not 1967. I've already passed this test, and I don't have to worry about pleasing any judges. And because I'm dreaming, I can skate with wings on my blades. I then start to skate again, but this time I can do anything. When I jump, I am weightless, and I fly as I turn in the air. When I spin, my balance is perfect. I feel a happiness that is one of the most profound I have ever known, and I am at one with the world. I feel all the forces of the harmony of the universe in my skating, and the intensity of my joy knows no bounds. ("Quickstep Becomes Free Skating")

This dream deeply impressed me with the way I restrict my enjoyment of skating by being a picky, perfectionistic judge of it. The dream has brought about a significant, enduring change in my attitude toward skating. The morning after the dream, I skated with my partner and secretly decided not to work but to play at it. Bob is something of a perfectionist himself, and when he began to comment on how much better my skating was than usual, I knew that my dream had had a tangible effect. I think that our dream producers' most powerful agents of change are not threat and fear (which are powerful) but pleasure and peaceful, yet exhilarating, joy. A dream producer can show you what it is like to let go of an attitude or complex which limits you. Then, once you've seen Paris, it becomes awfully hard to keep yourself down on the farm tending old and comfortable, but limiting, attitudes. This is especially true in lucid dreams, where the intensity of perception can be so marvelously heightened.

After finding the incongruous elements in dreams, one is tempted to say, "This is not real, it is only a dream." Such a mental exclamation can be effective in precipitating a lucid dream. However, I prefer the response, "This is not waking reality; this is dream reality." This response better prepares the dreamer to operate within the dream state, which is, after all, real in its own way and follows its own laws.

Celia Green states that almost all the lucid dreamers she studied stressed "the importance of emotional detachment in prolonging the experience and maintaining a high degree of lucidity."[15] Garfield also suggests that the lucid dreamer not allow himself to become too emotionally involved with the dream action because this might disrupt the lucid state.[16] However, both Garfield[17] and I have experienced strong emotional involvement in some lucid dreams without losing our lucidity. It may be that lucidity depends not on avoiding the experience of strong emotion but on maintaining a constant awareness or observation that you are experiencing it. This would be similar to being both the witness and the experiencer of your emotions and thoughts, as is suggested in several forms of meditation. It would seem that one of the greatest advantages of dream lucidity is the clarity and intensity of perception and expression it makes possible. You can maintain lucidity while experiencing this if you learn to observe your dream thoughts and feelings as you experience them. This "witness principle" or critical faculty would seem to be at the base of even the vaguest prelucid dream experiences, in which one reflects upon the process or incongruity of the dream.

Before we go on to other ways of inducing consciousness in dreams, it might be good to consider one of the major factors inhibiting many people's efforts in attaining consciousness of the sleep state.

One clear night in 1970, I was in the French Alps at a ski resort called Chamonix. I had skiied to the point of "first day on the slopes" exhaustion. I dragged myself out of the hot tub and tumbled into bed. I was so tired, I wondered why I wasn't asleep after a few minutes. Then I heard myself practicing my French. Then I noticed a short dream that seemed to be happening while I was wide awake. This was like a real dream not like the plotless, brief hypnogogic images so common just before sleep. Then I seemed to be reviewing the day and practicing both skiing and French. After quite a while of this, I became very impatient to fall asleep. I was tired and had a full day's skiing ahead of me the next day. This was no time for insomnia. Another dream intruded upon my more normal thoughts. Finally I came to the conclusion that my body had fallen asleep but "I" hadn't! I watched the next dream with renewed interest. Then it occurred to me to replay it, changing one dream event so that the dream would terminate with a resolution which would help me accept the inevitable fact that after this week I would never again see a certain Mr. X who had made a deep impression on me. It worked. The dream gave me a sense of peaceful acceptance that we would never be free to get to know each other, and I was grateful for that. This lucidity was very beautiful and helpful in the dream state, but it was irritating and boring in between dreams where I witnessed the endless chatter of another part of my mind that just wouldn't stop practicing French. I felt like a captive audience at a spelling bee. What a time to become lucid. I wanted to sleep, to go *un*conscious. I wanted to awake refreshed to a new world. I had seven days to enjoy in Chamonix. Why couldn't I experiment with my consciousness while I was back home in New Jersey? Try as I might, I couldn't go unconscious. Why it never occurred to me to move my body and so break the spell puzzles me. At any rate, several dreams and many mundane thoughts and pronunciation exercises later, the sun came up and I dressed for the ski slopes.

Although I expected to feel a great fatigue skiing, I seemed as rested as I usually do after a good night's sleep. During the following two nights, I had the same impression that I was wide awake and fully conscious. I seemed to be witnessing several other levels of consciousness operating simultaneously. While my daily review and "normal chatter" thoughts would occur, so would my French and ski practice sessions. On another level, dreams would periodically occur; on yet another level things were happening which I couldn't quite perceive. While all this was going on, I was also conscious of my reflections on this unusual state of consciousness and of my increasingly adamant desires to go unconscious. I really just wanted to be relieved of all this awareness. I kept wishing I could "pass out" of this witness role and not have to attend to it. I told myself that this was no time to be fooling around with my sleep; that no matter how much I had hoped for and tried to achieve consciousness of my sleep states, this was not the time for it. I kept telling myself to "fall asleep." On the fourth night, I finally had a normal night of mostly unconscious sleep. Years later, some of the dreams I had during those "lucid nights" are still amazingly vivid in my mind. I found that I could not willfully produce lucid nights upon my return to the United States. I have had such experiences only four times since Chamonix, and each time I was in a very high-altitude ski resort and had gone to bed physically exhausted.

Since my first experience with lucid nights, I have learned a little about meditation techniques of quieting the mind and have used these to reduce somewhat the seemingly endless "chatter thoughts" in my mind at such times. Although my experiences with lucid nights has consequently become more agreeable, and in spite of the fact that the lucid dream states of these nights are fascinating and sometimes very pleasurable, and in spite of the fact that I do not seem to lose any physical rest from them, I *still* resist staying conscious. I have become aware of attitudes I had not recognized I held about the desirability of not taking conscious responsibility for my sleeping activities. Although I lust after lucid dreams and expanded awareness of all of my experiences, I am willing to go only so far before I've had enough and seek escape in the refuge of unconsciousness.

The Tibetan yoga of dream control teaches that one can willfully and regularly allow the body to sleep while the mind remains fully conscious and free to manipulate in both dream and other sleep consciousness.[18] You might ask yourself how much you really want to become conscious in your dream or sleep states. Of course, you needn't go as far as remaining conscious through most of the night. But if you become aware of your own desires not to attain consciousness in dream states, you will be better equipped to deal with them if and when they inhibit your progress toward lucid dreaming. Ambivalence toward new growth and awareness in both waking and sleeping states is natural and is best dealt with when it is confronted and understood.

Learning How to Wake Up and How to Fly

False Awakenings. A curious experience which you may have had is that of apparently awakening from sleep or from a dream, and then actually awakening and realizing that the first time you "awoke" you were still dreaming. These experiences are called *false awakenings.* If you can become aware that a false awakening is indeed that, you may become lucid. The next time you suspect that you are experiencing a false awakening, test your environment to see if you are truly awake or not. See if you can look at the bed you went to sleep in. If it is empty and you can touch it, and if all other things seem normal, then you are probably awake in waking reality. However, if you look back to your bed and your body is still in it, then you will know you are in a dream state having what is called an out-of-body experience (OBE). (OBEs will be discussed at length in the next section, but, briefly, they are experiences in which one seems to perceive the environment from a vantage point outside of the physical body.) It is not always possible to think of or to find one's bed during a false awakening. In this case, the best way to explore the reality of your present environment is to see how it compares with waking reality. Is something out of place? Are basic laws of gravity and placement in space being violated? Do the lights go on when you flip the switch? Tests like these should tell you if you are awake in day or dream reality.[19] If you realize that you are in a dream state, you may then either have a lucid dream experience or choose to conduct other experiments on your abilities in this state.

Several of us in the Dream Meetings have experienced two kinds of false awakenings. In the first, the dreamer, apparently awakening from a dream, then has another dream while under the impression that he is awake. This impression is then corrected by the actual awakening. In the other sort of false awakening, the dreamer, after having completed a dream, seems to awaken into the normal environment of his room. Sometimes the dreamer looks at the clock to see if there is enough time to go back to sleep before beginning the day's activities. Sometime later, the actual awakening occurs. When I have a false awakening of this nature, I seem quite able to read the clock, which in fact may be in another room or in my own room in extreme darkness.[20] Sometimes I am vaguely aware that I am still asleep and am checking the time to see if I must awake my physical body or if I can go on sleeping. Usually this occurs within an hour of the time for which the alarm is set to go off. I have always had the impression that my sleep reading was accurate upon awakening.

Another sort of false awakening described by Celia Green is apparently awakening to the awareness that something is amiss. Usually the dreamer lies still in bed and is rather frightened. There is suspense in the air. The dreamer may hear voices talking about her or breathing. Then, if the dreamer does not awaken in fright, she might explore the situation by saying to herself, "What's going on here?" or by seeming to reach out to locate the source of the sounds.[21]

Virginia had an experience like this. She seemed to awaken from a dream and was lying in her bed when she felt a threatening darkness or shadow come over her. She tried to open her eyes but couldn't. She tried to scream but couldn't. Then she wondered what was happening and heard two men talking about making some use of her body. She realized that she was dreaming and knew that she could not be harmed. Now she could open her eyes. The intruders became friendly. One was her brother, the other a friend of his. The three of them had a pleasant encounter dealing with their relationships, and the experience ended when Virginia started laughing so hard that she awoke. Whatever else this experience may suggest, it demonstrates once again how fear in sleep and dream states acts as a distorting lens. Whenever you can overcome fear in these states, you will almost always find that a frightening experience then becomes a nonthreatening one that may be enjoyable.

Dream Flying. An easier route to lucid dreaming seems to be flying. In these dreams, one can fly like Peter Pan or Superman without any mechanical assistance. If you have had flying dreams, you know how pleasurable they are. Many people consider them to be their most enjoyable dreams. It is possible to induce flying dreams through incubation and other techniques and thereby begin or increase your experiences with dream flying.

When you fly in a dream, you have a perfect opportunity to become aware of your dream state if you recognize that you are engaging in an activity that is impossible for you in waking reality. Sometimes you will notice that, while you are flying, your mind seems especially clear and you may be vaguely aware that this is one of your favorite dream activities. If you can push this awareness into the full realization that you are dreaming, you will become lucid and able to consciously direct your flight and other activities in this state.

Sometimes, after having become lucid in a dream, you may choose to fly simply because it's so much fun. In my "Quickstep Becomes Free Skating" dream, I chose to use my lucidity to fly in the context of my favorite activity of ice skating. Some lucid dreamers choose to see if they can visit friends, favorite places, or guides, or just practice their flying technique. Some dreamers report that they learn to improve their flying techniques with each new flying dream.[22] The angle of an outstretched arm or leg or the rate of flapping the arms might be altered to improve the control of flight. I have had dreams in which I am instructed to remember the feeling of twisting my body, using my arms as helicopterlike propellers. The impression is that what I need to recapture in order to fly well is the *feeling* not the specific body movements, which seem to be symbolic. As other lucid dreamers and I have found, the body movements we make to fly seem finally unnecessary once we have confidence that flying is directed by our thoughts and emotions.

Many dream flyers, lucid and prelucid, have practiced their flight to see how high or how far they could fly. Some have experimented with aerobatics as they develop their agility and confidence in flight. Judging from the accounts available to me, flying dreams tend most often to take place in outdoor environments. I have noticed that about half of my flying dreams (lucid or not) occur in a dance studio or an ice-skating rink. I am often practicing controlling my flight so that I can use it in my skating and dance. I may hit my head on the rafters, bump into a wall, or overshoot the ice surface in too long a jump. These experiences are always rather humorous and carry with them the knowledge that I am just a beginner and have much to learn. Over the past seven years of such dreams, I have clearly made progress in controlling and directing my flight, and this has brought with it enormous satisfaction. A number of dreamers have commented that, during a false awakening after a flying dream until they actually awake they are certain that they could fly in waking reality. I have had flying dreams (lucid and nonlucid) in which I was told by dream teachers or guides that I could learn to fly in my skating and dance in day life. I have said things like, "Do you mean that I can really learn to use this ability and actually use gravity for my own artistic purposes in the physical world, the world where I skate with steel blades on real ice?" The answer has always been *yes.* I awake to physical waking reality after such dreams with a sense that I could fly on earth if I could just master the skills and acquire the confidence. Rationally, I know that reports of levitation have never been scientifically verified and that what my dreams portray has never been done before in the three-dimensional world. Yet the dreams impress me so deeply that I will often follow them up by trying to recapture the flying states of mind and trying to fly or levitate in my dance or my skating. It hasn't worked yet, but insofar as the feeling of flying has inspired me to skate or dance better, it has had a welcome influence.

Surely the fact that flying dreams can seem so convincingly real as to encourage sane and rational people to think that flying is in fact possible suggests something of their intensity. Many dream fliers are entirely convinced that they do indeed have the ability to fly, at least in nonphysical dimensions of reality, which they consider every bit as "real" as waking reality.[23]

There are several ways to induce flying dreams either for the sheer pleasure of them or to precipitate lucid dreams. The methods described will require practice and patience, but flying dreams are well worth the effort.

First, you can use dream incubation to request a flying dream. In your incubation discussion, describe how much and why you want to fly in your dreams. Recall and describe past flying or floating dreams and savor their delights. You might choose a location in which or to which you would like to fly. Describe it in your journal. Then formulate an incubation phrase such as, "I want to fly," or "Tonight I fly," or "Tonight I fly to the beach." Hold the phrase vividly in mind as you fall to sleep. Successful incubations for flying are more difficult to achieve than those for problem solving or inspiration. Perhaps this is because, in incubating a dream to solve a problem, you are already quite involved with the issue and your producer is freer to deal with it as he or she likes. Producing a specific dream action such as flying may require far greater conscious control of the dream process.

You can reinforce your dream incubation efforts by focusing upon the desired activity during the day. Tell yourself that tonight you will fly in your dreams. Look at birds, study their flight. Study photographs of birds, draw and paint them. If airplanes fascinate you, focus on their flight during the day.[24] All your day thoughts about flying will increase the likelihood both of your flying in a dream and of your recognizing that you are dreaming while doing so. You may have dreams of flying freely in your own weightless body, or you may dream of flying in planes or floating in water. The sensation to look for is one of weightlessness. Dream friends may guide you in leaping higher or higher, or in floating in the air or water without fear. You may dream of showing others how to leap or fly or float. In demonstrating the art, you may recognize the wonderful, weightless, joyous sensation and realize that you are dreaming. You may also dream of falling. If you do, tell yourself not to be afraid and let yourself fall. Usually you will begin to float or fly and can continue the dream, perhaps becoming lucid in the process.

Exploring the Feeling of Freedom from Your Physical Body.   The Freudian theory[25] that flying dreams represent the dreamer's desire either to recapture childhood pleasures of swinging and rocking or to enjoy sexual pleasure or prowess seemed to fit Joe's dream about his trouble in maintaining an erection, discussed in Chapter 5. Adler's theory that we use flying dreams to express our will to dominate and be superior to others may apply to some flying dreams.[26] Steckel's theory that flying dreams represent death because suspension in air suggests ghosts and angels[27] seems useful when the dream includes images or feelings which connote death to the dreamer. Jung saw flying dreams as a symbolic representation of the dreamer's desire (or actual achievement) of breaking free of restrictions or a problem that he wishes to or has overcome. This interpretation makes sense in many cases where the dreamer's life situation corresponds to it. In such dreams, the flying may be used to escape from pursuers or overcome obstacles in one's path.

In interpreting flying dreams,[28] it is important that you consider the feeling tones of the experience and your associations to it. Traditional psychological theories will help you to understand one level of many flying dreams; however, there may be a whole level of significance to these dreams which traditional approaches miss entirely. It may be that we really are flying, albeit in another dimension of reality and perhaps in another body. Many people throughout history and in the present have claimed to be able to leave their physical bodies in bed while a part of their conscious selves was free to travel to other places. These people further claim that, while their consciousness is away from the physical body, it seems often to be clothed in a lighter, more subtle "second body," which seems ghostlike to witnesses who have reportedly perceived it.

The second body, or double, is a phenomenon which has been studied by scientists since the 1920s. Hector Durville and other French experimenters used chemical screens and other devices to try to detect its presence. Durville used hypnosis both to "project" the double out of the physical body and to sensitize an observer who was to try to see the double. He claimed that the double not only caused physiological changes in the hypnotized subject but could consciously observe and feel and even move objects at a distance.[29] More sophisticated research is being conducted at the Psychical Research Foundation in Durham, North Carolina; the Division of Parapsychology at the University of Virginia; The American Society for Psychical Research in New York; the Stanford Research Institute in Menlo Park, California; and in Russia. Although this research has not yet provided scientific "proof" that the double exists in physically detectable form, it has renewed scientific interest in the phenomenon. It is hoped that, as more sensitive devices to measure minute changes in the physical body and in the environment are developed, some tangible evidence for the existence of the double will be found.

One method of inducing an out-of-the-body experience (OBE) is becoming lucid in the dream state and choosing to fly. Another method involves the theory that flying dreams are metaphoric representations of actual traveling in the second body. Those who have practiced inducing OBEs say that, by becoming conscious while flying in a dream (either in a plane or in the body), one can become aware of the fact that her physical body is in bed and that she is in her second, lighter body.[30] This double is also known as the *astral body*.

One model of OBEs suggests that in some sleep states the intuitive portions of consciousness leave the body while the "physically oriented portions of consciousness" remain in it. This event is apparently not perceivable by present technology such as EEG machines. At first, the absent consciousness is passive. It receives information from the "sources of its being" and from other "nonphysically oriented consciousnesses." Then this "absent consciousness" becomes active and participates in actions which serve as examples to clarify and reinforce concepts perceived in the passive state. Here the personality is rejuvenated. Guides, teachers, angels, or images of the higher self may instruct the absent consciousness. Often when this part of the personality returns to the body, other layers of the self, the body consciousness, and the subconscious interpret the information into dreams that will relate directly to, and in images of, the waking consciousness. It is at this point that the dream producer can translate general teachings into practical advice on a particular matter. This theory also states that the dream translations are not always necessary.[31] The dream formation process is described as symptomatic of an unwillingness to accept the original experiences in their nonphysical form, so the dreamer translates the experiences, which seem too intense or simply unbelievable, into dream imagery which she can more easily relate to.

This theory seems very plausible in light of so many dream accounts that comment: "There was very much more to this dream, but I can't remember what." or "I understood things about myself on a very deep level, but I can't put it into words." or "Some wise people explained things to me which I can't remember exactly, although I *feel* that I remember them in my heart." Perhaps we have difficulty remembering not only things we want to repress but also information we perceive in nonphysically oriented images. Among those who have been conscious of out-of-body experiences, there is the "almost universal belief that [OBEs], particularly when they are on higher planes, bring sharper clarity of mind and more vigor to the physical body."[32] Ernest Hemingway; Carl Jung; the poet Walter de la Mare; St. Ignatius of Loyola; J. H. M. Whiteman, a physicist and mathematician in South Africa; Camille Flammarion, the French astronomer;[33] and literally thousands of others have had conscious awareness of out-of-body experiences.[34]

The original accounts of OBEs and the studies conducted to explore them suggest many exciting possibilities for the out-of-body traveler. Perhaps it really is possible to visit friends while you and they sleep in your bodies. Perhaps it is possible to communicate with people who are dead and exist now in other dimensions of reality. Besides visiting alive and "dead" friends and relatives, what I have enjoyed most about becoming conscious while apparently out of my body has been the incredibly vivid and intense contact I have had with states of consciousness which seem extremely wise and intelligent and which give me much understanding and peace at very basic nonverbal levels of my being. Many lucid dreamers have reported the same attitude toward some of their out-of-body experiences. It may be that what feels like an OBE is instead an altered state of consciousness (perception and expression) that "takes place" within the physical body.

In our Dream Meetings, OBEs have been reported by several members who had never before encountered the idea that such things were possible for common mortals. A few members have reported dreams which, judging from the literature on astral travel and from the dreamer's later experiences, appear to have been precursors to lucid experiences of being out of the physical body.

Virginia had this dream before her first conscious OBE:

I see a little pale white transparent wisp come out of the center of my body. Then a larger one wells up from the perimeters of my body. It is as if I see them out of the corner of my eye. I question what they are. Then I realize the big one's me. I'm not sure of the small. Then it seems as if this lift out of the larger one is repeated over and over so that I can get the hang of it. ("Ghost Practice")

I had a similar experience in a prelucid dream (about which Virginia knew nothing):

I felt myself falling, slipping into my body, then rising out of it again and being filled with love. My friend Henry is present, sometimes watching or helping, or doing this himself and showing me how. I had a very strong feeling of increasing self-knowledge and self-understanding. I stopped. I was out of my body and enjoyed it so much I didn't want to go back into it again. Henry encouraged me to reenter, and at that I fall back into my body through the head. It feels like I'm slipping into an old, familiar, and very comfortable piece of clothing. Then, as I continue the practice of going in and out of my body, I begin to understand it better. I awoke very relaxed and happy in "the understanding of things." ("In and Out, In and Out")

Dreams which seem to portray learning how to get in and out of the body and operating outside of it may represent the dreamer's early encounters with the experience or may be a dream representation of his efforts to become conscious of an experience he has unconsciously and skillfully achieved many times before. The dreams themselves may be normal, prelucid, or lucid. The motifs of such dreams often include flying in an airplane or helicopter, floating in the air or water, rising upward in an elevator, or any number of activities that might simulate the feeling of flying. In some dreams, I seem to practice operating out of my body through learning how to water-ski. Typically, friends who are wiser and stronger and more skilled than I instruct me. In one dream, I failed to get up out of the water because the undercurrents were too strong, and my instructor said it was too late in the day for a good practice session. Had I gone to sleep too fatigued, or was I too close to morning-waking consciousness to maintain my focus in the dream state? In another dream's practice session, the water-ski instructors gave me a shorter cord to hold on to because I seemed to wobble and lose control with the longer one. Was this a dream representation of the silver cord referred to by many people skilled in the art of leaving their bodies? The silver cord has been described as the elasticlike cord which connects the two bodies. Sylvan Muldoon noted that it could stretch infinitely as the second body traveled away from the physical body.[35] Two of the pioneer experimenters with OBEs, Muldoon[36] and Oliver Fox,[37] felt that dream action often parallels the movement of the second body as it leaves or enters the physical body and travels outside it. Each suggested that, by becoming conscious in such dreams, the dreamer would realize he was in his second body.

When you find yourself flying in a dream, or doing something that would give you the sensation of weightlessness, tell yourself that you are dreaming. Some astral travelers describe the double as leaving their physical bodies through the head, some through the center of the body, some through the feet; others describe it as welling up from all parts of the physical body at once. You may dream of trying to squeeze out of a skylight into the great outdoors as a symbolic representation of leaving the body through your head. Dreams of getting stuck half way in or out of a room or box might represent the actual position of your double in relation to your physical body. One way to become conscious during such dreams is to suggest to yourself during the day that, when you meet similar conditions in your dreams, they will trigger in you the realization that you are dreaming. This is a form of dream guidance. Using dream guidance, neither my students nor I have ever had any unpleasant experiences in this apparently out-of-body state. There are a few techniques for inducing OBEs from the waking state, but they may result in rather frightening experiences and seem more complicated than the following OBEs experienced in a lucid dream state.[38]

Sonia had a dream experience which involved a false awakening that may have been precipitated by the appearance of her father in his second body. Though she could not verify that her father had had an OBE the same night (because he had no dream recall that night), she did learn something important from this experience, which had the characteristics of a nonlucid encounter between two astral bodies. Here is her written account:

In waking life, my parents had just visited me and stayed overnight. I experienced a lot of old feelings and tensions having them in my house. I was nervous and could feel old habits and interactions happening again with them. I had a very restless night's sleep on the couch and missed my own bed, in which they were sleeping.

The next day I went to bed quite early, and sometime between 7:00 P.M. and 1:30 A.M. I dreamt:

My father was suddenly standing next to my bed as I was sleeping having the dream. His presence was so real it was startling (when I woke I looked for him to be there). I dreamt he was standing there. He touched my shoulder, saying, "This is your father." Then as I sat up, I could see him, and my mother behind him. They had returned to my house again, and were again going to stay the night. I sort of groaned to myself, because I did not want to leave my nice bed and go sleep in the living room again. My father quickly said there was no problem and that he and my mother would make a place to sleep in the living room and that I did not have to move. They were quite cheerful about it. I saw them making up a place to sleep in the living room. ("Mom and Dad Visit")

I took this dream to mean that my father was "waking me up" to the fact that my parents *are* willing to accept my life and do not want me to feel pushed around by them. They *are* willing to compromise. I think this is in fact the case. I had forgotten this the day before when I was so nervous and acting in old ways. The dream was so startling I was forced to remember the real situation of cooperation. I wonder if we were all out of our bodies by the end of the dream when I saw them in the living room.

I once had the distinct impression that, just after becoming lucid at the end of a dream, I found myself in the body of a good friend! It felt wonderful to experience what I thought was his state of mind, peaceful and very happy in a way that was peculiarly his:

I am aware that John has just returned from an OBE and has invited me into his body to see what it would be like. Inside, I am fascinated to learn that the way he experiences happiness is typical only of his personality. I am glad to see this from the inside. I am also fascinated at the experience of having such big lungs. As I participate in his breathing, I seem to have a sense of what it is like to have his muscular body instead of mine. Very interesting. I then move out of his body and into mine via the top of my head. I am awake and feel that I have been since the moment when I entered John's body. ("Muscles!")

As I lay in my sleeping bag (we were on a camping trip with seven friends) I was dying to awaken John and ask him if he had just reentered his body and had some memory of my "visit." Before I could give in to my impulse, his daughter started to cry out for him. John seemed uncharacteristically irritated at this abrupt awakening. After he had tended to his daughter, I asked him why. He told me he had just returned to his body after an extremely pleasant OBE. I asked him if he had noticed my presence, but he had not. To my knowledge, this is an unusual OBE, and I present it here so that, if you find yourself apparently in someone else's body you will be less likely to panic and more likely to enjoy the experience.

After our first experiences of marveling at the awareness of being outside the body, my students and I choose to experiment with contacting other day-life friends who, themselves, might be in or out of the body. One student, Diana, incubated six dreams asking for a lucid OBE in which she would visit Sue, a friend thirty miles away. Each trial was on a different day over a period of one month. Sue had agreed to the "visits" but on only two occasions did she know what days Diana would try to visit her. On four of the six occasions, Sue had a distinct feeling of Diana's presence at the approximate time that Diana was sleeping after an OBE incubation. Three times Sue was awakened in the middle of the night by what seemed to be Diana's presence. On one of these nights, when she had been expecting Diana's visit, Sue was startled by a purple spiral she saw floating above her bed. She immediately thought it was a representation of Diana. Another time, Sue, who was wide awake and in a conversation, was suddenly vividly aware of Diana's presence. This was during a mid-day sleep period before which Diana had telephoned Sue to tell her she was about to attempt another visit. Curiously, Diana had no recall of any dream activity during two of the nap periods when Sue noticed her presence. Diana became lucid in only one dream about visiting her friend.

Another Dream Meeting member, Eileen, writes:

Some dreams which I have fairly often are of myself floating toward the ceiling in a room. Usually I am teaching other people how to accomplish this themselves.

Most of Eileen's lucid dreams of being out of her body have been pleasant, but one was not. She writes that "the scariest dream I ever had was apparently shared by my husband Jony":

I was out of my body. A man dared me to get farther and farther from it. Finally he took it over. I was in a state of panic when Jony entered into my dream and helped me get back into my body. I woke up and had a feeling of terrible heaviness and evil in the house. ("Taken Over")

This was her commentary on the experience:

Just then Jony woke up and said (without my offering anything) that he'd just had a terrible dream and asked if I were okay. At that moment Kim, my four-year-old daughter, started screaming. I went to her, and she said that something awful was in her room. She said, "A big monster is over my bed." She spent the rest of the night in bed with us. We all felt a very negative influence all night.

Robert Monroe[39] and some others who have had conscious OBEs have recounted similar stories of frightening out-of-body experiences. It may be, as Yram[40] and Fasher[41] suggest, that in the out-of-body dream state the dreamer attracts experiences which correspond to his expectations, fears, and level of psychological development, as well as to his current emotional state. The fact that Eileen had been involved with frightening occult studies around the time this dream transpired might explain why she had such a frightful experience. Perhaps her daughter tuned into the same dream frequency as her parents and thus had a similar experience of fear. One of the few frightening experiences I have had in lucid dreams came at a time when I was quite fearful of what other realms of existence might be like. I had little confidence in my ability to handle the forces of the unconscious. Since I have adopted the belief that I can always awake into day consciousness and that I am capable of dealing with any frightening dream images, I have not had any frightening lucid or prelucid OBE dreams. A confident attitude toward dream experience tends to result in pleasant lucid dreams. One source suggests that, if you find yourself in a dream or OBE, confronted with unfriendly figures or images, you need only say "Go in peace" to be freed of their influence.[42] The idea is not to deal with a negative force on its level, fear. It seems that, if you can overcome fear, unpleasant OBEs as well as normal frightening dreams will lose their fearful quality.

To wind up our discussion of lucid experiences of being out of the body, here is an example of a romantic OBE. A year ago, during a three-week vacation in Switzerland, I missed my fiancé, Steve, very much. On four different nights, I incubated a dream, asking for a lucid OBE in which I would visit Steve in California. I hoped to assuage the longing in my heart and bring him cheer as well. After two of the nights I tried this, I had no dream recall at all. On a third night, Steve came to visit me in a happy dream. On the fourth try, I had what felt like success. I had a prelucid dream in which I was hugging Steve and feeling very happy to see him. I suspected that I might be out of my body, but I did not pursue the thought. Steve told me that he was glad to see me, and we talked about how we had missed each other. I awoke refreshed, as though we had just been together. Steve wrote me that, on that evening at the same time I had been sleeping for two hours in Switzerland, he had a "visitation" from me: "[I was] standing in the kitchen. Then without any precursor, I suddenly felt as if you were really there with me. I talked to you, felt warmed by you, and thanked you for coming." The only time Steve had this experience of my presence was the same night that I felt I had actually succeeded in visiting him. We were both less lonely after this experience.

Now that you have had a glimpse of some experiences which can result from increasing your conscious awareness of dreaming, let's review a list of some of the possible areas of exploration open for the adventurous dreamer. Increased consciousness in the dream state might be used to:

1. turn frightening dream figures into helpful, informative ones.

2. come to a clearer understanding of dream images.

3. consider and solve problems more easily and vividly than in normal dream states.

4. produce dream experiences desired by the dreamer.

5. initiate pleasurable flying dreams.

6. closely examine objects of artistic interest.

7. visit and bring cheer to, or learn from, people in both the physical and the spiritual worlds.

8. explore other dimensions of reality, including the possibilities of out-of-body existence, and experiences of a nonverbal, imageless nature which may be the source of some dreams and even of our being.

As we have seen, you can increase your conscious awareness by using dream incubation and dream guidance. For those who would like to experiment specifically with out-of-body experiences, I have one more suggestion to add. If you choose as your goal in having an OBE not only exploring the experience but also bringing cheer to someone you would like to visit, I think you will find your first experiments less difficult. In our experiments, the use of this suggestion in an incubation request for an out-of-body visit has never been followed by an unpleasant dream. In fact, the nights on which we have used incubation phrases like "I'd like to visit my sister and bring her cheer" have generally been filled with exceptionally pleasant dreams and lucid and prelucid experiences of wonderful and warm visits.

In Startrekking, you increase your conscious awareness of whole realms of your experience which have been largely unknown to you. Startrekking is for those who want to expand their awareness of the multidimensionality of their being and of the different realities in which they have that being. Rainer Maria Rilke has written that:

. . . Only someone who is ready for everything, who excludes nothing, not even the most enigmatical, will live the relation to another as something alive and will himself draw exhaustively from his own existence. For if we think of this existence of the individual as a larger or smaller room, it appears evident that most people learn to know only a corner of their room, a place by the window, a strip of floor on which they walk up and down. Thus they have a certain security. And yet that dangerous insecurity is so much more human which drives the prisoners in Poe's stories to feel out the shapes of their horrible dungeons and not be strangers to the unspeakable terrors of their abode. We, however, are not prisoners. No traps or snares are set about us, and there is nothing which should intimidate or worry us. . . . We have no reason to mistrust our world, for it is not against us. Has its terrors, they are *our* terrors; has its abysses, those abysses belong to us; are dangers at hand, we must try to love them. And if only we arrange our life according to that principle which counsels us that we must always hold to the difficult, then that which now still seems to us the most alien will become what we most trust and find most faithful. How should we be able to forget those ancient myths that are at the beginning of all peoples, the myths about dragons that at the last moment turn into princesses; perhaps all the dragons of our lives are princesses who are only waiting to see us once beautiful and brave. Perhaps everything terrible is in its deepest being something helpless that wants help from us.[43]

11

Network Special Reports

*Exposés and Commentary on Progress
in Meditations, Affirmations,
and Achieving Goals*

You may be involved in various disciplines aimed at furthering the development and growth of your personality. You may practice meditation or prayer, or be in some sort of individual, group, or family therapy. Perhaps you are attending classes and workshops or just reading at home with the aim of broadening your horizons and increasing your understanding of yourself and others. As dream study becomes a natural and regular part of your life, you will find that your dream producer can provide you with invaluable feedback, advice, and inspiration regarding all these disciplines, including your dream study itself.

In our Dream Meetings, we have hit upon a number of ways to use dream incubation to elicit dreams which provide helpful insights regarding our efforts to further our personal growth. We have also used incubation to reanimate our motivation to practice disciplines which we felt important but which we "never got around to."

Our dream producers seem to have access to resources of wisdom and good sense which can help guide us along our journey of self-discovery. Without our ever asking for it, our dreams comment upon our experiences with different self-development techniques, and we have found that specific requests for dream feedback have enhanced this spontaneous function of dreams. In this chapter, we shall look at a few of the ways we in the Dream Meetings have used incubation to obtain these "Special Reports" on our psychological growth "network." This will give you ideas for your own use and will also help you recognize your spontaneous dream feedback reports, which often escape many dreamer's notice.

A housewife in her thirties, Marishka was impatient to get out of school and begin her career because she felt guilty about not contributing money to her household. She had no children and wished to share with her husband the responsibility of earning a living. She had taken odd jobs now and then but felt she should do more, even though she did not want to take a full-time job since this would retard her academic progress considerably. Marishka incubated a dream, asking, "How should I bring a significant amount of money into our good life?" She dreamed:

A lady my age is criticizing a little girl three years old. I can't take it anymore and tell the lady to stop defacing her daughter. I tell her she is being cruel to criticize a little girl who can't be expected to act like a grown-up. I tell her to stop, or I'll pull her eyes out if I have to. She begins to realize what she is doing to the little girl, and I begin to like her. ("Sadistic Lady")

Marishka understood the dream to mean that she had been using her self-appraisal sessions as opportunities for excessive self-criticism. When asked what part of herself or area of her life was three years old, she responded that she had begun her career training in school exactly three years ago. Her dream helped her see that she was heartlessly criticizing her career-self for not earning money after three years when she needed to understand and accept the fact that it would be at least two more years before she would be in a position to earn a good income in her field.

A Dream View of Psychotherapeutic Relationships.

Jim, who was in individual psychotherapy, incubated a dream, asking, "What is the value of my working with this particular analyst?" Jim dreamed of taking a trip into his childhood. There he was to review and understand the dynamics of several of his present-day conflicts which stemmed from attitudes he adopted as a child. In the dream, he saw himself as a child reliving highly charged experiences. Jim realized he would not be able to understand all this at once nor recall it completely for later study. Therefore, in the dream he rented a movie camera to record the sights and sounds so that he could review them later. Upon his return to present time in the dream, Jim went to the camera shop to return the movie camera. He told the saleslady that the camera did not work well and that he was displeased. The saleslady began giving all sorts of excuses for the camera's poor performance. Jim lost his temper. He told her that the camera was a lemon and that he had one at home just like it that worked very well. At the end of the dream, Jim was wondering why he had not used his own camera.

Jim was puzzled by the dream until he was asked by a class interviewer to define and describe a movie camera. As he described its function as observing and capturing a significant moment or feeling, Jim was struck by the realization that he had used the camera to represent his analyst. He came to the "aha!" conclusion that he was depending on the rented services of his analyst to explore and understand his psyche. He felt his dream producer was not only calling his analyst a lemon but was also encouraging Jim to depend more upon his own analytic and observational skills. Jim considered this evaluation during a few more weeks of analysis. He decided to terminate the analysis and explore the possibilities of a program of self-observation and analysis. After a few months of working on his own, Jim felt that he had made the right choice for this period in his life.

Sometimes your spontaneous dreams will give you pointers on specific issues and dreams which were not well understood in a particular analytic session. Once a dream sage told me to go over my dream of August 25th again because my analyst and I had missed its meaning. My dream sage proved to be quite right. I was once in therapy with a kind but not highly skilled therapist. At the time, I was just beginning my journey of self-discovery and did not know how to distinguish a good analyst from a mediocre one, yet I had had my doubts about this analyst's abilities and about his attitudes toward women and psychological explorers under the age of forty. I felt he was not taking me or my desire to know my inner self very seriously. I never told him of my critical thoughts, and unfortunately he never fished for them or encouraged me to share them. My dream producer knew better than I that it is crucial in a good analysis that the analysand inform the therapist of judgmental reactions, as these can so easily allow her to disqualify important insights the therapist may offer. Then again, feelings that the therapist is not very good or appropriate for a given analysand may be quite accurate.

Later, in the following dream, I received interesting feedback on my analysis. My analyst was cast in the role of "The Professor":

I have long been on a journey to confront the Dark Lord. My company and I have rested at many simple shelters, inns, and what is now left of us rests—waits in the house of the Light Lord. I am in my room when I receive the strong premonition that I must take the blue confrontation handbook (like a collection of Edgar Cayce readings) and the Cayce book of Revelations, also bound in blue. With these in hand, I knock on the door of an oldish professor, the only one to accompany me on this next and last part of my journey. I tell him to come with me into the blue room. I know my time has come; I am scared but prepared. I wait for a sign, half expecting a bomb to drop in another part of the house to signal the commencement of battle. As I wait, I look at the Revelations book and wonder how this will help in the battle—not obvious, yet surely vital.

The Professor, meanwhile, has taken off his blue tennis shoes. I say, "Put your shoes back on! He is coming any minute. We will have to be on our toes and move fast." He does so. Just then the Dark Lord knocks at the door downstairs. The Light Lord goes to the door. The Dark Lord asks if I will come with him (be under his power). The Light Lord answers with a long "Noooo." This is the moment I must go to battle with the Dark Lord. ("Dark Lord Battle")

The mere sharing of this dream with my analyst led me to tell him what I thought of his therapeutic style and how I felt that he was just lounging about "barefoot" in the analysis. Discussing honestly my reactions to him allowed for more openness in our work together. My analyst assured me that he was keeping his "action" shoes on and was ready to assist me in my confrontation with my unconscious (Dark Lord). His assurance was not convincing, however, and after a few more sessions I changed analysts. The second analyst helped me to recognize much more of my own power and responsibility in my journey of self-development. He reminded me of what the "Dark Lord Battle" dream had suggested—that vital to my excursions into the unconscious would be my willingness to prepare and arm myself with self-study (represented by the blue Cayce do-it-yourself books), which would reveal to me a great deal of my inner life. The feedback dreams I spontaneously recalled and incubated on my work with this second analyst were very positive.

A few of our Dream Meeting members have had beautiful, positive dream responses to requests for an evaluation of their work in psychotherapy. In these dreams, the motif most often involves the therapist's showing the dreamer a new room, house, country, or vantage point, from the top of a hill, for example. In some dreams, the therapist will guide the dreamer into new levels of feelings and understanding. It is good to judge the meaning of feedback dreams in light of their feeling tones and in light of an honest discussion of them with your therapist. Used in this manner, your spontaneous and incubated Network Special reports will significantly further your therapy goals.

Centers of Psychological Insight or of Psychobabble?   Ever-increasing numbers of people are flocking to major centers of psychological study throughout this country. Such centers as Esalen, the Naropa Institute, the Jung Institutes, the Freudian psychoanalytic institutes, the Edgar Cayce Association for Research and Enlightenment, and countless other organizations attract seekers of wisdom to courses of study aimed at helping the seeker on the journey. A few of my students have received dreams encouraging them to take advantage of such courses, and others have dreamt of arriving at a mecca of some sort (psychological, sport, or religious) only to find that the goods or services for sale there were outdated, rigid, or just didn't fit. One seeker who traveled for two years' study at the mecca of her favorite psychotherapy dreamt:

I arrive at a ski resort and am looking for someone who can give me good advice about which skis are best for me. A salesman shows me his selection. He has only a very small selection, and it is not top quality. It's a bit outdated. The skis are like the old-fashioned rigid ones in wood and steel. I am awfully disappointed. I had not bought skis in the city, thinking the selection at a resort designed especially for skiing would be extensive. I had hoped to buy the really good, flexible fiberglass skis. As I awake, I realize that this dream portrays my true feelings about my experience so far with the institute. The quality of teaching has been very disappointing. I wonder if I should change my plans. ("Ski Resort")

How Am I Doing?   Skiing often comes up in dreams as an image of learning or mastering the challenge of psychological development. Viv had undertaken an independent program of getting to know herself. She had been exploring her life for a few months through extensive journal writing when she recognized that she often found (or put) herself in situations where she felt obliged to do whatever or go wherever her dates wanted. This was because she was afraid that, if she were more honest with her own desires, she would risk offending her date and not see him again. Viv had come to the conclusion that she had been underestimating both herself and her dates and that, if she lost one because he didn't like her honesty, then that would be just as well. On her next date, she let her feelings be known and did not play the role of the sweet, agreeable-no-matter-what young lady. Sure enough, her date was not pleased. Viv had not yet learned to choose and attract men who would like her as she was rather than as she had been accustomed to pretending she was. "But no matter," she thought. "If I want to have a good relationship, I've got to be myself from the first." That night she dreamt:

I am on a snow-covered mountain slope. I am skiing down leisurely yet fast, and doing large carved turns. I really feel the edges catch. I have very good control of my skis and feel good. There are jumping ramps. I take them often and get lots of fresh air. I am surprised at the ease and skill with which I am skiing. ("Skiing Well")

In her commentary, Viv wrote that skiing connoted to her "pleasure, mastery, challenge" and added, "Perhaps this represents the small success I made last night!"

Dream producers will also be responsive to questions about work with dreams. A woman from San Diego, after reading an article inviting her to try incubation and send me the results for an article about the experiment, wrote me this in a letter accompanying her dream accounts:

. . . I incubated a dream, asking, "Should I permit my name to be used in connection with your project?" I normally would not want to. This dream followed: I called someone in the Chancellor's office at the University of California, San Diego. I identified myself. "Oh yes," she said, "I just saw your name in an article I was reading."

On the basis of this dream, please feel free to use my name! . . .

(signed) Dorothy

Psychic Reading. Other dreamers have used incubation to obtain their inner selves' responses to the worth or meaning of their experiences with psychic experiments and psychic readings. These dreams can provide insight into motivations for such explorations which might surprise you. They can offer you guidance in the use of your own psychic skills or those of others. At times, these dreams seem to rate the quality of those from whom you receive "readings." Is it possible for your dream producer to accurately assess another person's performance? Or would such an evaluation be a reflection only of your feelings about the reading? Look at your dreams closely and compare your psychic's reading with your own reading a few months later. Then you will probably find the answer.

Frequently, on the nights following a growth class or therapy session, your dreams will spontaneously offer you important feedback regarding your experience. Keep your eye out for these dreams or make a point of requesting them.

In our Dream Meetings, we have used dream incubation to ask for feedback commentary on a variety of topics. Here is a list of a few more incubation ideas that have given us valuable insights into our network of growth experiences:

Ask for guidance in your prayer, meditations, and affirmations.

Ask for guidance in choosing a method of self-development.

Ask for inspiration in making the best possible use of a given discipline.

Ask for commentary on your progress in losing weight or kicking other habits that work against you.

Ask what is your major block to psychological, artistic, or spiritual growth.

Ask what is your major asset in these areas of personal growth.

Ask for guidance in reinforcing your assets in and overcoming your blocks to self-discovery.

Ask for an exposé of your attitudes (toward a certain problem area) which, if altered, could solve the problem.

Ask for an exposé of old, antiquated attitudes and beliefs which no longer work for but against you. (You may discover many beliefs you were unaware of but which still influence you strongly.)

Ask for birthday dreams or New Year's dreams which will review your past year and inspire you for the next.

Our dream study has underscored the importance of becoming aware of basic assumptions and beliefs about ourselves and our world. As you explore your attitudes toward certain events, people, and experiences, you will discover how these attitudes determine, to a large extent, your perception of and reaction to the world. As you know, many of your dreams deal with attitudes which need to be changed and updated or encouraged and reinforced. Dreams dealing with your efforts at psychological or spiritual growth will be especially rich with insights into rigid unchanging attitudes, which, when changed or made more flexible, will no longer be obstacles in your path but wind in your sails during your lifelong adventure in self-discovery.

PART FOUR

Getting Your Show

On the Road

12

The Producers' Workshop

How to Start a Dream Group
or Put on Your Own Show

In deciding to study your dreams, you are embarking upon a marvelous mystery tour of the deepest recesses of your being. This voyage is, and must be in part, a solitary quest for wisdom. Among all mortals, only you will "be there" to taste and know the actual adventures along the way. And yet sharing what you can of these adventures will help you to understand them better and to recall and experience future episodes more vividly. By forming a dream study group, you can significantly accelerate your learning about dreams. At the same time, you will discover a new level of understanding and acceptance of others, as well as of yourself. In this chapter, you will find guidelines for starting a dream group. You will also find suggestions for dream projects which, added to the other material in this book, will help you evolve a well-rounded approach to the understanding and enjoyment of your dream life. Whether you choose to study your dreams in a group or individually, you will derive important benefits from experimenting with the dream projects and readings described below.

Group Setting and Procedure.   Exploring your dreams with just one other person will be a great boon to your efforts in understanding your dream shows. However, sharing your dreams in a group of four to six dream producers seems to be ideal. Each member of your "producers' workshop" should begin keeping a dream journal (see Part V) and exploring his or her dreams not only in the group but individually, more or less daily. Ideally, the group should meet regularly for two or three hours from one to four times a month. If your meetings are too frequent to fit easily into each member's schedule, they will begin to feel like obligations rather than welcome occasions for sharing dream interests and talents. If your meetings are irregularly scheduled and too infrequent, the members will miss out on the benefits of an exciting and well-paced group momentum. One of the major benefits of shared dream study is the increased motivation it provides each member in making the most of dream explorations. A dream group can be composed of two or more friends, colleagues, family members, church or literary group acquaintances, and the like.

The ambience in the group is of utmost importance. Your group will go well if a nonjudgmental atmosphere of trust and joint adventure is established from the beginning. Each member must respect the others' feelings and rights to privacy at all times. While each member should be willing to share his dreams, sensitive issues may be difficult for some people to talk about at first. In time, as the members learn to know and trust each other better, inhibitions will almost disappear. Be patient; encourage yourself and others to get the most from the group experience by opening up; but remember that pressuring and insisting upon full openness from each member, especially in the first meetings, will be counterproductive. Of course, each dreamer should agree during the first session to keep utterly confidential all the proceedings of the group meetings. This includes not discussing another member's dream or day affairs even with other members of the group unless the dreamer is present.

It is a great privilege to share in another human being's experiences with self-exploration. You will learn much about him, about your own feelings, and about humankind. Cherish and use this privilege wisely and well. Humor is a very natural part of group sharing of dreams. As long as laughter does not take on the quality of ridicule, enjoy it. Humor helps the free flow of associations and makes the whole process of exploring dreams more fun. Often the group's perception of humor in a dream which the dreamer could see only as ugly, embarrassing, or frightening can open the dreamer's eyes and heart to the comical side of his dream show.

Each member should bring his dream journal to the group meetings. A good way to open a group meeting is with a brief discussion about dreams in general and about various members' experiences in reading books or attending classes on dreams. During your first meeting it is a good idea for each member to introduce himself to the group, summarizing his life and dream-life interests and what he hopes to gain from the group meetings.

After the preliminary discussions, each dreamer should have the opportunity to tell a dream story to an attentive audience. The dreamer should have reviewed his dream account before the meeting so that he is able to tell the dream in a flowing and engaging manner. If the dream is told in the present tense and first person, the immediacy of the dream experience will be enhanced for both the producer and the audience. It is best not to interrupt the dreamer in the original telling of the story. Comments like "I had a dream like that in which I. . . ." or "Oh, I have a car (lamp, dog, etc.) just like your dream one!" or "Something like that happened to me once in real life!" are very distracting to the dreamer who is trying to relive the dream feelings. Such comments are also very distracting for the other group members who are trying to "dream along" with the dreamer's narrative. Try to participate actively but silently in the dream saga being recounted.

After the dreamer has finished telling a dream story and telling the group what he has thought and felt about the dream since having it, the dreamer describes any private efforts at interviewing his dream producer through journal work. After this, the dreamer is usually ready to choose another group member as interviewer. The suggestions for conducting a dream interview described in Chapter 3 will lead to very fruitful exchanges, which will teach each class member something new about his own dreams whether he plays the role of producer, interviewer, or audience. At any point during the interview, the producer is free to change interviewers if he wishes.

Either the producer or the interviewer may ask for ideas and feedback from the audience when that would seem helpful. It is better for the audience not to interrupt the interview with uninvited commentary, because this often has the effect of disrupting the train of thought or line of questioning in process during the interview. The interview should be pursued until the dreamer has an "aha!" or esthetic experience of the dream, unless, of course, this does not occur before the dreamer or his interviewer runs out of stamina. You can work on a dream for only so long before your attention begins to drain the life from it rather than animate it. You will learn through experience when it is time to end the interview. In the beginning, understanding and insight come more slowly, but as you gain experience in working with dreams, your interviews will move much more quickly. After the interview, the members might comment on their ideas about and reactions to it. Then allow the producer to relive his dream either silently or by telling it one more time with feeling. After this, move on to the next member who would like to tell a dream. Continue interviewing different dream producers until the group decides to move on to other things or adjourn.

Sometimes group members complain of having so many dreams they would like to discuss that they don't know which one to choose. As a rule of thumb, the best dreams for group work are those with the most highly charged feelings or those which most baffle the dreamer. Dreams which have occurred within three days of the meeting are generally the easiest to work with because the associations to them are still fresh in the dreamer's mind.

In meetings made up of a family group with a mixture of adults and children, it is crucial that the adults not push the children to interpret their dreams. There is nothing worse than to tell your special dream and have a know-it-all adult tell you what you should do with it. As an adult, you must put yourself in the place of the child. As a child, almost everyone around you has more power than you do. Almost everyone can do almost anything better and more easily than you can, but your dreams are your own. They are your own very special productions, which are as intense and exciting as any adult's dreams. You can do what you will with your dreams for only you need know them. If an adult seems to push you into learning from your dreams, so that they then become lessons that teach you to be good, how will you feel? If adults want to encourage a child's interest in dreams, they must never correct or criticize the child for behaviors or thoughts reflected in the dream.

The surest way to help a child enjoy dreams is to show that you are interested in them. Let the child know that you enjoy hearing of night adventures and encourage her to enjoy the pleasant and even scary experiences of dreams. Encourage the young dreamer to confront and understand dream monsters, adding the assurance that in the dream world one cannot be hurt. Tell her to call upon the Bionic Woman, Superman, God, or a favorite guardian angel to help out in threatening dream situations. Children can confront and conquer their frightful dream figures.[1] Expecially after a nightmare, a child may eagerly go back to sleep if she can look forward to calling on her own strength and courage (backed up by a favorite hero or heroine) to claim a victory over intimidating dream figures. However, gentle suggestions that dream enemies are really disguised dream friends who are asking the child to love them result in even more satisfying resolutions to dream fright. The child can experiment and see which approach fits best for a given dream. Adults are wisest to follow the child's lead in discussing dreams. If a young person asks for help in interpreting a dream, offer it; if not, it is probably best to limit your comments to encouraging and congratulatory remarks regarding the dream action itself. Dream guidance gently and amusingly presented will appeal to many youngsters. If a child is not interested in dreams, she should not be pushed into talking about them. Young dreamers need the same respect you would show an adult dreamer. Because dream interviewing involves asking simple questions anyone can answer, it will work as well with young people as with adults.

In discussing dream shows with adults or children, remember that your appearance in their dreams may or may not have very much to do with you. Another dreamer's representation of you may tell you a truth about your relationship with the dreamer, or it may reflect the dreamer's feelings about you. *Or* the dream producer might have used your image in caricature to represent a part of the dreamer which corresponds to one of the dreamer's images of you. If you take other people's dreams too personally, it will be difficult for you to see what their dreams are saying. If you never take them personally, you will probably miss interesting insights into how others see you. Again, experience will be your guide.

Projects to Try Alone and in Group Settings.   There seems to be an endless variety of projects which people studying dreams alone or in groups can undertake. Some of these dream projects are easily adaptable to an individual program of study. Most of them however, will be more interesting when shared with one or more fellow dreamers.

It is very satisfying and sometimes quite revealing to draw, sculpt, or paint your unusual or special dream images. You can also give physical form to your dreams by acting them out. As you play the part of your dream friends or enemies, you can get a very immediate feeling about what part of your personality they represent. Pretend, too, that you are the lions, dogs, shoes, cars, and the like in your dreams. Because every dream image is a part of you and your feelings, you have the ability to be any of your dream images. Invite other dreamers to play supporting dream roles if you like and experiment with creatively altering the action of the dream in your waking reproduction of it. Fritz Perls has described this method of working with dreams in *Gestalt Therapy Verbatim.*[2]

If you enjoy jigsaw puzzles, you might be interested in the following idea. I have discovered that the intense concentration I lavish on a difficult picture puzzle is a kind of meditation where I clear my mind of almost everything but the shape and color of the puzzle pieces and their relationships to one another. When I spent four days working on the puzzle of the Buddha, I dreamt several extraordinarily meaningful dreams about piecing together the Buddha of my psyche. Another time, I chose a puzzle in colors which I had never liked, hoping that, by requiring myself to look very closely at the gradations of these browns and tans in this very difficult puzzle, I might learn to appreciate the colors better. I assumed that a dislike for a color represents a lack of appreciation not only for the color but also for some aspects of life. My dreams picked up on my puzzle work and helped me to enjoy the rusty browns and tans in the dream state. These experiences have added to my appreciation of life's colors. Whether or not there was a more general effect on my personality, I cannot say. Painting, drawing, or sculpting subjects you would like to dream about would have the same effects as "puzzling" if you were to concentrate intensely upon the activity.

Besides sharing incubated dreams on matters of concern to individual dreamers, our groups have experimented with choosing one particular topic which all the members would use as an incubation issue on a given night. For example, one week each dreamer was to incubate a dream on Tuesday night with the question, "What is it like to be dead?" Comparing notes during the next session was very interesting. A more difficult group exercise would be to incubate lucid dreams in which all the members would gather at the usual meeting place for an out-of-body dream meeting. Of course, members participate in group incubations only if they want to.

Dream producers can be very helpful to each other in the waking state. In making and comparing lists enumerating each member's attitudes toward various subjects, we can gain insight about the nature of our expectations and of our self-fulfilling prophecies. In the Dream Meetings, we have made lists of our positive and negative attitudes toward issues of common interest such as male-female sex roles and psychological differences, marriage, children, middle age, old age, death, afterlife, reincarnation, good and bad luck, and so on. Also revealing has been an examination of our conscious attitudes and beliefs regarding our parents, siblings, children, and friends. If you list all the negative and all the positive characteristics of the people who are close to you, and add to this list of your own assets and foibles, you may be very surprised by a comparison of the lists.

Your group may be interested in inviting members' spouses and family to meetings now and then. If everyone invites guests on an appointed guest night, you may find that your family will be more interested in, or (in some cases) less condescending toward your study of dreams.

As you may have noted in Chapter 4, having spouses as regular members of the same dream group can open new and important pathways of communication and shared experience. Frequently, however, husbands are disinclined to study their dreams. They may say, "Dreams are frivolous fantasy that don't mean anything. Why should I study them?" or "I never remember my dreams anyway." or "I have enough problems to contend with in my *real* life with spending time on dreams." In our society, men even more than women have been brought up to believe that only the reality of waking consciousness is valid. Even this reality tends to limit itself to tangible objects, actions, and "practical" ideas, and it often excludes most intuitions and feelings. Men, having for so long been charged with earning money, often have not had as much experience with the feeling side of life as have most women. In order to recall dreams, one requires a moment in which to reflect upon what was going on just before awakening. Most men have strong habits of thinking about what is to be done today the minute they awaken. Women more frequently recall their dreams than most men, in part because they feel less constrained to meet standards of achievement in the first moments of wakefulness.

People who know little about what they feel and what they dream and who devalue dreams as unreal fantasies can hardly be expected to take a sudden interest in dreams at a spouse's or friend's suggestion. If you would like to encourage such a person to study dreams with you, the best way can be through an appeal to his (or in some cases her) intellect. Tell the reluctant spouse why you would like to study dreams together, then challenge him to read a few good books on the subject before making a final decision. After looking into the literature on dreams, few will continue to describe dreams as unreal or meaningless fantasies, and few will be able to resist recalling a dream or two in the same week as reading the book. Then, if his curiosity is sufficiently aroused and if his needs to remain unaware of the feelings living in his dreams are not too great, you will have gained a dream partner.

Finally, your group could throw a dream party to which all guests come in costumes and play the role of one of their favorite dream figures. Impromptu dream skits can be hilarious.

You will no doubt discover many other ideas for dream projects. I would love to hear about these and would welcome letters from those who have experimented with them.

Information from Outside. A dynamic dream group takes advantage of opportunities for research and new input into their fund of knowledge about dreams. One of the major resources available to every group is a study of the literature on dreams. Your libraries will provide information on books and journals which deal with dreams. Begin your reading on various dream theories with an open mind. Rather than deciding to agree or disagree with different ideas on dreams, try first to understand the ideas and then keep them in mind as you explore your own dreams and those of your friends. See if a given idea helps you to understand dreams better. Look for what you can use in a wide variety of dream theories. Read each dream specialist's work carefully before judging it. Try to remember that even the most outlandish conceptions of well-known dream theorists come from long years of sincere study. Though many dream theories are not very plausible by today's standards, almost every decent book on dreams has something special to offer—a new idea, an interesting historical note, or even a whole new way of looking at your dream life that makes its dynamics much clearer. Reading the theorists of opposing schools of psychology, such as the Freudian and Jungian schools, is an enlightening process which will allow you to benefit from the good ideas in each. You may think one school's dream theories for the birds, and it may be. Yet there is always something in each that is worth knowing. Dreamers who are dogmatically opposed to particular dream theories usually have dreams at some point dealing with their (the dreamers') rigidity and closed-mindedness. It is a shame to miss out on helpful insights because of unexamined prejudices.

To get you started in your dream reading, I would suggest Carl W. O'Nell's book *Dreams, Culture, and the Individual.* Also very good are *The New Psychology of Dreaming* by Richard Jones and *Dreams and Nightmares* by J. A. Hadfield. Patricia Garfield's *Creative Dreaming* and Ann Faraday's *The Dream Game* are also highly recommended by almost all the novice students in my classes. Another of my favorite books is Jane Roberts' *The Nature of Personal Reality: A Seth Book.* The chapter and other comments on dreams in this book contain some of the most provocative dream reading I have come across.

Other books I highly recommend are: *Dream Telepathy,* by Montague Ullman, Stanley Krippner, and Alan Vaughan, for an excellent treatment of the history of psychic dreaming and a description of recent laboratory research in dream telepathy; Raymond De Becker's *The Understanding of Dreams and Their Influence on the History of Man;* Harmon Bro's *Edgar Cayce on Dreams;* and R. Woods and Herbert Greenhouse's *The New World of Dreams,* an anthology of articles on a wide variety of dream-related issues. For information on lucid dreaming and out-of-body experiences read Celia Green's books reviewing both topics: *Lucid Dreams* and *Out of the Body Experiences;* Oliver Fox's *Astral Projection;* and Herbert Greenhouse's *The Astral Journey,* a very good analysis and collection of the astral travels of many of the best known of history's astral travelers as well as of contemporary cases of out-of-body experiences.

For an overview of Gestalt dream theory, read Fritz Perls' *Gestalt Therapy Verbatim* and Jack Downing and Robert Marmorstein's *Dreams and Nightmares: a Book of Gestalt Therapy Sessions.* For the Jungian view on dreams read *Dreams,* by C. G. Jung; and for Freud's view read *The Interpretation of Dreams.* Good basic books on the field of psychology in general are *Personality and Personal Growth,* by James Fadiman and Bob Frager; and *Psychology: What's in It for Us?* by Lewis M. Andrews and Marvin Karlins.

For the serious student, I heartily recommend *The Handbook of Dreams* edited by Benjamin B. Wolman (Van Nostrand Reinhold, 1979) and *The Dream in Clinical Practice* edited by Joseph M. Natterson, M.D. (Jason Aronson, 1980). Dick McLeester has written a good sourcebook for readings on dreams called *Welcome to the Magic Theater: A Handbook for Exploring Dreams.*

If each member in your dream group reads even a few of these books, your group experience will be much enriched.

Employing good professionals in the field of dream study to participate in your dream meetings from time to time can also animate and enhance your skills in working with dreams. Professional assistance is, of course, very helpful in individual dream exploration as well.

Beyond this, I would suggest that each group member attend lectures, classes, and workshops on dreams and share his or her experiences with the group. Sustaining a constant flow of fresh ideas into a shared or private program of study will keep you on your toes in this open-ended area of human existence.

A Model Agenda for Your First Dream Meeting. How do you initiate and conduct a dream meeting? Here is an outline of steps you can take to make your dream groups a success.

The Arrangements.

1. Contact interested friends or family members and form a group of from two to fifteen members who will meet at regularly scheduled meetings.

2. Decide who will be the group organizer for the first few months of meetings. The organizer should have a list of the names and telephone numbers of all the members. If a meeting is cancelled at the last minute, the organizer can thus notify the members. A member who is unable to attend a scheduled meeting should notify the organizer.

3. Each member should begin keeping a dream journal, before the first meeting if possible. The journal model presented in Part V is a good form for all members to follow.

4. Decide at whose home you will meet. Fix the time the meeting will promptly begin and end. Two or three hours is long enough in most cases. You may wish to rotate the meeting place from one member's home to another's, but this can be confusing and it is ususally preferable to meet at the same place for several weeks in a row.

5. If each member reads at least the first three chapters of this book, your first meeting will be more unified and will proceed more smoothly.

At the First Meeting.

1. The dreamer who plays host to the group should provide a room which affords the group complete privacy for the duration of the meeting.

2. The host dreamer may decide to provide snacks and drinks (nonalcoholic ones work best if they are consumed before the end of the dream interviewing). If so, the rest of the group can chip in to reimburse the host for all expenses. Some groups prefer pot-luck snacks, and some prefer not to have any refreshments. If refreshments are to be part of the meetings, experimentation is often necessary to determine the best time to serve them so that they will not dissipate the energy generated by the group.

3. The smoking issue can be surprisingly irritating, and it should be settled as soon as possible. The group must decide whether or not smoking is to be permitted and, if so, under what conditions.

4. The group should affirm that the proceedings will remain completely confidential.

5. Even if all the members know each other, it is interesting for each person to introduce his dream self by summarizing his experience and interest in dreams.

6. A brief discussion on what each member hopes to gain from the dream meetings will be useful in organizing future meetings and projects.

7. After the preliminary discussions, the group organizer can initiate the dream telling by asking, "Who would like to tell us a dream?"

8. When the first dreamer has finished telling the dream, he then chooses an interviewer, who follows the instructions on interviewing in Chapter 3.

9. Work with as many dreams as time and interest allow. The organizer can insure a good momentum in suggesting when to move on to the next dream and when to bring the dream telling to a close.

10. This is a good point to suggest readings on dreams. This book has been arranged for group study. Each member should read it through once at the begining of the dream meetings, preferably before the first meeting. Then the group can read one chapter a week and open the meetings with a discussion of the shared reading. When the group studies chapters on specific kinds of incubations, it may choose to focus the week's efforts in incubation and dream telling on those areas or issues. Conducted in this manner, the first cycle of meetings would last for fourteen weeks. Before the first meeting, the members read the whole book. Then each week the dreamers read one of the twelve chapters and the appendix. The discussion of model dream interviews will be quite instructive.

11. In later meetings, the members may want to try some dream projects or invite guest speakers. A good time to discuss plans is in the last ten minutes of the meeting.

12. However you decide to conduct your dream meetings, remember not to make them seem like work. The meetings will be most successful if their tone is one of serious but also humorous adventure.

Studying your dreams with one or more dreamers will allow you to pool talents and exposure to dream insights and thus accelerate the process of learning about the meanings and uses of dreams. But there is another benefit in sharing your dream explorations which could be considered a side effect of group dream study. You will discover that sharing dreams is a wonderful way to get to know a fellow human being. Even people you don't like at the beginning of your dream group will become very dear to you after you have shared in their private dream worlds, which so poignantly portray their deepest and most sincere loves and hates, struggles and victories. As you come to understand each group member's internal struggles and visions, I think you will find yourself loving each one in a very meaningful way. Your appreciation for each dreamer's uniqueness will be enormously heightened as you hear the dream stories which only that dreamer could create. As you all grow and learn to love your negative dream images, you will love yourselves better and thereby will more easily accept the displeasing characteristics you see in others. This side effect of shared dream exploration is priceless.

Whether you share your dreams or not, look to them for understanding and compassion toward yourself and the people you love and don't love. If you learn to understand and make good use of your dreams, you will be rewarded with the most coveted prize of all: happiness in knowing and loving yourself and the world around you.

*You'll Never Remember the Script
if You Don't*

Write It Down!

Fear and Forgetting. Many people have complained to me that they can't remember their dreams or that they remember them only very infrequently. They will go on to tell me how left out they feel. They know they are missing something, but they find it impossible or difficult to grasp their dreams. They ask me to tell them the "tricks" of dream recall.

Almost every time this happens, our discussion reveals that the dream forgetter has never made a concerted effort to recall or record her dreams. She may never have considered dreams important enough to record, perhaps not important enough even to look for and recall. The dream forgetter may think dreams fascinating but may never find the motivation to write down those great productions which now are faded or lost.

The most important remedy for dream forgetting is the actual recording of dreams in a dream journal. The decision to record your dreams is the first step; actually doing it is the second step. If you really want to remember and use your dreams, you will find the time to write them down. When you have found the time to record your dreams, they will usually come.

Later in this chapter, I will describe the method of journal keeping my students and I have found most useful. It will get you started or give you ideas as you develop your own journal style. But now that you've decided to record your dreams, the *sine qua non* of dream study, we have to deal with the major block to good dream recall: fear. The fear of one's own inner life, shown in dreams, may manifest itself in many ways. It may show up as an obvious fear in waking or dream consciousness, or it may appear to an observer as simply a lack of interest in dreams.

Ed, a member of one of the Dream Meetings, really wanted to remember and work with his dreams. He kept a journal, came to the meetings, and tried all the tricks we knew. In six weeks he remembered only two dreams. One was just a fragment: He dreamed that he was at a soul food restaurant. His friends were encouraging him to try what they said was a great sauce that really made the flavor of the food come alive. They kept offering it. He kept refusing. He was afraid the sauce was LSD. He was afraid it was dangerous, but he didn't want to admit his suspicions to his friends.

Ed told us that the restaurant scene was like the dream meeting. We were all encouraging him to bring the productions from his soul to life by remembering his dreams. He had not realized how afraid he was that his dreams might "blow his mind." He was afraid to find out what his soul tasted like.

Some people who don't recall their dreams very often are glad they don't. They say that most of the dreams they do remember scare them to death or are, at the least, very unpleasant. Unfortunately, the expectation of unpleasant dreams can act as a self-fulfilling prophecy. Telling these people that, if they would remember more of their dreams, they would find many to be pleasurable and pleasant is not too effective. Instead, I suggest that they write down every nightmare. They will thereby be greatly relieved of the hangover feeling left by a bad dream even if they don't care to interpret it. I found this out for myself ten years ago.

At that time, I was living alone in Paris for a year as a student. I had just gone through two broken engagements to the same handsome Dane. I had fallen in love not only with him but also with his family and his country. Both times he had suddenly changed his mind. I had not yet met any close friends in Paris. I was broken-hearted and very lonely. For an entire month, every night brought nothing but nightmares of my own death and torture. I awoke in great fear and went to bed dreading the night to come. Finally, I bought a book on dreams and began to record my horrible dramas. Immediately after I wrote out the nightmare, the terrible feelings of fear subsided. Though I had no idea what the dreams meant, this much was a welcome development! In written form, I saw the dreams as interesting and puzzling. Before I recorded the dramas, they frightened me so much that all I cared about was forgetting them. About a week later, the obvious struck me. I was suffering from a good, old-fashioned death wish. My existential philosophy of the world was becoming nihilistic and was not very satisfying. It certainly didn't help me cope with the pain of a broken heart and loneliness. I saw no purpose in suffering, and the dreams made me admit that a good part of me wanted to die and escape. Once I admitted my wish to die, I remembered how much I loved living. I decided to give up my victim role and get out and enjoy life in Paris. My dreams had made me take a good look at my life, and they moved me to change it. Their mission accomplished, the nightmares disappeared. My study of dreams had begun.

What about those who record dreams only very rarely because "it's such a bother" and because "dreams aren't that important"? "Besides," they may say, "it's more important to pay attention to real life than to spend so much time on dreams." Some therapists, psychologists, and psychiatrists feel this way. They say there is enough going on in the conscious mind and our daily behavior to tell us what we need to know about ourselves and our patients. What they don't appreciate is how dreams can speed up and enrich the whole process of self-discovery and growth.

To remember our dreams is natural. Not to remember at least one dream every day or two can be a symptom of purposeful forgetting.[1] Our culture has conditioned some of us to forget our dream life, labeling it irrational and meaningless. With a bit of research, we can inform ourselves of the inaccuracy of that belief. With a few tips and a little practice, we can change this belief and the habit of forgetting that results from it.

We can discover what it is that we are trying to avoid by forgetting our dreams through exploratory discussions with ourselves and others. Nicholas, a Santa Barbara psychiatrist, found a clue to his forgetting and resistance to recording his dreams in the following dreams show:

I'm with Dirk. We're at the second large part of a big show which takes on a psychedelic air of incredible quality. There unfolds before me a rapid transformation of a somewhat bent woman amid vapors, echoes, voices, and lights into a virgin. She becomes several beautiful Michelangelo sculptures, then the Pieta; *then she is erect before me, a virgin statue in marble. I am in awe of the great beauty of this work of art. Now I move to another scene, where I keep repeating, "Jesus is God," at first with solemnity, then with doubt, then in laughter. It's as if I'm stoned. I ask Dirk if he put any drug (LSD) in something I ate. He assures me he hasn't. We are leaving the show building, in front of which is a black couple. The woman wants me to play the part of a doctor. She asks me to put an intake note on 100 patients' charts in the building because they are using the patients in an art show. I tell her I am in fact an M.D. and would be liable for their care. So I can't do that. She says, "Oh, then you each have to pay 20¢ for the show." I laugh but pay with a $1 bill since I don't have exact change. I play with them and teasingly say, "This is the same as someone stopping you on the road, holding a gun to your head and saying 'pay up'." They laugh and want to return the money, but I insist they keep it. ("Intake Notes")*

Nicholas was enchanted by the beauty of this dream. When asked what the dream made him think of, he said:

Well, the second part of a big show . . . I think of a conversation I had yesterday with a colleague who was telling me how Jung said that the second half of life is a time of turning inward to spiritual and higher values and creativity. In the first half of life, one is occupied with learning the tools of culture, profession, and having a family. I'm in my second half of life now, and in the dream I must be at that show. In fact, now that I think of it, the first half of the show was more real and concrete in comparison to the second half.

Asked who Dirk is, he replied that Dirk was a fellow doctor, a good friend who was very wise in a basic, natural way. The psychedelic transformation of the woman was a textbook example of an anima image, the ideal of feminine beauty and values which Nicholas thought of as intuition, creativity, and harmony of emotions. These were all aspects of himself which Nicholas hoped to develop in his second half of life. In the dream, he had an experience of great appreciation of and oneness with this woman. He felt deep admiration for Michelangelo's ability to create such beauty and said, "Michelangelo must represent my creative self or my ability to create such beauty in my life."

"What about the 'Jesus is God' part?" I asked. "I'd say it reflects my religious history: of faith, then doubt, then less somber, more joyous experimentation with religion." Nicholas repeated the phrase as he remembered doing it in the dream. I commented that he seemed to accentuate the word *Jesus*. Nicholas said, "Yes, it almost sounds as if I could be meaning *Jesus* is God, not *I*." Dirk, a friendly, trustworthy ally, told Nicholas that he did not drug his food, thus reassuring him that he was having these ultravivid and pleasurable perceptions on his own and that they were real.

Asked to elaborate on the black couple outside, Nicholas seemed to think that the woman was like a bright, high-powered, very competent, black woman psychiatrist he had read of the day before. She was the more assertive, outgoing one of the couple. The black man was kind, gentle, and intelligent. This couple's relationship paralleled Nicholas' with his girlfriend. Asked why he might cast the couple as black, Nicholas said, "That would signify the part of me and of my lady that is better connected to the earth, more natural and easygoing."

"What are intake notes?" I asked. Nicholas replied, "They are notes the doctor takes to formalize a patient's entry into therapy or the hospital. They force you to organize your thoughts about the patient, but they are a pain in the neck to write." (It happened that Nicholas' girlfriend had been encouraging him to record his dreams, which he resisted doing because there were so many, it was a bother, etc.) The black woman wanted to use these patients in an art show, in other words, display their beauty and interest. The black woman reminded Nicholas of his girlfriend.

Perhaps the black woman was saying, "Organize your thoughts on your 100 [many] dreams, give them form, write them down!" But Nicholas refused for fear of being vulnerable to lawsuits:

I'd have to take responsibility for the patients if I wrote the intake notes. Hmm. Patients are disturbed, my dreams are disturbing, but both have beauty. I am reluctant to take responsibility for them, in part because, as an M.D., a psychiatrist, I feel vulnerable to attack on my self-esteem and status. If dreams are so important and if I have been neglecting to explore that area of experience, my competence might be attacked, as in a lawsuit. Anyway, since I won't "play" (I take being an M.D. seriously), I'm charged 20¢. Now what about that!

"What can you buy with 20¢?" I asked. "A newspaper," answered Nicholas, who is addicted to reading the paper daily, the *whole* paper. In fact, he said that was something he felt driven to do in an effort to learn and know as much as he could. He felt he must read everything relating to his many interests, that he must become wise. To this end, he subscribed to many journals and magazines. He saved them for years, feeling he must one day read them all. Instead, of course, the reading material piled up everywhere into insurmountable piles. So instead of tackling that mass, he kept reading the newspapers and watching news programs. These strivings for omniscience dampened enjoyment of play and spontaneity because there was always so much work to be done, so much to learn.

Nicholas' self-image as the wise M.D. exacted its price. The cost was 20¢, or a personal sense of having to learn more than would ever be possible. Then, in the dream, Nicholas played with the couple and teased them about holding a dramatic gun at his head. To this, they responded by trying to return his spectator's fee, but he refused to accept the money, preferring to stay in the role of a "real M.D." He was thus (in the logic of the dream) a spectator.

Nicholas summed it up this way:

Insisting on my M.D. title, I refuse to play, to be in this great show of my life. Therefore, I am charged to be a spectator. However, when lighter and less serious, I can enter as a participant. My self-image as an M.D. is getting in the way of my being part of the show and of recognizing some of the actors of parts of my self who play in my life. This also points out some of the reasons for my resistance to my girlfriend's suggestion that I record and study my dreams.

We can all learn to be part of the show. Learning to remember our dreams is an important first step.

The Strategy of Improving Your Dream Recall.   Once you have resolved to explore your dreams, to keep a dream journal and to examine your motivations for forgetting dreams, you will find some or all of the following suggestions very useful in increasing the number, detail, and intensity of the dreams you remember.

1. *Be sure to have paper and pen by your bed at night BEFORE you go to sleep.* This is very important. It acts as a definite suggestion that you will recall a dream in the morning. If you awaken from a dream and have to get out of bed to find the paper, you may not bother. If you do get up, the dream may have vanished by the time you find the pen.

2. *Go to bed with a clear head.* Extreme fatigue, drug or alcohol intoxication, and certain medicinal drugs such as sleeping pills tend to leave you with their characteristic hangovers but few dream memories.[2] If you feel that you need Valium or sleeping pills to get to sleep, consider breaking that habit. You will probably find that, as you become more and more interested in what happens in your sleep, you will no longer need the pills.

3. *Learn the habit of thinking backward when you first awaken.* The moment you are awake, keep your eyes closed, lie still, and start thinking, "What was happening a moment ago? What was I feeling and doing?" Don't insist on instant recall of a full dream. *Feel* your way backward. Relax. Take a minute. A feeling or a fragment of a dream may come to you. Follow it. See where it takes you. Soon you will remember dream scenes. Sometimes the last scene will come to you first, and the first scene last; recall of dream scenes in reverse order is very common. Instead of dreams, you may awaken with a poem or a song in your mind. Enjoy it and record it.

4. *Allow yourself peaceful time upon awakening to recall and record dreams.* Dreams can be fragile. One concrete thought about what you are going to do today can demolish a dream memory. So can the startling sound of an alarm clock or the chatter of an alarm radio. When the alarm goes off, use it as a signal to remind yourself not to wake up but to remember your dreams. Better yet, suggest to yourself that you will awaken five or ten minutes before the alarm goes off. With a little practice, this will allow you to awaken gently, usually having just finished a dream. A natural awakening, without alarms, will avoid both the interruption of a dream in process and the addition of images formed in response to the alarm.

5. *Watch out for the treacherous fragment trap!* Like everyone else, you will probably awaken some mornings with the memory of only one part of a dream. You may say to yourself, "This is only a fragment, not enough to do anything with," or "Why bother to record it?" *Beware!* You are about to fall into the fragment trap. In a second, the "fragment" will be gone. Just after you awaken from a dream is the worst time to make any judgements about it. What you disparagingly call "just a fragment" might lead you to recall an entire dream or perhaps several dreams. The "fragment" may in fact appear to be an entire dream itself, as many dreamers have discovered upon reviewing the journal entry later in the day. The fragment may remain a brief segment of a largely forgotten dream. Sometimes fragments will provide the missing link to other dreams that puzzle you. Ed's soul food dream "fragment" served the important purpose of opening his eyes to unrecognized attitudes he held toward dreams.

6. *Record your dreams as soon as possible after you wake up.* The memory of most dreams will start to fade as soon as the dream ends. This is not a tragedy, as you have at least four of five dreams on a typical night, the last one being the longest.[3] If you retain a good memory of only the last dream of each night, you will have plenty of dreams to keep you busy. Some sources consider the last dream, which will usually last from thirty to sixty minutes, the most important dream of the night.[4] Waiting to record your dreams until the evening or even until after breakfast will result in various degrees of loss of detail and vividness. One dream a day is good enough. But three dreams a day might be better. Often dreams of the same night will treat the same issue from different angles. One dream will help in the interpretation of another.

Almost all your dreams are useful. However, laboratory tests have shown that, even when you remember the dreams that you had earlier in the night, by morning your recall of them will be far less detailed and vivid than it would have been if you had awakened right afterward.[5] Just imagine being fully conscious and watching four of five dream movies over eight hours. How well would you be able to recall each one? If you would like to capture the full impact of your earlier dreams, the surest way is to awaken after each one and record it immediately.

Optional Dream Recall Strategies.

7. *Teach yourself to awaken after each dream.* By monitoring brainwaves on an EEG machine in sleep laboratories, researchers have found that most dreams occur during the period called REM sleep,[6] which is distinguished by rapid eye movements (REMs), increased physiological activity, and characteristic brainwave patterns. If you were to sleep in a dream laboratory, scientists using an EEG machine could awaken you after each REM period and ask you to report your dream. Using this method, you would probably be able to recall four to five dreams each night you slept in the dream lab. There is however an easier way to achieve almost total dream recall. By simply giving yourself the suggestion for several nights before sleep, you can learn to awaken after each dream. Set your internal alarm. You will be rewarded with richer experiences of many more dreams. This practice is not as fatiguing as you might think. If you leave yourself an extra half hour or so to sleep, you will awaken perhaps even more refreshed than if you had slept straight through the night.

8. *Sleep for shorter periods, two or three times a day.* I have found that changing my sleep habits so that I sleep about five hours at night and one or two during the day has had wonderful effects on both my dream life and my waking life. I feel much more alert when I awaken from these sleep periods and less fatigued when I enter them than when I sleep all in one stretch. I need one to two hours less sleep per twenty-four hours than I normally require. Dreams are easier to recall and more vivid. I feel that wonderful refreshment of sleep twice a day. My energy levels are unmistakably higher.

9. *Read about and study intensely any subject, especially dreams.* You will recall more dreams when you are in the process of studying a subject that excites you. This will be true especially when you read and talk about and attend lectures on dreams. When your waking mind is alert and active, dream recall increases. The more you occupy your mind with thoughts of dreams, the greater the access you will have to them.

If you follow the above strategies, welcome your dreams, and record them, you will soon have plenty of dreams to explore.[7] However, the dreams you do not remember are not wasted. An unrecalled dream must surely affect us as does any event. The dream is already a reaction to and translation of a more basic deeper experience. That original experience touches us at very deep levels, of which we usually are not conscious. As you become more aware of your various sleep states, you will understand why I fell so sure of this even though no brainwave machine exists that could prove it. Some rather common experiences do, however, suggest that forgotten dreams have their effect. For example, we can imagine that the mood we wake up in is a result of our sleep and forgotten dream experiences when it differs markedly from how we felt when we went to sleep. You may have noticed that, when you sleep on a problem, the next morning it may be solved. You may not remember a dream but suddenly have an idea or insight that unravels the issue. Ballet masters, when teaching a difficult sequence of steps, know better than to push too hard. They work on it for awhile in class and then tell the dancers to go home and sleep on it. Some unrecalled dreams will leave you with distinct impressions that can be very valuable.

For example, in April of my junior year of college, an unrecalled dream changed my life. In high school, I had decided that my college major would be international affairs. I was about to finish my junior year in an excellent undergraduate international affairs department. I had worked hard to be there and was very glad to be in the school. Or was I? Actually, I seemed to have lost the zest I used to feel for economics and politics. I felt that I was misusing my liberal arts education by filling my head with information, data, and concepts of international law. I found myself wanting to read all about philosophy, psychology, and religion. But that seemed frivolous when I had so much "serious" reading to do. Still, I couldn't forget that the theoretical ideal of a liberal arts education is that it should provide for learning new ways of perceiving the world, for the expansion and broadening of understanding. I was already specializing my interests, training for a good graduate school, aiming for a good job. I did what philosophical reading I could on the side, and I continued along my chosen path.

I was not planning to do much else about this state of affairs when I had a dream—a dream which I couldn't remember. It left me only with the impression that "today" I had to do something about it. The school was just not the place for me. My interests had changed from international to internal affairs. I had the feeling that I should get up (it was about 9 A.M.) and go to the student center "just to see who is there." This was very strange, as I had been to the student center only twice before and did not particularly enjoy its atmosphere. But I knew I should go there that morning. When I arrived, whom did I see but Dr. Eisenberg, who taught in the Religion Department and whom I had met just one week before. I said, "Hi, what are you doing here?" He replied by asking, "What are *you* doing here?" "Oh, thinking of changing departments to religion," I said. He actually seemed to think this was not an impossible move to make, even at such a late date. He told me whom I should see about it. That was just the encouragement I needed to make the change.

Three days later, I was in the Religion Department studying different ways of understanding the world, really educating myself instead of training myself for a job.

I was as surprised as Dr. Eisenberg when I heard myself saying that I was seriously considering changing departments. The experience of a dream that I couldn't even remember must have prompted me to take courage and make a big change that would dramatically alter my choice of careers.

How to Record Your Dreams and Other Important Events. The method I use to record my dreams has evolved through ten years of recording my own dreams and of teaching others how to record theirs. I hope you will give it a try; later, you may want to adapt it as you develop your own style.

If at first glance this journal format looks too complicated, remember that it is presented in its ideal form. On days when you don't want to spend much time, a mini-entry will do. But keep in mind that a clear and complete journal will afford you the maximum opportunity to reexamine your sleep experiences and learn from them. As you become more skilled in understanding your dreams, a review of past dreams will take you on a voyage full of discoveries. Sometimes you will discover that, one month or a few years after a puzzling dream, rereading it will trigger sudden understanding that may be very relevant to your present life.

This happened to me a few months ago. One day after a week of reviewing the last four years of my dream journal, I was sitting on the couch thinking of nothing in particular. I was abruptly struck by the meaning of a dream I read the other day which I had dreamt in 1973:

I had forgotten my beautiful diamond watch at the ice-skating rink. I was getting out of the car when I realized that I was wearing a very plain, though functional, man's watch. I was very upset and afraid that the watch would be stolen by the time I could return to retrieve it. ("My man's watch")

Now, sitting before the fireplace in the living room, I realized the dream was a warning that I was losing *precious* time not ice-skating! I had spent most of my precollege days in training for skating competitions. When I started college in 1968, I gave up skating, telling myself I couldn't both skate and study well. By the time I was twenty, I began to tell myself I was too old to be a skater. Four years after that, my dreams were still taunting me. I had left my most precious times at the ice rink while I drove myself to become a conventional psychologist. The watch I wore in the dream was just like the one worn by a very conventional psychologist I knew at the time. The way he used the time in his life was admirable but seemed too work-oriented. I had been trying to ignore my first love, my creative, artistic needs, so that they would not distract me or tempt me away from my studies. It took yet another month, but my dreams finally got it through my thick head that just a few days of skating a week would go a long way and wouldn't tempt me into being a mindless "jock." I started skating again, to the enormous enjoyment of my creative self. If I had had the habit then of reviewing my dreams monthly, I would not have taken so long to get the message.

If you have to plow through a haphazard collection of scribbled dreams, you will be much less likely to review them. Especially in the beginning, it is by reexamining your dreams over and over that you will learn your own dream language. Here is my favorite dream journal formula:

Materials.

Two fine-point pens.

Loose-leaf 8½″ × 11″ notebook paper with reinforced holes.

A 15″ clipboard. You may use the night table or the floor or the bed to write your dreams on. The clipboard will firmly support the paper wherever you do it. The extra length will support your hand as you write to the bottom of the page.

A tiny lamp or a battery-lighted pen (optional).

Some people feel that recording their dreams on a tape recorder is preferable to journal recording, because it takes less effort and does not require as much concentration as writing. A recorder does make a detailed, more flowing description possible, and you might like to experiment with this method. The reasons I prefer a written journal are: (1) I find it easier to write than to talk clearly in the middle of the night. (2) The benefits of actually *seeing* my dream description before me, with all the revealing puns, would be diminished on tape. (3) Reviewing a taped journal is difficult, and transcriptions can be tedious.

Looking at a page from Maria's dream journal will give a concrete example of how students in our Dream Meetings record their dreams. Then we will proceed step by step to explore the ways you can use this format.

May 3/77
Sat.

Day Notes. Today was a productive day. Slept til 12:00, did six loads of laundry, tons of ironing, shopping, became a natural blonde again, made a fabulous meat loaf, and went to see *Godfather II* with Jim. I feel productive, exhausted, and relaxed.

ID *Incubation Discussion.* I'd like to gain some insight into my relationship with Tom. I feel as if I'm really getting tired of it but at the same time am somewhat lonely for him sometimes. I enjoy him. But will it develop into the kind of relationship I'm looking for? I really want to find a man I could share a home and children with. What place does Tom have in my life?

★ What place does Tom have in my life?

\# *MAPLE TREE BLAHS*

Tom is sitting under a rather blah maple tree with yellowing leaves— almost like the fall but not rich or warm like the fall. I go up to him and bring a picnic basket. I think it is full of cheese and French bread, fruit, and goodies like that. I open up the checked cloth and find peanut butter and jelly with coke and chips. It's all wrapped in McDonald's hamburger paper. We have a good time, make love, and eat all the junk food. Yet I feel a little disappointed about the whole thing. End.

Commentary. What a trip! I really just kind of see Tom because of the sex. He isn't really the kind of man I want. I felt surprised when I opened the picnic basket—like expecting steak and getting hamburger. Analogy enough, I think I've run my course with Tom.

Dream Journal, Step by Step. This example from Maria's dream journal is brief, informative, and easy to read. The paragraph headings and the margin symbols make clear what was on her mind that Saturday and that she incubated a dream that night. It is easy to see where the dream ends and where her commentary about the dream begins. You can set up a journal like this by following the instructions below.

Day Notes. Before going to sleep, record here what the day was like for you. Make this as short or as extensive as you like. Maria's entry was brief but to the point. The main purpose is to summarize your day's thoughts, feelings, and actions. This will help you to review your day and to orient you to the journal process. Be sure not to list only what you did during the day; write at least one line on what you *felt* and *thought* during the day. These notes often provide the key to the meaning of the dreams that follow. They are especially helpful when you try to interpret a dream more than two days after you produced it. In the left margin, place a bracket around these paragraphs.

Incubation Discussion (optional). If this is a night you decide to incubate a dream on a particular problem or question, this is where you discuss the issue with yourself before going to sleep. For example, Maria discussed her feelings about Tom. Examine and stir up your thoughts and feelings on the matter you want your dreams to help you with. Write ID in the margin to the left of and on the same line as the paragraph heading.

Incubation Phrase (optional). If this is an incubation night, write here a one-line question or request that expresses your clearest desire to understand the dynamics of your predicament. Maria's incubation phrase was, "What place does Tom have in my life?" Write your phrase before going to sleep. Draw a large star (★) in the left margin on this important line for later reference.

Title of Dream. Leave this line blank until the morning. Then after recording your dream below, write in big letters a three- to five-word title that highlights the dream plot. Maria chose as her dream title, "Maple Tree Blah's." Dream titles are good reference aids as you work with your dreams and review them. Sometimes the title you create for a dream will give you a clue to its meaning.

Dream Entry. Record here as much of the dream as you can. Be as accurate as possible. Describe the feelings you experience during the dream and upon awakening. Record also any impressions, feelings, fantasies, or songs that fill your mind and heart upon awakening. These can be interpreted like dreams and can sometimes tell the tale. Be sure to write down any specific quotes, songs, or poems immediately. Describe and sketch any unusual dream images first. Specific words seem the most difficult elements of a dream to recall. If you record them right away, before the rest of the dream, you will have the best chance of capturing them. Watch out for the notorious dream traps! There is the one that lurks in the middle-of-the-night awakenings: "I'll just repeat this dream to myself to make sure I don't forget it. Then I'll write it down in the morning." You may lose out on a lot of very meaningful dreams this way. Remember that the worst time to judge a dream is just after you awaken from it. This is the time to record not to judge. This trap is sometimes set by your own desires to avoid certain dreams. Sometimes you may even catch yourself in that state between sleeping and waking, deciding to forget the dream you just had. Then, of course, there's the very popular treacherous-fragment trap discussed earlier. It lurks in the mind of the most experienced dream recorders, ever threatening to swallow up some of the most interesting productions.

In most dream dramas, you will be using images that act very much like their daily counterparts. This is the case in Nina's dream with the image of the bon voyage party and in Nicholas' dream with the image of the black couple who ask for intake notes. However, many images do not follow the usual laws of three-dimensional reality. Normal cause-and-effect and logical sequence don't apply. For example, Nicholas' image of the crippled old woman transforming into beautiful Michelangelo-like sculptures indicated that the reality assumptions of day life are not of this sort of dream experience. As you record your dreams, or better yet as you dream your dreams, take a close look at transforming images. These will remind you that you are operating in a different kind of reality, with laws of its own. In dreams, logic and meaning follow laws of association; as feelings change, images often change. Time and space as we know them don't apply.

Learn to appreciate and enjoy the freedom your dreams offer you. You are free to act and perceive in a reality not limited by gravity, cause-and-effect, or time and space. Try to capture this freedom of expression in your screenplay. Try not to force your dream descriptions to conform to the restrictions of waking reality any more than is necessary. As much as you can, write in the style of the dream. Note when you are aware that you are dreaming or are aware of two dream scenes occurring simultaneously. Note also times when you notice nondreamlike events taking place in your sleep, such as seeming to be floating above your body or feeling or seeing light of unusual brilliance.

Use the margin beside the dream entry to write in flash associations to dream images or actions. You may also find it useful to sketch likenesses of unusual dream images here. Place the symbol for number (#) in the margin to the left of the first line of each dream entry to clearly mark the beginning of the dream.

Commentary. Record here your dream interview and any other associations you have to the dream. Add dream-associated events from yesterday as you think of them.

Because you will be writing each dream entry on a separate page, you can always modify and add to your commentaries as new ideas and associations come to you in later dream reviews. This is also a good place to describe visual, auditory, or feeling experiences you might have in the drowsy, hypnogogic state just before sleep.

This is the basic model for the dream journal most of the dreamers mentioned in this book have used. Some days you will be able to work with your dreams in such detail; some days you will find it difficult enough just to record one dream. If you "work" too hard on your journal, you will lose the excitement of your dreams. If you do too little with them, you will miss their meaning. Aim for a balance that satisfies you.

Dream Glossary. Some dreamers find it helpful to build a glossary of images that recur in more than one dream. These can teach you a good deal about your own symbol system if you study them. Remember that the significance of some images will change as your associations to them change, and some dream elements will show interesting and revealing evolutions through several or even many dreams. Your glossary is not exactly a dictionary of your symbols. It can be more of a thesaurus, an aid to associations and to the examination of perplexing, recurring dream elements.

Reviews. If you carefully file your dreams in yearly notebooks, you will have easy access to one of your most valuable natural resources. Monthly and yearly reviews of your dreams will provide you with surprising insights. If you have kept revealing day notes, even inscrutable dreams many years old can be interpreted and related to your life in light of new skills and insights you gained subsequently.

As you review your journal, you will notice recurring themes that can be seen to develop in both your day and your dream notes. Write a dated review of the last month's or last year's dreams. Describe the themes that recur in your day notes and in your dreams. Describe also the different ways you have responded in dreams and in day life to situations of fear, intimidation, aggression, kindness, attack, exploration of the unknown, and so on. In the period under review, how often did you play the role of the victim, the heavy, the resister, the passenger, the driver, the helper, the asserter, or the initiator? Look at your dreams first, then at your life, to see when you play these and other roles.

In our Dream Meetings, each student is encouraged to rewrite or retype and review an entire eight weeks of dreams. After completing their reviews, the students almost always notice a new level of experiencing their lives. They see their dreams and their lives more clearly. Several students, recognizing how frequent were their complaints about their daily lives and how often they played victim roles in both their days and their dreams, decided to do something about it. One dreamer said, "I got so sick of rewriting my day notes! The same old gripes day after day. What a drag! I hadn't realized how often my thoughts travel in negative circles. I'm going to have to do something about this." And she did. She quit the job she hated and started her own business. She lost the twenty pounds that she despised. Telling her old friends that she wasn't going to sit around talking about "problems" anymore, she found new, more positive friends. This dream producer apparently had decided to become the creator instead of the victim of her life. Her dream journal review had triggered this change.

Dream reviews are exciting events in which even the dreams you previously thought trivial and boring spring to life and show themselves to be part of a fascinating, ever-chaning, never-complete life mosaic. A few of the writer-producers in our Dream Meetings make yearly journal reviews about a week before their birthdays. Then, on the birthday itself, they ask their dreams for a review of the past year and a preview of the one to come.

The following pages from the dream journal of a psychiatrist named Ginger summarize the principles we've been discussing.

July 10/75
Sat.

Day Notes. Carole, my sister, came to town today. I'm a little hurt that she won't have time to visit till tomorrow, since I see her perhaps a total of about five days a year. I miss her and wish we lived closer to each other. Spent most of the day reading. Had a great time Greek dancing with Victor tonight. A pretty good day, but I am disappointed at the lack of birthday dreams.

ID *Incubation Discussion.* My birthday was on the seventh. For three nights I have been trying unsuccessfully to elicit a birthday dream that would give me a preview of the next year of my life. Actually, I've been asking for advice and counsel so that I can make the best of it. I feel that in this past year I've not accomplished much in the way of professional or personal goals. I want to get moving again in my twenty-ninth year. Whereas my past birthday dreams have clearly centered around motifs of future goals and challenges, my recent incubations have not resulted in any dreams of this sort. Further, the dreams I have recalled lately have neither the vividness nor the impact I have come to expect from birthday dreams.

Since incubation is usually very easy for me, I guess I must be blocking that level of dreaming or at least the recall of it. I must be resisting, but I don't know why or how to stop it. What don't I want to see or accept about what is likely to come up for me next year? Maybe I should just ask why I've been blocking.

★ Why have I been blocking my birthday dreams?

KEEPING THE PROSELYTIZER OUT

In a meeting room. I am wearing a white doctor's coat signifying (I realize in the dream) that I am a doctor of psychiatry. I am in a meeting with professional people who have gathered to share their songs, each one having his or her own. I start to sing mine, but my voice is shaky and off-key. Another doctor cuts in and sings my song as if it were her own. I am disappointed but realize that she sings better than I and deserves the recognition for that. As the meeting ends, I leave feeling a bit dejected. On the way out, I meet one of the group, a very kind and gentle young doctor, perhaps a resident not yet out of training. We chat. He seems to understand how I feel and offers me comfort by just chatting with me. It turns out that he's a "born-again" Christian. Upon discovering this, I say, "Oh, one of those! Then let me tell you right now, don't lay your trip on me. I am not into the fundamentalist bit. Besides, I'm a woman, and the chauvinism of it all just infuriates me!" He says, "O.K." He doesn't talk to me anymore.

This doctor has a graduate student–like office right under my office. An old woman who used to work for me and who is now senile comes into my office. She is brandishing two metal clawlike instruments and is threatening to maul me with them if I don't do something (I forget what). The young doc-resident-graduate student downstairs hears this and comes upstairs to help. (I then realize that he and I had earlier made a deal. I had agreed to talk with him if he could find the way to approach me other than the judgmental proselytizing "new Christian" one. To this end, he had been practicing walking all over his office, even over desk tops with his eyes closed. We both wanted to understand and get to know each other, but I couldn't tolerate his style. Therefore, he had been trying to figure out a way to communicate with me that I would accept when he heard the old woman threatening me and came upstairs to help.

Meanwhile, here I am, losing a terrible struggle with this big old lady. The young doctor appears at the back door of my office, in front of which the lady and I wrestle. He can see through the glass in the door that she is about to maul me with her metallic claws. I say, "Do some-thing!" He can't get in. The door is locked. Then I say, "Then you hold her (arms), and I'll unlock the door and let you in" (physically impossible but possible in the dream).

He holds her. I unlock the door. Together, we subdue and disarm the lady.

"Now Lillie. . . ," I begin. She corrects me, saying, "My name is Jean." "Oh, forgive me, dear!" I say, as I hug her warmly and tell her not to do this any more. I feel compassion for her and say, "Here is what you need; now you go home with your hubbie." I am trying to understand her. She feels this and appreciates it, saying, "But that other woman won't even try." I reply, "Yes, it's too bad, isn't it?"

Commentary. What an intense dream! I feel sure it is an answer to my question about why I'm blocking my birthday dreams. The born-again Christian, the locked door, and the fact that the doctor doesn't talk to me any more are all elements that seem to confirm this feeling. I am trying to keep something out of my awareness, but what? Surely I'm not about to turn into a Jesus freak. . . .

The setting (professional meeting room and my office): Suggests that I'm dealing with professional concerns. The fact that Sue, a colleague, steals my song reflects my concern that she will do just that, and since she has published long before I, her voice is stronger than mine. It seems that this dream is dealing with my concerns about my professional status and achievement.

Who is the young doctor? A resident, graduate student–type who is not as far along as I in the professional world. He's about to graduate.

What's he like? At first I am struck by his kindness and goodness. He seems a very friendly, giving, understanding soul. I am attracted to him as a friend. Then when I discover that he is a born-again Christian, I treat him like a stereotype not an individual. Actually, he hadn't said a word that fit the stereotype before I jumped on him. I just assumed that he would go into the same love-God-but-hate-the-devil and follow-your-man trip the Jesus people I knew at college had parroted. To avoid this, I shut him up. He stopped talking to me. My inspirational dreams have stopped talking to me lately. . . .

The old woman who used to work for me: An old part of myself, a set of old ways of seeing the world. Old beliefs and behaviors that used to work for me but now are senile, worn out, and threaten to maul and scar me.

Who is Lillie? A woman I see at parties now and then.

What is she like? She's an eccentric, chatterbox hysteric. Maybe depressed underneath but is clever, bright, and amusing.

Jean? A psychiatric patient I've heard a lot about but have never met. She's very dependent, hostile, depressed, suicidal and has been for many years. A very sad lady. Oh, dear! Is there a Jean in me that I don't recognize and who I think of only as Lillie? Looking through my day notes for the last twelve weeks, I've just realized that I've been sick with a continuous series of flus, colds, and viruses for the last eleven weeks! Suddenly I noticed several dreams which I resisted looking at with suicide motifs centering around an unknown young woman. I know I've been depressed lately. Who wouldn't be after constant congestion, fevers, and sore throats? Jean reminds me of my mother's way of dealing with the world—as a victim of circumstances beyond her control. Jean is a very troubled Lillie. I've been considering my recent depression as not very serious and largely related to feeling guilty about not disciplining myself to complete my book on my research.

Now I can feel that my depression has been far deeper than I was willing to admit. Perhaps that is why I avoided reviewing this year's journal until this morning. The dream suggests that a part of me is depressed, as Jean is. Dreams exaggerate, but this does make sense now. My mother, a Jean-type, has been depressed for as long as I've known her. She sees herself as a martyr and as a victim of circumstances beyond her control. A part of me has always known that she could make a happier life if she would stop playing the victim and *do* something for herself. Yet another, less conscious, part of myself has adopted her victim strategy to avoid taking responsibility for certain things. Perhaps I allowed myself to stay sick so long to excuse myself from doing my writing and launching my career. Jean may represent this depressing belief in myself as a victim of circumstance. I have consciously rejected (fired) this belief, although it still shows up in my professional life (office) now and then.

Action. My old victim attitudes and the depression that comes with them are represented by Jean, who is barging into my professional life (office) and is threatening to maul me to death. My Jean-attitudes are sabotaging my work. The way to save myself is to open the door to the doctor I've locked out. The minute I do this in the dream, things get better. I am then able to give this poor, suffering lady what she needs (understanding?) and send her out of my office in peace. The impression is that she will go to her own home where she belongs and die peacefully.

I have been locking out the very thing (the doctor) that could help me to understand and thus free myself of the Jean within. What does the doctor represent? Who or what do I need to let into my life? How do I feel in conversations with proselytizing Christians? At one level, I feel irritation at their insensitive agressiveness and judgmental pronouncements. But at another level, I envy their feeling of being reborn, even if into a set of beliefs that offends me. These Christians want to change me.

I recognize in my chest a pang of fear at the idea of being changed, even into my own image of my ideal self. I can really feel a resistance to changing at all. Who would the new me be? Would I still be myself? What if some life experience really changed me, even for the better? What parts of myself would I have to give up? What attitudes or habits would change? Perhaps after the change I'd be glad to be freed of limiting beliefs and behaviors. But now those that I have are dear to me and comfortable, even if they work against me!

The reborn Christian in the dream is really not at all the way I stereotype him. He is an embodiment of patience, kindness, brotherly love. He represents the best of Christian beliefs, ones I would very much like to be reborn into. Because of my fear that he will try to change me, I prefer to stereotype him instead of listening to him. He is a resident. He resides in my psyche, just beneath my awareness. He has been trying to communicate with me by walking about with his eyes closed. A tactile, or feeling, communication. If I were to *feel* what he has to offer me, I would feel great love, acceptance, and understanding. As I allow myself to feel him within me, I begin to really understand how my mother developed her helpless-victim attitudes from a depression which started in her childhood when she never felt she was cherished by her family or accepted as she was. As a child, she felt criticized, pushed aside, at times abandoned. Such were her early, formative years—not mine, for I have been very well loved, and life has been a beautiful challenge for me. Yet I seem to have adopted some of my mother's depressive personality habits and attitudes without realizing it. When they pop into my life in the form of severe procrastination and escapism through illness or "the blues," I have rather ineffectively chastized myself for laziness and continued to feel guilty for not being very productive. I am beginning to understand that I've been blaming myself for my laziness and procrastination instead of recognizing them as manifestations of very passive, dependent, antiachievement attitudes I unconsciously copied from my mother. Seeing this frees me to see through the facade of laziness to the passive, depressive habits of thinking that keep me from enjoying my work. My tendency has been to see myself as a victim of school or professional authorities who "make me" do my work. There really is no reason that I couldn't start today to change that attitude. Instead of seeing my writing as a task imposed upon me, I am quite free to see it as it is—something I have *chosen* to do for my own reasons. If I could really see my writing in this light, I could enjoy the writing process itself, communicate my ideas, and enjoy the pleasure of achievement.

I hope "that other woman" (the judgmental part of me who struggled with the old lady, locked the door, and struggled unsuccessfully with Jean) will listen to the new self I became when I let the proselytizer (changer) in. As long as "that other woman" (my old self) refuses to understand Jean, I'm going to be in trouble. If I can learn to stop judging myself when Jean-like attitudes and habits cause me trouble, and start understanding their dynamics, I really will be reborn. I'll be free then to create my own attitudes toward work and achievement, and I'll feel a lot better about myself too. Well, there's my challenge for my next year.

In the two years since Ginger had this dream, she has begun to really enjoy her writing and has changed her self-image to include a belief in herself as a productive and creative psychiatrist. She reports that her whole life feels better now that she does not spend the greater part of it feeling guilty about the work she is putting off. These changes did not come overnight. Ginger had to keep these dream insights close to her heart as she went through her daily work-related conflicts. Gradually, she found herself able to understand the Jean within her. Only then could she send her away in peace. Jean still shows up now and then, but Ginger has learned how to disarm her with understanding.

When Ginger awoke from this dream, she had little intuitive understanding of it, as is usually the case with dreams treating issues we are trying to lock out of consciousness. She used her dream journal to explore the dream images and action, and this led her to some very useful insights.

NOTES

1. 1. See Gay Luce and Erick Pepper, "Biofeedback: Mind over Body, Mind over Mind," *The New York Times Magazine,* September 12, 1971, pp. 34ff; D. Shapiro et al., "Effects of Feedback and Reinforcement on the Control of Human Systolic Blood Pressure," *Science* 163 (1969):588–590; and T. Weiss and B. Engel, "Operant Conditioning of Heart Rate in Patients with Premature Ventricular Contractions," *Psychosomatic Medicine* 33 (1971):301–321.

2. Raymond de Becker, *The Understanding of Dreams and Their Influence on the History of Man* (New York: Hawthorn Books, 1968); C. Kerenyi, *Asklepios: Archetypal Image of the Physician's Existence* (Princeton, N.J.: Princeton University Press, 1959); S. Lorand, "Dream Interpretation in the Talmud," in R. Woods and H. Greenhouse (eds.), *The New World of Dreams* (New York: Macmillan, 1974); C. Meier, *Ancient Incubation and Modern Psychotherapy* (Evanston, Ill.: Northwestern University Press, 1967).

3. As cited in Henry Reed, "Dream Incubation: A Reconstruction of a Ritual in Contemporary Form," *Journal of Humanistic Psychology,* #4, no. 16 (Fall, 1976):52–70. See also M. Eliade, *Myths, Dreams, and Mysteries* (New York: Harper & Row, 1960); A. Kiev, *Transcultural Psychiatry* (New York: The Free Press, 1972); and G. E. von Gruenbaum and R. Caillois (eds.), *The Dream and Human Societies* (Berkeley, Calif.: University of California Press, 1966).

4. Emile Durkheim, *The Elementary Forms of the Religious Life,* trans. J. W. Swain (Glencoe, Ill.: Free Press, 1947; originally published 1912).

5. Edgar Cayce was a trance psychic who, during his lifetime, gave thousands of psychic readings concerning many areas of human experience. His readings on the process of dreaming and its use are among the most interesting of all sources of ideas on the subject. These readings are on file at the Edgar Cayce Association for Research and Enlightenment, Virginia Beach, Virginia. See especially reading #294–42. See also Harmon Bro, Edgar Cayce on Dreams (New York: Paperback Library, 1968); Elsie Sechrist, *Dreams: Your Magic Mirror* (New York: Dell, 1969); and John Sanford, *Dreams: God's Forgotten Language* (Philadelphia: Lippincott, 1968).

6. For example, Ann Faraday, *The Dream Game* (New York: Harper & Row, 1974),

pp. 142–143. Faraday suggests petitioning dreams for help in problem solving and clarification through mental request, prayer, or self-suggestion. Many Jungian analysts plant the suggestion in their clients' minds that they will have a dream on a specific issue by saying, "Let's see if you have a dream on it this week." Robert Lifton, a research psychiatrist at Yale University, describes an exercise in which he, Eric Olson, and a number of research subjects participated. The exercise consisted of concentrating on a life struggle just before sleep, and "willing" a dream that would address that struggle. Without citing what percentage of such exercises was successful, Lifton states that "altered perspectives" and "directions of resolution" resulted from the dreamer's associations to these dreams. See R. Lifton, *The Life of the Self* (New York: Simon & Schuster, 1976), p. 102.

7. For example, D. M. Gregg, *Hypnosis, Dreams, and Dream Interpretation* (San Diego, Calif.: Medical Hypnosis Center, 1767 Grand Avenue, Suite 107, San Diego, Calif.; 1970).

8. Henry Reed, "Dream Incubation: A Reconstruction of a Ritual in Contemporary Form."

9. Laboratory research has demonstrated that we do most of our dreaming during cyclic periods of rapid eye movements (REM) in sleep. REM periods occur about every ninety minutes, lasting ten minutes just after the onset of sleep and about forty-five minutes to one hour in the last period just before awakening. However, subjects have been found to produce reports of mental phenomena in other non-REM (or NREM) stages of sleep as well. These NREM phenomena tend to be described less as dreams and more like thoughts of a less bizarre and more daylike nature than dreams. Both Freud and Adler felt that we dream in proportion to the number and gravity of our personal conflicts, and that we dream only when we must to cope with problems. Physiological dream research has shown this theory to be incorrect. We dream approximately twenty percent of the time we spend in sleep. This percentage of REM sleep remains quite stable in almost all people studied, regardless of the degree of conflict or problems in their lives. See D. Foulkes, "The Psychology of Sleep," *Psychological Bulletin* 62 No. 4

(1964); or, in book form, *The Psychology of Sleep* (New York: Scribners', 1966).

10. Faraday, *The Dream Game*, pp. 204–230.

2. **1.** Gayle Delaney, "Secular Dream Incubation," Master's Thesis, Sonoma State College (California), 1974 (unpublished).

2. Carl G. Jung, *The Collected Works*, 2nd ed. Vol. 8: *The Structure and Dynamics of the Psyche* (Princeton, N.J.: Princeton University Press, 1969).

3. Charles Tart, "Conscious Control of Dreaming: I. The Post-Hypnotic Dream." Original manuscript of an article later shortened and published under the same title in the *Journal of Abnormal Psychology* 76 (1970):304–315.

In Tart's (1970) study of the use of post-hypnotic suggestion in the conscious control of dreaming, he found that, the greater the overall hypnotizability of the patient, the more able he was to follow suggestions that he dream about the story or movie presented to him before sleep. Because of this positive correlation to hypnotizability, Tart hypothesizes that posthypnotic dream control is a relatively difficult hypnotic procedure. I did not test the hypnotizability of the incubants studied, but the frequency of their success in recalling dreams dealing with the desired issue suggests that, unlike hypnotic suggestion, dream incubation is a form of suggestion that is rather easily accomplished when practiced in the manner presented.

As to whether the process of focusing upon the incubation phrase with the expectation of receiving a helpful dream constitutes an autohypnotic suggestion or not is a matter of how one chooses to define autohypnosis. I do not present, nor do I think about this technique, in terms of hypnosis but rather in terms of positive self-direction. In any case, it may be of interest to note that the incubated dreams which flow from this technique are experienced as normal dreams, although generally more vivid than most. Tart observed that the parts of hypnotically influenced dreams which incorporated scenes from the target stimulus narrative seemed to be out of context with the rest of the dream, which itself seemed to be interrupted by the inclusion of the suggested content. The incubants who used this technique focused on matters of relevance to themselves and made no reports of this phenomenon, nor could I detect evidence of it in the dream reports I heard and read.

4. Joseph Murphy, in *The Power of Your Subconscious Mind* (Englewood Cliffs, N.J.: Prentice-Hall, 1963), pp. 80–82, suggests using Charles Baudoin's technique of selecting a short phrase and repeating it in the drowsy state before sleep as a lullaby. He did not suggest this specifically to elicit a dream but rather to achieve healing or problem solving. Tart ("Conscious Control of Dreaming") and Reed ("Dream Incubation") encouraged their subjects not to focus on the desired goals of the dreaming suggested in the last few minutes before sleep. Yet presleep focusing on the incubation phrase seems very important for good, dependable results. The subjects using the phrase-focusing method of incubation report that, if they can focus clearly on the incubation phrase, they can be sure to recall a relevant dream even if they omit the other steps preceding the choice and use of the phrase.

3. **1.** Fritz Perls, *Gestalt Therapy Verbatim* (Moab, Utah: Real People Press, 1969).

2. Faraday, *The Dream Game*, pp. 169–229.

3. Jane Roberts, *Seth Speaks* (Englewood Cliffs, N.J.: Prentice-Hall, 1972); the Edgar Cayce dream readings.

4. Erika Fromm and Thomas French, "Formation and Evaluation of Hypotheses in Dream Interpretation," in Woods and Greenhouse (eds.), *The New World of Dreams*, pp. 228–235.

5. Jung, *The Structure and Dynamics of the Psyche*.

4. **1.** Virginia Satir, *Conjoint Family Therapy* (Palo Alto, Calif.: Science and Behavior Books, 1967).

5. **1.** Meier, *Ancient Dream Incubation and Modern Psychotherapy*.

2. Lorand, "Dream Interpretation in the Talmud."

3. Woods and Greenhouse (eds.), *The New World of Dreams*.

4. Lorand, "Dream Interpretation in the Talmud," p. 46.

5. O. Carl Simonton and Stephanie S. Simonton, "Belief Systems and Management of the Emotional Aspects of Malignancy," *Journal of Transpersonal Psychology* 7, No. 1 (1975).

6. David Sheehan and Thomas Hackett, "Psychosomatic Disorders," in *The Harvard Guide to Modern Psychiatry*, ed. Arman

Nicholi, Jr. (Cambridge, Mass., and London: The Belknap Press of Harvard University Press, 1978).

7. Tart, "Conscious Control of Dreaming."

8. Kenneth Altshuler et al., "Dreams of the Aged," in Woods and Greenhouse (eds.), *The New World of Dreams,* pp. 35–37.

9. Helen Keller, quoted in Altshuler et al., "Dreams of the Aged," pp. 34–35.

6. 1. San Francisco *Chronicle,* March 24, 1978.

7. 1. See Richard Corriere and Joseph Hart, *The Dream Makers* (New York: Funk and Wagnalls, 1977), p. 10.

8. 1. For interesting accounts of dream inspirations in the lives of artists, scholars, and scientists, see Woods and Greenhouse, *The New World of Dreams,* 46–64. Also see Havelock Ellis, *The World of Dreams* (Boston: Houghton Mifflin, 1911); Edwin Diamond, *The Science of Dreams* (New York: MacFadden Books, 1963); and Norman MacKenzie, *Dreams and Dreaming* (London: Aldus Books, 1965), p. 281.

2. Jacques Maritain, *The Dream of Descartes,* (London Editions Poetry: 1949), pp. 9–23. See also Maxime Leroy, *Descartes le Philosophe au Masque Paris: Editions Rieder,* 1929, pp. 79–96.

3. Marie Francois Arouet de Voltaire. "Somnambolists and Dreamers" trans. J. G. Gorton quoted in Ralph Woods ed. *The World of Dreams,* New York: Random House, 1947, p. 230.

4. Mohandas K. Gandhi, *An Autobiography: The Story of My Experiments with Truth* (Boston: 1957), Beacon Press, pp. 459–460.

5. M. D. Fagen, Ed. *A History of Engineering and Science in the Bell System: National Service in War and Peace (1925–1975),* Murray Hill, N.J.: Bell Telephone Laboratories, Inc., 1978, p. 135.

6. Ibid.

7. Ibid, p. 136.

8. Ibid, p. 133.

9. M. D. Fagen, Ed. *A History of Engineering and Science in the Bell System Vol. II: National Service in War and Peace (1925–1975),* Murray Hill, N.J.: Bell Telephone Laboratories, Inc., 1978, p. 148.

10. Prescot C. Mabon, *Mission Communications: the Story of Bell Laboratories,* Murray Hill, N.J.: Bell Telephone Laboratories, 1975, p. 145.

11. Robert Louis Stevenson, "The 'Little People' in an Author's Dream," in Woods and Greenhouse (eds.), *The New World of Dreams,* pp. 51–56.

12. Norman MacKenzie, *Dreams and Dreaming,* p. 135.

13. David Foulkes, "You Think All Night Long" in Woods and Greenhouse (eds.), *The New World of Dreams,* pp. 298–302.

14. Carl G. Jung, *Dreams* (Princeton, N.J.: Princeton University Press, 1974); and Jung, *The Archetypes and the Collective Unconscious, Collected Works,* Vol. 9i (1968).

15. Carl G. Jung, *Aion, Collected Works,* Vol. 9ii (1968), p. 7.

16. See Gayle Delaney, "The Religious Process Manifest in Dreams as Seen in the Works of Carl G. Jung and Edgar Cayce," senior thesis submitted to Princeton University, Department of Religion, 1972, p. 105 (unpublished) for more examples of tutorial dreams.

17. Rainer Maria Rilke, *Letters to a Young Poet* (New York: Norton, 1954), p. 19. Translation by M. O. Herter Norton.

9. 1. Alan Vaughan suggests the comprehensive term *psychic dreaming* for dreams which display clairvoyance (mental perception of events at a distance); telepathy (mind reading, one mind's communication with another mind); precognition (perception of future events in the present); or any combination of the above. This is a useful term because it is usually difficult to determine which kind of psychic perception operates in any given event. For example, in Ullman and Krippner's experiments (see M. Ullman, S. Krippner, and A. Vaughan, *Dream Telepathy* [New York: Macmillar., 1973]), in which the dreamer was supposed to dream about a randomly chosen picture which a person in another room was to concentrate on and send to him while he was in REM sleep, it seems impossible to determine which extrasensory faculties were used by the dreamer in "receiving" the message. Though some dreamers clearly had dreams which used the imagery of the target pictures, how can we know how they did it? Did they telepathically read the mind of the sender, who was concentrating on the picture? Did they use precognition to perceive ahead of time the picture which would be chosen for a given night's experiment? Or did they use clairvoyance to perceive the picture, by-passing the sender's efforts?

2. Quoted in Arthur Koestler, *The Roots of Coincidence* (New York: Random House, 1972), p. 14.

3. *Extrasensory perception (ESP)* is another term for the psychic perception described in note 1 above.

4. George Devereux (ed.), *Psychoanalysis and the Occult* (New York: International University Press, 1953); and Jan Ehrenwald, *New Dimensions of Deep Analysis* (New York: Grune and Stratton, 1954).

5. Faraday, *The Dream Game*, pp. 316–336.

6. The psychic readings of Edgar Cayce; and Jane Roberts, *Seth Speaks* and *The Nature of Personal Reality*, Englewood Cliffs, N.J.: Prentice-Hall, 1974, emphasize this function of psychic dreaming, going so far as to say that we dream of every important event in our lives before it occurs.

7. Roberts, *Seth Speaks*.

8. Alan Vaughan, the psychic researcher, author, and parapsychology editor of *New Realities* magazine, has also found this suggestion to be very effective.

9. *The Sundance Community Dream Journal.*

10. *Astral travel* is a term for the experience which some people claim to have of leaving their physical bodies, usually during sleep, to travel in a weightless body which can fly and enter other planes of reality. This will be discussed more fully in Chapter 10.

11. Hornell Hart, "Reciprocal Dreams," *Proceedings of the Society for Psychical Research* 41 (1933):234–240.

12. Faraday, *The Dream Game*, pp. 131–136; James Donahoe, *Dream Reality* (Oakland, Calif.: Bench Press, 1974).

10.

1. Celia Green, *Lucid Dreams* (London: Hamilton, 1968).

2. Patricia Garfield, *Creative Dreaming* (New York, Ballantine, 1974).

3. Kilton Stewart, *Creative Psychology and the Dream Watchers* (New York: The Stewart Foundation for Creative Psychology, 144 East 36th Street, New York, NY); Stewart, *Creative Psychology and Dream Education* (New York: The Stewart Foundation for Creative Psychology); Stewart, *Pygmies and Dream Giants* (New York: Norton, 1954). See also Garfield, *Creative Dreaming* for the most engaging and informative treatment of Kilton Stewart's dream theories.

4. In an unpublished paper titled "Report on a Trip to Malaysia," researcher Peter Bloch states that he and a fellow filmmaker could find little if any evidence to support Stewart's "findings" regarding the elaborate dream systems among the Temiar (Senoi) of Malaysia. Bloch and his friend had gone to Malaysia to seek out and film the Temiar, whom Stewart had described as a primitive tribe which based much of its private and communal life on the sharing of dreams and the control of dream processes. Bloch was in the jungles of Malaysia for only five weeks, and this forty years after Stewart had studied the tribe. Bloch also points out that he was not permitted by the government to meet with any "Tiger" shamans (the most powerful ones), nor to visit any deep jungle stations. Bloch therefore suggests that Stewart's findings may be valid, or that the tribal dream practices described by Stewart may have died over time or may remain hidden in the deep jungle. However, Bloch's reference to "Temiar Religion," an unpublished Cambridge Ph.D. thesis by Richard Benjamin which suggests that Stewart's claims were exaggerated, raises questions as to the validity of Stewart's reports.

5. Stewart, *Creative Psychology and the Dream Watchers* and Stewart, *Creative Psychology and Dream Education.*

6. Ernest Rossi, *Dreams and the Growth of Personality* (New York: Pergamon Press, 1972).

7. Stewart, *Creative Psychology and the Dream Watchers*, p. 25; Stewart, *Creative Psychology and Dream Education*, p. 28.

8. Stewart, *Creative Psychology and Dream Education*, p. 28.

9. Ibid., p. 29.

10. Carlos Castaneda's "spiritual guide" Don Juan (*Journey to Ixtlan* [New York: Simon & Schuster, 1972]), suggests focusing on certain images in an effort to stabilize dream imagery and maintain lucidity.

11. See the published accounts of lucid dreamers such as Oliver Fox, *Astral Projection* (New York: University Books, 1962); Mary Arnold-Forster, *Studies in Dreams* (New York: Macmillan, 1921); P. D. Ouspensky, "On the Study of Dreams and on Hypnotism," in *A New Model of the Universe* (New York: Vintage, 1962); Frederick van Eeden, "A Study of Dreams," *Proceedings of the Society for Psychical Research*, XXVI (1913):431–461; J. H. M. Whiteman, *The*

Mystical Life (London: Faber and Faber, 1961), and Garfield, *Creative Dreaming.*

12. Hervey de Saint-Denys has written a book on dream direction called *Les rêves et les moyens de les diriger (Dreams and Ways of Directing Them),* which is being translated by Patricia Garfield.

13. As quoted in Garfield, *Creative Dreaming,* p. 224.

14. See especially Roberts, *Seth Speaks;* and Roberts, *The Nature of Personal Reality* for an extensive and provocative discussion of the idea that thoughts create physical reality. See also W. Y. Evans-Wentz, *The Tibetan Book of the Dead* (New York: Oxford University Press, 1960), for a description of the yoga of dream control, which encourages the manipulation of dream objects and events as an exercise to teach the dreamer the illusory nature of dream reality.

15. Green, *Lucid Dreams,* p. 90.

16. Garfield, *Creative Dreaming,* p. 130.

17. Ibid., pp. 142, 143.

18. W. Y. Evans-Wentz, *Tibetan Yoga and Secret Doctrines* (New York: Oxford University Press, 1958).

19. Green, *Lucid Dreams.*

20. Apparently "seeing with eyes closed" during sleep states has been reported by such lucid dreamers as Garfield, *Creative Dreaming,* p. 131; and Oliver Fox and Ernst Mach in Green, *Lucid Dreams.*

21. For examples of such false awakenings, see Garfield, *Creative Dreaming;* Green, *Lucid Dreams;* Fox, *Astral Projection.*

22. Arnold-Forster, in *Studies in Dreams;* and Garfield, *Creative Dreaming,* report practicing and learning how to fly in dreams, as have several of my students.

23. For example, see Roberts, *The Seth Material* (Englewood Cliffs, N.J.: Prentice-Hall, 1970); Sylvan Muldoon, *The Case for Astral Projection* (Chicago: Aries Press, 1936); Fox, *Astral Projection;* Muldoon and Herewood Carrington, *The Phenomena of Astral Projection* (New York: Samuel Wiser, 1969); Celia Green, *Out-of-the-Body Experiences* (Oxford: Institute of Psychophysical Research, 1968); Robert Monroe, *Journies Out of the Body* (Garden City, N.Y.: Doubleday, 1971); and Herbert B. Greenhouse, *The Astral Journey* (New York: Avon Books, 1974).

24. Garfield, *Creative Dreaming,* p. 136.

25. Sigmund Freud, *The Interpretation of Dreams* (New York: Basic Books, 1965); and Havelock Ellis, *The World of Dreams,* p. 133.

26. Alfred Adler, "Dreams Reveal the Life Style," in Woods and Greenhouse (eds.), *The New World of Dreams,* pp. 213–216.

27. Emil A. Gutheil, M.D., "Universal (Typical) Dreams," in Woods and Greenhouse *The New World of Dreams,* p. 220.

28. For other opinions on the interpretation of flying dreams see Ellis, *The World of Dreams,* p. 133.

29. Greenhouse, *The Astral Journey,* p. 276.

30. See, for example, the published accounts of astral travelers such as Fox, *Astral Projection;* Muldoon, *The Case for Astral Projection;* and Yram (pseud.), *Practical Astral Projection* (London: Rider, 1935).

31. Roberts, *Seth Speaks,* p. 291; paraphrase.

32. Greenhouse, *The Astral Journey,* p. 263.

33. Greenhouse, *The Astral Journey,* pp. 178–186.

34. For good descriptions of a wide variety of out-of-body experiences, see Greenhouse, *The Astral Journey,* and Robert Crookall, *Casebook of Astral Projection* (New Hyde Park, N.Y.: University Books, 1972).

35. Muldoon and Carrington, *The Phenomena of Astral Projection.* Muldoon noted that his double would zigzag when it did not have sufficient control to act on its own, but that, by learning to move further away from his body, he could gain stability and direct its actions. My dream experience suggests that I gained more control as a novice when my cord was shorter and I was not so far away from the body.

36. Muldoon and Carrington, *The Phenomena of Astral Projection.*

37. Fox, *Astral Projection.*

38. See Fox, *Astral Projection;* Monroe, *Journies out of the Body;* Muldoon, *The Case for Astral Projection;* Yram, *Practical Astral Projection;* and Greenhouse, *The Astral Journey.*

39. Monroe, *Journies out of the Body.*

40. Yram, *Practical Astral Projection.*

41. Greenhouse, *The Astral Journey,* pp. 228–236.

42. Roberts, *The Seth Material.*

43. Rilke, *Letters to a Young Poet,* pp. 68–69.

12. 1. See Garfield's description of Leonard Handler's work with children's nightmares in *Creative Dreaming,* pp. 5–6; and Leonard Handler, "The Amelioration of Nightmares in Children," *Psychotherapy: Theory, Research, and Practice* 9 (Spring 1972).

2. Perls, *Gestalt Therapy Verbatim*.

Part Five. 1. Calvin Hall, in *The Meaning of Dreams* (New York: McGraw-Hill, 1966), p. xiii, states that the average person remembers about one dream in three days. This does not necessarily mean that the normal is the ideal.

2. Certain substances, such as alcohol, amphetamines, and barbiturates, seem to decrease REM time in sleep. See H. Greenhouse, "The Effect of Drugs on Dreaming," in Woods and Greenhouse (eds.), *The New World of Dreams*, pp. 391–392.

3. Edward Wolpert and Harry Trosman, *AMA Archives of Neurology and Psychiatry*,

described by Edwin Diamond in *The Science of Dreams* (New York: MacFadden Books, 1963), p. 90.

4. For example, see the Edgar Cayce readings on dreams, and Roberts, *Seth Speaks*.

5. Wolpert and Trosman, *AMA Archives*.

6. See for example, Donald R. Goodenough, et al., "Dream Reporting Following Abrupt and Gradual Awakenings from Different Types of Sleep," *Journal of Personality and Social Psychology* 2 (1965):170–179.

7. For a further discussion on various tricks of dream recall, see Garfield, *Creative Dreaming*, pp. 172–191; Henry Reed, "Learning to Remember Dreams," *Journal of Humanistic Psychology* 13 (Summer 1973):33–48; and Diamond, *The Science of Dreams*, p. 89, for a description of Herman Rorschach's work in dream recall.

INDEX